HIGH SCHOOL BASKETBALL

OFFICIALS MANUAL 2023-25

DR. KARISSA NIEHOFF, Publisher
Lindsey Atkinson, Editor
NFHS Publications

Published by the
NATIONAL FEDERATION OF STATE HIGH SCHOOL ASSOCIATIONS
PO Box 690
Indianapolis, IN 46206
Phone: 317-972-6900, Fax: 317-822-5700
nfhs.org

Printed in the United States of America

Table of Contents

2023-25 Mechanics Changes

Signal Change

Officials Signal 7 – Throw-in designation and free-throw designated spot violation signal has been amended to include both throw-in and free-throw violation.

Arm and hand pointing toward the spot on the floor where throw in is to be made. Arm should be straight with palm extended.
• Designate spot throw-in following a time-out, fouls or violations following a held ball situation, or following any foul that will not include free throws.
• Designated spot is 3 feet wide, with no depth limitation. Spot is established by the official.
• Verbal communication of the "designated spot" is required.
• Used when a player leaves the designated spot on a throw-in to indicate a violation.
• Used to identify the designated spot for a free throw and a violation by the free thrower.

Officials Signal 19 – Bonus free-throw signal has been removed. New signal 19 (previous signal 20) will be used to signal all free throws by indicating the number of free throws awarded.

Part 1

Officiating Principles

1.1 BASKETBALL OFFICIATING

1.1.1 Purpose of Rules: The basketball rules allow two teams to play so that neither team has an unfair advantage. The role of officials is to enforce the rules. Mechanics are the necessary tool that place officials in the proper position to enforce the rules and communicate infractions. This manual is written with those purposes in mind. The rules book and manual are the constant to which everyone has access. Officials should enforce the rules as written and follow the manual as written.

1.1.2 Game Officials: Game officials are responsible for creating public confidence in sports and are critical to the well-being of athletic competitions. Officials ensure games are played fairly, by the rules, within the spirit of the rules and in a safe manner. Officiating takes a great deal of preparation, continuing education and commitment of time. This is facilitated through the registration, promotion and training programs available to officials through the NFHS and state associations.

1.1.3 Rules Knowledge: Complete knowledge of the rules is essential. To know the rules thoroughly requires constant and analytical study. Rules should be studied before the opening of the season and continuously reviewed throughout the season. For educational purposes, the following aids are helpful: rules book, case book, simplified and illustrated rules, handbook, preseason guides, Part I and II examinations, officiating mechanics exam, interpretations, PowerPoint presentations, video play review, discussion at state-sponsored and local meetings, clinics and periodic releases by the state association office. Good officiating is dependent on a thorough knowledge of the basketball rules.

1.1.4 Language: The language of basketball must be fully understood, such as: bonus free throws, common foul, double foul, fumble, multiple throw and many other terms as found in the definitions. The technical meaning of “team in control” and understanding of technicalities such as when “continuous-motion” provisions apply are essential. The same thing applies to a clear and definite understanding of exactly when the ball becomes dead and when an act such as a dribble or a free throw ends. The definitions portion (Rule 4) of the NFHS Basketball Rules Book should be thoroughly studied.

1.1.5 Signals: Knowledge of the rules alone does not ensure competency. Understanding and using approved signals and mechanics are necessary to administer the game. Proper NFHS signals, as outlined in this manual and the rules book, are to be used exclusively. Signaling is an essential aspect of officiating and, through proper use, decisions and information are relayed to players, coaches and spectators. These official signals are informative and meaningful. Clear signals establish the understanding that the officials are in control of the game.

1.1.6 Proper Court Coverage: A good system of mechanics is required to ensure the officials will be at the proper location on the court at all times. The movements must be such that an official moves with a purpose to monitor activity within the defined primary coverage area. An official who is not in the proper position on the court decreases the opportunity to make the accurate rulings. Officials must be proficient in good officiating mechanics.

1.1.7 Players' Welfare: Officials should be alert constantly to the possibility of player injury. Injured players should be attended to as outlined in the rules. In all situations, the welfare of an injured player has the highest priority.

1.2 PERSONAL CHARACTERISTICS

1.2.1 Conduct: Every member of the officiating profession carries a responsibility to act in a manner becoming of a professional person. The conduct of any official influences the attitude of the public toward the profession in general, as well as toward the official as an individual. Officials should constantly uphold the honor and dignity of officiating in all personal conduct and relations with student-athletes, coaches, athletic directors, school administrators and the public. Officials are entrusted to assist schools in the educational development of youth through athletics. Professionalism and politeness allow for an official to be independent, impartial and responsible to the people being serve. Officials should review the NFHS Officials Code of Ethics at the end of this manual, as well as in the NFHS Basketball Rules Book.

1.2.2 Communication: Communication is vital to being a successful official. Understanding non-verbal and verbal communication sends a message to players, coaches and fans. Good communication starts with accepting game assignments, contacting game administration prior to the contest and working with the table officials in preparing to start the game. During the contest, officials must communicate with their partners, coaches and players in a positive, professional manner. Officials must be aware of their non-verbal communication cues and body language. Officials shall not address fans and must refrain from derogatory comments.

1.2.3 Conditioning: Basketball requires a well-conditioned body and an alert mind. A physical examination should be taken at the start of each season and after any illness or injury that occurs during a season. Unless an official is in good physical condition, reaction time and the ability to concentrate in making decisions will be less than satisfactory. Hustle and energy have no substitutes. An official must develop the ability to move quickly and purposefully, and be in position to observe all game action.

1.2.4 Composure: During a game, if a head coach asks what happened on a certain play, your explanation should be the extent of the conversation; do not argue or lose your temper with a player or head coach. A diplomatic manner will foster positive interaction. Being tactful in responses encourages a cooperative attitude on the part of players, coaches and spectators. Tactfulness is a talent that will pay dividends in officiating. It is not desirable to be demonstrative when making a ruling. It is not the officiating, but the game that is the attraction. An official should not be overbearing, but perform as an integral part of the contest. An official cannot be overly sensitive about criticism.

1.2.5 Fair and Impartial: A good official will be courteous with players and coaches during the game. Conversations with the head coach before, during or after the game may give the appearance of favoritism. If conditions warrant a conference, both head coaches should be involved. Avoid physical contact with players and coaches. A player should be addressed by number rather than by name. In addressing the captain or head coach of a team, do so by title.

1.2.6 Decisiveness: Quick and positive decisions are essential aspects of officiating. Hesitation implies a lack of confidence. Self-confidence must be developed. Many decisions can be questioned no matter how are ruled. The practice of making concise decisions must be habitual. However, officials should not be hasty when there is a question at the table regarding scoring, timing, disqualification, fouls, the alternating-possession arrow, etc. Take time to try and prevent any mistake or error from being made.

1.2.7 Teamwork: Each official must give full cooperation to the crew and all personnel associated with the game. Officials must be willing to share the responsibility and execute their duties in a coordinated manner. Do not negatively or publicly comment about a game officiated by another official.

1.2.8 Prevention: An official must anticipate potential trouble. The presence of an official in whom the players have confidence will prevent most of these situations. Being in a position to observe any unnecessary contact will go a long way toward preventing such contact. Unsporting action is a circumstance that requires immediate attention before it gets out of hand. Communicate expectations and penalize if needed. Officials must not tolerate rough play or unsporting action. Decisiveness in ruling fouls when rough play begins will avoid later loss of control which often results when warnings are used as a substitute for penalties.

1.2.9 Integrity: Honor game assignments. Avoid conflict of interest situations whenever possible. Any situation that could potentially compromise the professional and/or personal accountability of the official should be a guide in determining potential conflict of interest. If an official accepts a game, that official should be there on time. If there is some good reason for cancellation, the official should inform the appropriate supervisor immediately.

1.2.10 Decision-Making: A quality official will be quick to rule violations and/or fouls when they occur. Do this consistently without regard to the score, position on the floor, whom it may affect within the game, the school or head coach. Regardless of pressure from fans, coaches or players, officials must have the professionalism to rule fouls and violations as they occur. Your honesty must be above reproach. It takes real commitment to resist pressure and intimidation. To a large extent, the personal reputation of an official will be based on performance.

1.3 GAME AWARENESS

1.3.1 General Provisions:

A. Awareness of all game activity is important to afford officials the best opportunity to make correct rulings.

B. Game awareness includes various aspects of judgment in making foul and violation rulings, and as importantly, handling dead-ball situations – players, coaches and bench personnel.

C. Creating an appropriate and professional relationship with players and coaches will facilitate officiating the game.

D. Understand the appropriate boundaries of relationships to ensure that officials are not and do not appear to be overly friendly with the players or coaches.

E. Approach the role as an official with professionalism at all times.

F. As a general principle, acknowledge head coaches and answer their questions at appropriate times – do not respond to statements.

G. If an unusual situation warrants a conference, both head coaches should be involved in the discussion. Both coaches should also be present for any discussion involving a fight, correctable errors or mistakes in timing, scoring or alternating possession.

1.3.2 Game Clock (and Shot Clock, if applicable):

A. Be aware of the game clock when possible.

B. Work to look at the clock on any whistle to ensure that the clock is properly stopped.

C. Similarly, when the ball is put back in play, the official, signaling to start the clock, should ensure that the clock is properly started.

D. Clock malfunctions occur; there are no provisions in the rules for "do-overs." Know the rules regarding these unusual situations and apply them appropriately.

E. Remember, an official's count (backcourt, closely guarded, throw-in, etc.) can be used to correct a timing mistake. Correction requires definite information.

1.3.3 Fights:

A. Game awareness and making correct accurate rulings are the best ways to avoid fights and player confrontations.

B. Be aware of matchups and rivalries both in individual games and during an overall season.

C. Should a fight occur, officials should use their voices and their whistles to gain the attention of players.

D. Do not touch, hold or grab players – both for the safety of the crew and for liability concerns.

E. One official should remain away from the action and observe non-participating players and bench personnel.

F. At the earliest point, get teams to their benches. Officials should then confer to determine appropriate penalties, if and how any free throws will be awarded and how play will be resumed.

1.4 UNIFORM AND EQUIPMENT

1.4.1 Official's Uniform: The uniform shall be clean and neat. State association patches or emblems shall be worn as specified. The standard uniform (unless modified by the state association) consists of the following:

A. Belt: If worn, it shall be black.
B. Jacket: Black, if worn. Recommended for wear prior to game.
C. Shirt: Standard black/white vertically striped:
Short sleeves – approximately 8 inches in length; with black cuffs
"V" neck shirt shall be worn and an undershirt should not be visible
Worn inside pants
Entire crew shall wear same design and style
D. Shoes: Predominantly black with black laces.
E. Socks: Predominantly black.
F. Pants: Entirely black slacks.
G. Whistle: Recommend black, pealess plastic whistle. Carry a spare.
H. Black lanyard.
I. Officials shall not wear jewelry, fitness bands or other items that are not necessary for performing their duties. Religious and medical-alert medals are not considered jewelry. A religious medal must be taped and worn under the uniform. A medical-alert medal must be taped and may be visible. Wedding rings are permitted.

1.5 OFFICIALS' PREGAME PROTOCOL

1.5.1 Arrival on Site: Officials should report to the proper athletic administrator at least one hour before game time.

1.5.2 Officials' Pregame Conference: A pregame conference is mandatory. The meeting affords an opportunity for the crew to develop confidence in each other and goes a long way in ensuring a smooth running game. The referee is responsible for conducting the meeting in a private and secure location. The umpire(s) should participate and contribute to the meeting. A sample of an officials' pregame conference can be found at the back of the book.

1.5.3 Duties of the Referee:

- Confer with scorer and timer before game time regarding their responsibilities.
- Recommend they be seated next to each other if they are not.
- Authorize the scorer to note and prevent any attempted illegal substitution.
- Designate the official timepiece and its operator, the official scorebook and official scorer.
- Check game clock and other timing apparatus.
- Check device to indicate substitutions and end of a quarter/period.
- Inspect ball, baskets, boundaries, placement of crowd and extraneous apparatus to see if special ground rules are necessary. Be sure the basket net is loose enough to permit the ball to go through.
- Crew of Three: Obtain from the umpires the number of team members warming up for each team and that starters are designated in the scorebook for each team.
- Crew of Two: Count the number of visiting team squad members. Check the visiting team uniforms and numbers and other apparel for legality, including undershirts and undergarments that extend below the pants. Check for jewelry, illegal casts or braces or any other illegal equipment. Check for illegal headwear or secure authorization from the coach, if the state association has approved. Players must be legally attired during the warm-up period.

• Conduct the coach/captain conferences at the designated time(s). Verify with the head coach that team members are legally and properly equipped and that all participants are expected to exhibit proper sporting behavior.

• Ensure the official scorer is wearing a black-and-white vertically striped garment.

• Verify the coaching box and X in front of the scorer are properly marked.

1.5.4 Duties of the Umpire(s):

(Crew of Three: U1 is responsible for the following duties with the home team and U2 for the visiting team)

• Count the number of home team squad members.

• Check the home team uniforms and numbers and other apparel for legality, including undershirts and undergarments that extend below the pants.

• Report to the Referee if any home team squad member is wearing jewelry, illegal casts or braces, or any other illegal equipment.

• Report to the Referee if any home team squad member is wearing illegal headwear or secure authorization from the coach, if state association has approved. Players must be legally attired during the warm-up period.

1.5.5 Sample Pregame Schedule:

A. 15:00 – Officials enter court and go directly to positions.

B. 12:00 – Referee goes to the table and checks scorebook(s), briefs scorer and timer, checks game ball.

C. 10:00 – Remaining official(s) go across the floor to join referee, greet the visiting coach, then greet the home head coach.

• Referee goes to area in front of scorer's table.

• U1 (and U2, if applicable) will get respective head coaches and captains from teams.

• Referee does introductions of officials, coaches and captain(s).

• Referee conducts pregame briefing to include discussing legal equipment and good sporting behavior with head coaches and captain(s). Also discuss: team color, proper basket, other appropriate items and answer any questions.

• Return to original positions.

• If teams return to dressing room, leave court, remove jackets, return to original position when teams come out, stand at attention for National Anthem.

1.6 DUTIES OF ALTERNATE OFFICIAL

1.6.1: When an alternate official is used, assigned duties shall include, but are not limited to the following:

A. Be present for pregame conference. Wear game uniform and jacket and be prepared mentally and physically to officiate in case of an injury, illness or other emergencies.

B. Be seated at the scorer's table as close to the scorer and timer as possible. Serve as an aid to both the scorer and timer.

C. Keep a written record of all fouls ruled, the number of the player fouling, the number of the free-throw shooter, the number of free throws and the time that the foul occurred.

D. Serve as an aid to game officials in case there is a scoring or timing error, a substitution error, a correctable error, etc.

E. Your role is as a "working observer." Use a data sheet to make appropriate notes and monitor any irregularities in order to report to the referee - do not make any rulings.

Part 2

Terminology

BACKSIDE: Refers to the area in the free-throw lane when a player moves away from the Lead into the lane.

BALANCE THE FLOOR: Refers to the positions of both the Lead and the Trail. When the floor is balanced, the officials are near their respective sidelines. That is the normal set position in two-person mechanics. The floor becomes un- balanced when the Lead moves ball side.

BALL SIDE: The location of the ball in the normal frontcourt offensive alignment of a team. In dividing the court down the middle, (using the basket as a Center point), end line to end line. The side of the court where the ball is located is ball side.

BALL SIDE MECHANIC: Refers to the Lead moving across the free throw lane to the ball side of the court, on the Trail's side, resulting in both officials being on the same side of the court. The Lead moves ball side when the majority of players and the ball goes below the free-throw line extended on the Trail's side of the court. This movement will allow the Lead to get a clear view of post play and eliminate being "straight-lined." Primary Coverage Areas (PCA) are adjusted when this occurs.

BOXING-IN PRINCIPLE: Refers to both officials, on opposite sides of the court, having all players between them, and having both sidelines and end lines covered.

BUMP AND RUN: A technique when one official "bumps" the other official out of that official's current position and the vacating official "moves" down the court into a new position.

CENTER OFFICIAL: The outside official, who is in the off-ball position, midway between a step below the free-throw line extended and the top of the circle. The Center official may be table side or opposite side.

CLOSE DOWN: Movement of an official (a step or two) related to movement of the ball to improve angles. On a try for goal shot attempt, the Trail and Center (3-person) closes down toward the end line; the Lead closes down toward the nearest lane line extended to improve positioning for rebounding action.

COMPETITIVE MATCH-UP: Opponents who are working/competing against each other as opposed to two opponents who are more than six feet apart.

DEAD-BALL OFFICIATING: Activity during the time immediately after the ball becomes dead. Don't stop officiating when the ball is dead. Continue to monitor the players and bench personnel.

DOUBLE WHISTLE: A situation in which two or more officials blow their whistles on a foul or violation.

FREE-THROW LINE EXTENDED: An imaginary line drawn from the free-throw line out to the sidelines. The area around the free-throw line extended is a significant guideline for 2-person officiating coverage and movements.

FREE-THROW LANE LINE: Refers to the free-throw lane lines perpendicular to the end line which intersect the free-throw line and the end line and run parallel to the sideline. During free throws, players are lined up in free-throw lane line spaces along the lane line.

LEAD MOVING TO TRAIL: Refers to the movements and changed positions of the Lead during a transition play. For example, when a play moves from one end of the court to the other, the Lead moves from that position to the Trail position at the other end of the court.

LEAD OFFICIAL: The official positioned along and off the end line. The Lead official may be table side or opposite table; will usually be on the opposite side of the court as the Trail (Crew of 2) or will be on the same side of the court as the Trail (Crew of 3).

LOW BLOCK: The area along the free-throw lane line closest to the basket but not in the lane.

MOVE TO IMPROVE: A technique that means to "move your feet" in order to "improve your angle" on the play. Helps to eliminate being "straight-lined."

OFFICIATING THE ARC: A technique that provides the Trail official with better court coverage. Trail will move in a motion that parallels the three-point arc in an attempt to be in closer proximity to the ball and also provides for better coverage of the three-point shot.

OPPOSITE SIDE: Away from the table.

PERIMETER AREA: The perimeter area is the area in a half-court setting away from the basket nearer the three-point arc.

"PINCH THE PAINT": Close down at the lane line in the close-down position. As the drive begins to move through the middle of the lane or from an angle on the weak side of the basket, the official should take a step or two into the imaginary extended free-throw lane to maintain an open angle for such a drive.

POINT OF INTERRUPTION (POI): Method of resuming play due to an official's inadvertent whistle, an interrupted game, a correctable error, a double personal or simultaneous personal foul. Play is resumed by a free throw or throw-in where the ball was located when the stoppage occurred.

POST AREA: The post area is around the low free-throw lane and in the bottom half of the lane nearest the basket.

PREVENTIVE OFFICIATING: Refers to actions by officials who prevent problems from occurring by talking to players and coaches. Preventive officiating is often related to dead-ball officiating.

PRIMARY COVERAGE AREA (PCA): Area of responsibility for each official. PCA is determined by ball location.

PRIMARY DEFENDER: Player who has initially guarded one's opponent.
R, U1, U2: Abbreviations for Referee, Umpire 1 and Umpire 2. All three have specific responsibilities during the pre-game listed in the rules book and officials manual.

ROTATION: A live-ball situation, whereby the location of the ball keys a change in coverage for the officials. In 3-person mechanics, this is implemented when the Lead official moves to ball side dictating a change of position by the Center and Trail officials. The Lead should not rotate until all three officials are in the frontcourt.

SCREEN: A legal action by a player who delays or prevents an opponent from reaching a desired position.

SECONDARY DEFENDER: A secondary defender is a teammate who has helped a primary defender who has been beaten by an opponent because he failed to establish or maintain a guarding position.

SELLING THE CALL: Placing emphasis on a ruling with louder voice and whistle, and slightly more demonstrative signals. Selling only occurs on close calls and should be used sparingly. It is designed to help the ruling gain acceptance and show the official's decisiveness.

SKIP PASS: A pass thrown across the perimeter from one side of the court to the other.

SPACING: Distance between the official and the play. If an official is too close or too far, the official cannot see the play clearly.

STAY DEEP: Refers to an official's position on the court away from the play, usually the Trail in a half-court setting. When the Trail stays deep, the Trail stays out of the passing lanes and avoids interfering with the play.

STRAIGHT-LINE: Refers to a situation that occurs when an official allows the vision to be obstructed by a player or players; having to look through a player's body instead of in between players. When a straight-line occurs, the official is not able to accurately see playing action. The situation is also known as getting "stacked."

STRONG SIDE: Side of the court determined by the location of Lead official.

SWITCH: A dead-ball situation created by an official who rules a violation or foul. After a violation is ruled or a foul is reported to the table, there may be a change in position of the officials. The switch will normally involve the ruling official moving to a new position on the court.

TABLE SIDE: The side of the court where the scorer's and timer's table is located.

TOP OF THE KEY: The top of the key is the area near the top of the free-throw circle.

TRAIL OFFICIAL: The outside official positioned nearest the division line, approximately 28 feet from the end line (near the top of the three-point arc). The Trail official may be table side or opposite side; will usually be on the opposite side of the court as the Lead in two-person mechanics. In three-person mechanics, the Trail is on the same side as the Lead official, positioned at approximately 28 feet from the end line.

WEAK SIDE: The side of the court opposite the Lead official; the Center's side of the court.

WIDE TRIANGLE: All three officials, when in the correct position, form the geometric shape of a wide triangle; keeping all players and activity within the triangle.

Part 3

Signals

STARTING AND STOPPING CLOCK (SIGNALS #1- #5)

#1 START CLOCK

Arm is moved into a straight, vertical position, with open palm extended. Move extended arm straight down and out, in a chopping motion.

• Used anytime the clock is to be started; i.e., when the ball is legally touched – by a player on a jump ball, by a player on the court after the ball is released by the thrower on a throw-in, or by a player on the court when a free throw is not successful and the ball is to remain live.

#2 STOP CLOCK

Arm is held straight up, with open palm extended.

• Signal timer to stop the clock on all violations, fouls and time-outs.

#3 STOP CLOCK FOR JUMP/HELD BALL

Stop the Clock (Signal 2), is given first, then both arms are extended straight out, at chest level, with fists clenched. Thumbs are displayed as a part of the signal. Signal is given with both arms moving in an upward motion. Should be followed with a directional signal (Signal 6) indicating team possession.

- Occurs when opponents both have their hands on the ball and neither can gain control.
- When an opponent places their hand on the ball and prevents an airborne shooter from passing or releasing the try.

#4 STOP THE CLOCK FOR A FOUL

One arm extended straight up and high above the head, with a clenched fist.

- Used on any foul situation.
- Should precede subsequent signal for type of foul ruled.

#5 STOP CLOCK FOR FOUL (Optional "bird dog")

One arm extended vertically straight up, with clenched fist.

- If using the "bird dog" signal the other arm is pointed straight from chest level, with palm facing down, and fingers extended, pointing toward the waistline of the player committing the foul. Use full hand. This is used to communicate from a distance, and when there may be doubt as to which player committed the foul. Take a step or two toward the offending player before giving the signal.

INFORMATION (SIGNALS #6-#14)

#6 DIRECTIONAL SIGNAL

One arm extended straight, from chest height. Palm is open, and pointing in the direction play is to proceed.

- This signal should be given with the same arm as used for stop clock.
- Indicates the direction in which play is to continue.

#7 THROW-IN AND FREE-THROW DESIGNATED SPOT/VIOLATION

Arm and hand pointing toward the spot on the floor where throw in is to be made. Arm should be straight with palm extended.

- Designate spot throw-in following a time-out, fouls or violations following a held ball situation, or following any foul that will not include free throws.
- Designated spot is 3 feet wide, with no depth limitation. Spot is established by the official.
- Verbal communication of the "designated spot" is required.
- Used when a player leaves the designated spot on a throw-in to indicate a violation.
- Used to identify the designated spot for a free throw and a violation by the free thrower.

#8 MOVE ALONG END LINE ON THROW-IN

Arm extended from chest, elbow bent at 90-degree angle, move hand and forearm from the elbow in a waving motion horizontally along the end line. Used after a successful goal when player may move along the end line during a throw in.

#9 VISIBLE COUNT

Extended arm, with palm flat toward the floor – use a back-and- forth motion from chest to full arm extension on a horizontal plane.

- Same signal used for all visible counts.
- Back-court counts, closely guarded counts, throw-ins
- Switch hands anytime new count is established.

#10 BECKONING SUBSTITUTES

Arm and palm (up) extended from shoulder level outward. Bend at elbow, then pull toward shoulder in one motion. Use the full palm in this signal, not individual finger(s). Do not use sweeping, overhead motions. Do not use both hands/ arms to beckon a player into the game.

#11 60-SECOND TIME-OUT

Hands together, palms in at the chest level. Arms are extended straight out, at shoulder level, palms remaining open.

- Visually and verbally state the jersey color and number of player who is granted the time-out.
- If a head coach requests and is granted a time-out, visually and verbally state the jersey color and the word "coach" along with the visual signal forming the shape of a "C" with the hand.

#12 30-SECOND TIME-OUT

Both arms bent, hands curled downward and touching the shoul- ders with fingertips.

- Visually and verbally state the jersey color and number of player who is granted the time-out.
- If a head coach requests and is granted a time-out, visually and verbally state the jersey color and the word "coach" along with the visual signal forming the shape of a "C" with the hand.

#13 NOT CLOSELY GUARDED

Both arms extended outward at shoulder level with cupped hands. The signal need not be held continuously – only when it is needed to clarify that no opponent(s) is within six feet of a player in control of the ball (holding or dribbling).

#14 TIPPED BALL

Point one hand vertically with second hand passing over the first and using a tipping motion.

- Used in a potential backcourt violation to indicate a defensive player was last to touch the ball in the frontcourt.

SHOOTING/SCORING (SIGNALS #15- #19)

#15 NO SCORE
(successful try for goal does not count)

Both arms are fully extended out from chest level and moved in a back-and-forth motion.

- Indicates that a successful try for goal, whether field goal or free throw, has been disallowed, due to a violation, a foul before the try for goal, etc.
- This motion is done one time.

#16 GOAL AWARDED

One arm extended vertically above the shoulder. Hand is "cupped." Arm is then brought down in a chopping motion.

- This signal is used to announce that a goal is to count, following a foul, goaltending or basket interference violation.
- Signal should be used at the spot of the foul and should be the first signal given when reporting a foul.

#17 POINTS SCORED
(follows Signal 16)

One arm held horizontally at shoulder level with either one or two fingers extended.

- Designates the number of points scored following a legally made goal.

#18 THREE-POINT SIGNAL

For the attempt, one arm held halfway between shoulder and head with three fingers extended.

To indicate a legal three-point goal has been scored, both arms are raised above the head with open hands, with both palms open and facing one another.

- The successful goal signal shall be mirrored by the non-ruling Center or Trail official. (Crew of Three)
- Lead official may communicate to the Trail official of the attempt in a fast-break situation but should not signal or mirror the successful try. (Crew of Three)
- When the Trail signals a successful three-point attempt, the Lead shall not mirror the signal. When the Lead signals a successful three-point attempt, the Trail official shall mirror the signal. (Crew of Two)

#19 SIGNAL FOR THE NUMBER OF FREE THROWS

Arm and hand are presented at chest level; either 1, 2 or 3 fingers are extended to indicate the number of free throw shots.

VIOLATIONS (SIGNALS #20- #29)

#20 DELAYED DEAD BALL VIOLATION

One arm fully extended, at shoulder height. The fist is held clenched.

- Used when opponent(s) of the shooting team violated on a free throw.
- No whistle is sounded unless the try is unsuccessful.
- If the try is successful, there is no whistle and play continues.

#21 TRAVELING

Preceded by stop clock (Signal 2). Arms are held at chest level, bent at the elbows, one under the other. Fists are held clenched. Arms are then rotated in a circular motion 2 to 3 revolutions.

- Used anytime there is a violation as per Rule 4-44.

#22 ILLEGAL DRIBBLE

Preceded by stop clock (Signal 2). Arms are held out at chest level, with palms flat and face down. An up-and-down motion with both arms is used to signify the dribble violation.

- Player dribbles a second time after dribble has ended.

#23 PALMING/CARRYING VIOLATION

Preceded by stop clock (Signal 2). One arm, with a flip of the wrist in a rotating motion.

- Allowing the ball to come to rest in one hand while dribbling a live ball.

#24 BACKCOURT VIOLATION

Preceded by stop clock (Signal 2). One arm held at chest level, swinging over and into a downward motion (similar to Signal 23).

• A player shall not be the first to touch the ball after it has been in team control in the frontcourt, if the player or a teammate last touched the ball in frontcourt before it went into backcourt.

#25 THREE-SECOND VIOLATION

One arm raised from the side to chest level. Palm remains open and flat with three fingers extended. Arm and hand are swung in a back-and-forth motion 2 to 3 times.

• Player shall not remain in any part of the free-throw lane while the player's team has team control in the frontcourt for more than three seconds.

#26 FIVE-SECOND VIOLATION

Preceded by stop clock (Signal 2). Hold one arm straight out from chest level with palm open and all five fingers extended.

• Violation on a throw-in when the ball is not released directly onto the court by the thrower-in.

• Player shall not hold the ball, nor dribble the ball for five seconds, when closely guarded in frontcourt.

#27 TEN-SECOND VIOLATION

Preceded by stop clock (Signal 2). Hold both arms straight forward from chest level with palms open and all 10 fingers extended. Same as Signal 26, except both arms and hands are used.

- When the offensive team does not achieve frontcourt location/status following the team gaining control in its backcourt.
- When a free thrower does not release the ball prior to 10 seconds expiring.

#28 EXCESSIVE SWINGING OF ARMS AND ELBOWS

Preceded by stop clock (Signal 2). If a foul preceded by Signal 4. One arm held at shoulder level and bent at the elbow. Arm, with clenched fist, is moved back and forth in a swinging motion.

- Player shall not excessively swing arms or elbows even without contacting an opponent.

#29 KICKING

Preceded by stop clock (Signal 2). Use one leg and foot in kicking motion.

- Intentionally striking the ball with any part of the leg or foot.

FOULS (SIGNALS #30- #38)

#30 ILLEGAL USE OF HANDS

Preceded by stop clock (Signal 4). Arms extended in front of torso, with fists clenched. One arm is chopped down on the other.

- Use of hand or arms (or hips and shoulders) to force through a legal screen or to hold a screener, then push them aside in order to maintain guarding position.

#31 HAND CHECK

Preceded by stop clock (Signal 4). Arm is extended straight out at shoulder level. Palm is flat, pointed up and out. Second arm is used to grasp the top of the wrist.

- Placing two hands on a player.
- Placing extended arm bar on a player.
- Placing and keeping a hand on a player.
- Contacting a player more than once with the same hand or alternating hands.

#32 HOLDING

Preceded by stop clock (Signal 4). Arm is held at the side, then bent at the elbow. Fist is closed. Second hand is used to grasp the first at the wrist.

- Illegal personal contact with an opponent which interferes with the player's freedom of movement.

#33 BLOCKING

Preceded by stop clock (Signal 4). Both arms bent inward, with hands resting on the hips.

- Illegal personal contact which impedes the progress of an opponent with or without the ball.

#34 PUSHING

Preceded by stop clock (Signal 4). Extend both arms straight out at chest level with the palms open and fingers pointing up. Use a one-time back-and-forth motion to indicate pushing.

- Illegal personal contact caused by pushing or moving into an opponent's torso.
- Player moving with the ball is required to change direction if defensive player has obtained a legal guarding position.
- Player with the ball may not push the torso of the guard to gain an advantage.

#35 PLAYER/TEAM CONTROL FOUL

Preceded by stop clock (Signal 4). The same hand used to stop the clock is placed at the back of the head. Show the directional signal (Signal 6) and then indicate the ensuing throw-in spot (Signal 7).

- A common foul committed by a player while that player is in control of the ball or by an airborne shooter, or a common foul committed by a member of the team that has control.

#36 INTENTIONAL FOUL

Preceded by stop clock (Signal 4). Both arms are raised over the head and crossed at the wrists. Both fists should be closed.

- A personal or technical foul that may or may not be premeditated, based solely on the severity of the act.
- Contact that is not a legitimate attempt to play the ball/player designed to stop the clock.
- Excessive contact with an opponent while the ball is live, or until an airborne shooter returns to the floor.

#37 DOUBLE FOUL

Preceded by stop clock (Signal 4). Both arms are extended horizontally at shoulder level, with closed fists.

- Situation where two opponents commit personal fouls against each other at approximately the same time.

#38 TECHNICAL FOUL

Preceded by stop clock (Signal 4). First arm is raised and inward, from shoulder level. Second arm and hand come together with the first arm and hand in the form of a "T." This "T" should be near the Center of the chest.

- A noncontact foul by a player.
- A foul by a non-player.
- An intentional or flagrant foul while the ball is dead, except a foul by, or committed on, an airborne shooter.
- Direct technical charged to head coach as a result of the actions of the head coach.
- An indirect technical foul charged to the head coach as a result of actions committed by bench personnel.

Part 4

Game Procedures for a Crew of Two Officials

The two-official system is designed to provide efficient and effective coverage by two officials. This coverage is generally used at the sub-varsity level, although some states do use two-person mechanics for varsity contests, and allows two officials to manage the administrative and adjudicating responsibilities required of game officials. The crew of two requires officials to be in proper positioning to see on-ball and off-ball action within their primary coverage areas as well as assist in secondary coverage areas.

Positioning is key. It is essential for officials to move quickly and efficiently within the Lead and Trail positions while maintaining proper sight lines to observe play within each PCA. In addition to proper positioning within each position, it is essential for smooth, seamless transitions from Lead to Trail and Trail to Lead. Dividing the playing court into two PCAs creates a challenge for crews of two.

Clear verbal and non-verbal communication during pre-game meetings and throughout the contest is a necessity for an effective two-person crew. Setting the expectations during the pre-game meeting allows crews to establish a baseline of understanding for a smooth game. When situations arise that require non-verbal or verbal communication, it is essential for crews of two to make frequent eye contact and communicate verbally when appropriate, so as to not interrupt the flow of the game.

While the two-official system is not as efficient as utilizing a crew of three, it can be effective when officials are diligent in maintaining proper positioning and open communication.

4.1 Pregame, Intermissions, Time-outs

PREGAME

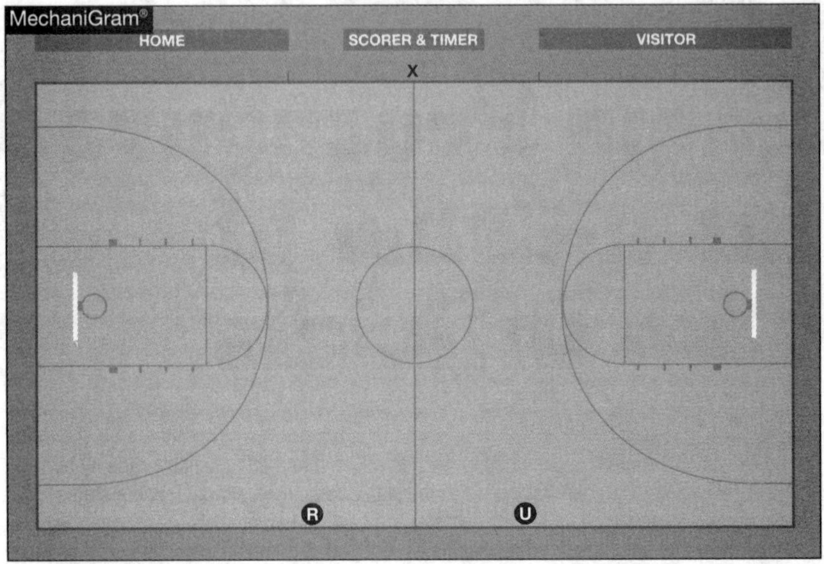

Both officials shall arrive on the court at least 15 minutes prior to game time and be positioned on the side of the court opposite the scorer's table. Each official should be approximately 28 feet from the nearest end line.

During that time, both officials observe team warmups and monitor the court for any illegal activity (dunking, etc.). The R observes the visiting team while U observes the home team. Both officials perform duties as prescribed in 1.5.

Optionally, after the R returns from the scorer's table, the R and U can switch positions in order to observe both teams.

HALFTIME

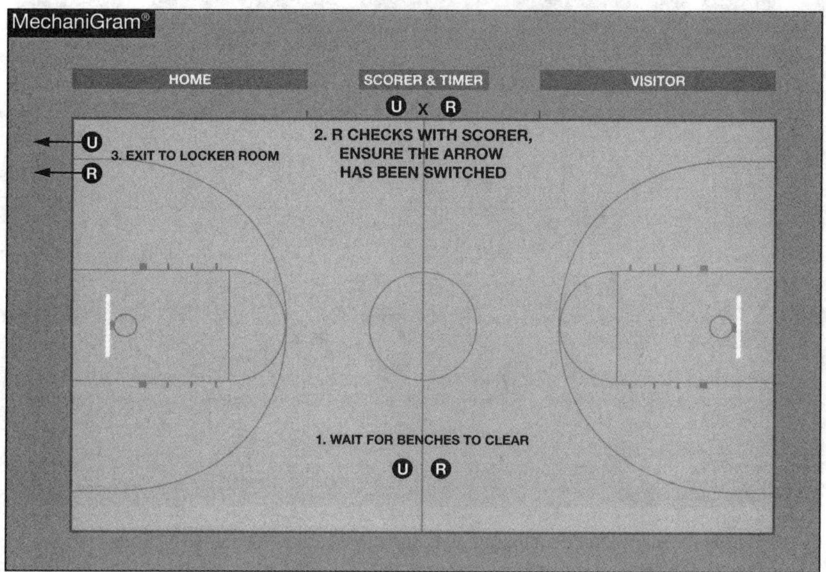

At the conclusion of play for the first half, the officials are now positioned halfway between the farthest point of the center circle and the sideline opposite the scorer's table (#1 in MechaniGram). After both teams have left their benches and gone to their respective locker rooms, both officials walk over to the scorer's table and the R takes care of specified duties (#2 in MechaniGram). After the R confirms the possession arrow is pointed in the proper direction to begin play in the third quarter, the officials leave together for their locker room (#3 in MechaniGram).

The officials should ensure both teams are notified three minutes prior to the start of the second half. During the halftime intermission, the officials shall return to the court for the second half, the officials will stand across the court until the one-minute mark. At that time, the U will secure the ball and bounce it to the R. The R will take a position with the ball at the division line on the sideline opposite the table indicating the direction of play with the placement of the ball. The U shall take a position on the division line on the opposite edge of the restraining circle until the first horn sounds.

BETWEEN QUARTERS

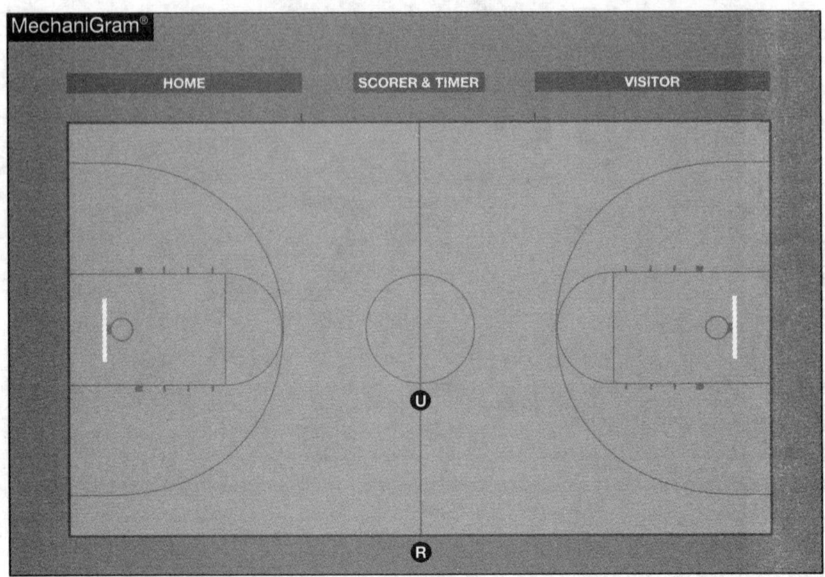

During the intermission between quarters and any extra periods, the R stands with the ball at the division line on the sideline opposite the table. The ball shall be placed on the side of the official that indicates the direction of play.

The U shall take a position on the division line on the opposite side edge of the restraining circle. The U is responsible for acknowledging substitutes and making sure that they report prior to the warning signal.

There should be no visiting with coaches or players unless it is to confer about a game situation. The officials are then responsible to count the players when the teams return to the court to begin play. Use preventive officiating to make sure there are five players on the court per team.

The throw-in to start the second, third and fourth quarters shall be administered by the R at the division line opposite the table. The R indicates jersey color and direction, designates the throw-in spot, sounds the whistle to alert players that play is about to begin and places the ball at the thrower's disposal.

TIME-OUTS PROVISIONS:

1. If a player or head coach requests a time-out while the ball is live, ignore it if the ball is in control of an opponent, not in control of an opponent or not in control of either team.
2. If the request is during a dead ball or during a live ball that is in control of the requesting player or a teammate, it shall be granted.
3. No time-out may be granted during an interrupted dribble.
4. The opponents may not be granted a time-out once the ball is at the disposal of the thrower for a throw-in or the ball is at the free-thrower's disposal.
5. Do not grant a time-out after a foul until the necessary information has been reported to the scorer.
6. Do not grant a time-out until an injured, disqualified or player directed to leave the game has been replaced.
7. After the free thrower has the ball or the ball is at the disposal of the thrower on a throw-in, the thrower or a teammate may request and be granted a time-out, but the opponent may not.
8. After a successful free throw or field goal, any player or head coach may request a time-out, until the non-scoring team secures the ball for the throw-in. Once the official begins the 5-second count, the scoring team cannot be granted a time-out.
9. If an official erroneously grants a time-out request, it is not a team infraction. The time-out will be granted and charged but there is no other penalty assessed.
10. A request for an excess time-out shall be granted, but it is penalized with a team technical foul.
11. If opponents simultaneously request a time-out during a dead ball, charge a time-out to each team (or better, hear or see one request before the other).
12. The official may suspend play to permit a player to correct or replace displaced eyeglasses or contact lens without charging a time-out.

REPORTING PROCEDURES:

1. Sound the whistle while giving the stop the clock signal.
2. While moving to the reporting area, look for verification from the head coach as to what type of time-out is to be charged. Communicate the type of time-out using the proper signal.
3. A non-ruling official should ensure that the non-ruling team is aware of the type of time-out being granted.
4. Within the reporting area, then signal the type of time-out being granted, Signal 11 for a 60-second time-out and Signal 12 for a 30-second time-out. Verbally indicate the team color, verbally and visually give the player number or head coach (indicate by forming the shape of a "C" with the hand) making the request. Allow players reasonable time to get to their time-out areas, then point to the timer and verbally instruct the timer to begin the time-out period.
5. Notify a coach when that team has used its allotted time-outs.

INJURY/BLOOD:

1. If a player is injured, an officials' time-out shall be declared when necessary. When appropriate, bench personnel should be beckoned at the first opportunity. If bench personnel enters the court (beckoned or not), the injured player must leave the game

until the next opportunity to re-enter by rule (game clock properly starts) unless a time-out is requested and granted by that player's team.

2. Officials should not touch an injured player.
3. Any player who exhibits signs, symptoms or behaviors consistent with a concussion (such as loss of consciousness, headache, dizziness, confusion or balance problems) shall be immediately removed from the game by the officials and shall not return to play until cleared by an appropriate health care professional.
4. If a player is apparently bleeding, has an open wound, an excessive amount of blood on the uniform or has blood on their person, that player shall be directed to leave the game and may not re-enter until the bleeding/blood has been taken care of. The same re-entry procedures as above apply.

60-SECOND TIME-OUT

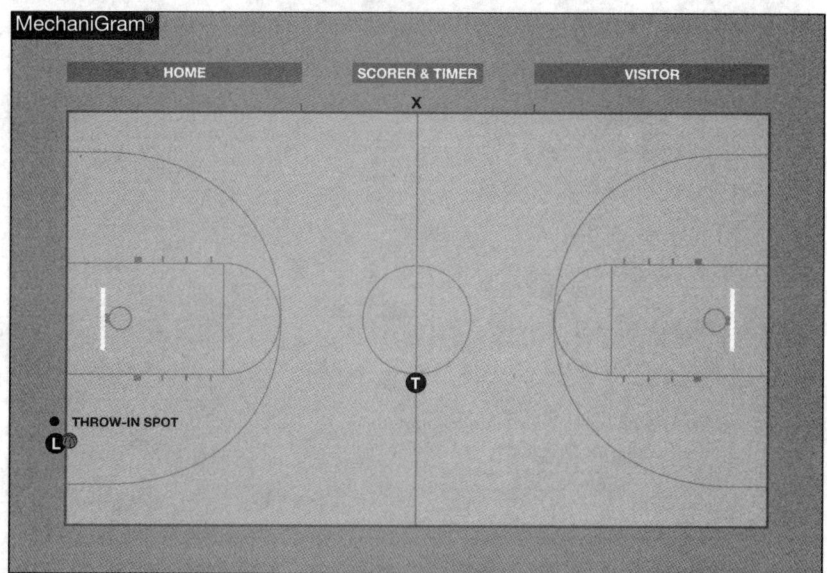

During any time-out, the administering official should take the ball to where it will be put in play. If that official needs to leave the administering spot, that official should have the partner hold the ball at the throw-in spot where play will resume. If play is to be resumed near the scorer's table or team benches, move straight out onto the floor in line with the other official. If play is to be resumed with a free throw, take a position on the free-throw line, in line with the partner.

During a 60-second time-out, the non-administering official should be on the division line on the circle farthest from the team benches. That official is responsible for beckoning substitutes into the game and should be prepared to give the scorer or timer any necessary information. During any time-out, the officials should remain in good posture and be alert.

If activity on the court makes it necessary to move, the officials should move to a safe location and move back to the designated spots at the conclusion of the activity.

At the first horn (15 seconds remaining), the non-administering official will step toward the nearest team huddle and notify that team by raising an index finger and saying "first horn," before moving to the other team horn to repeat the process.

30-SECOND TIME-OUT

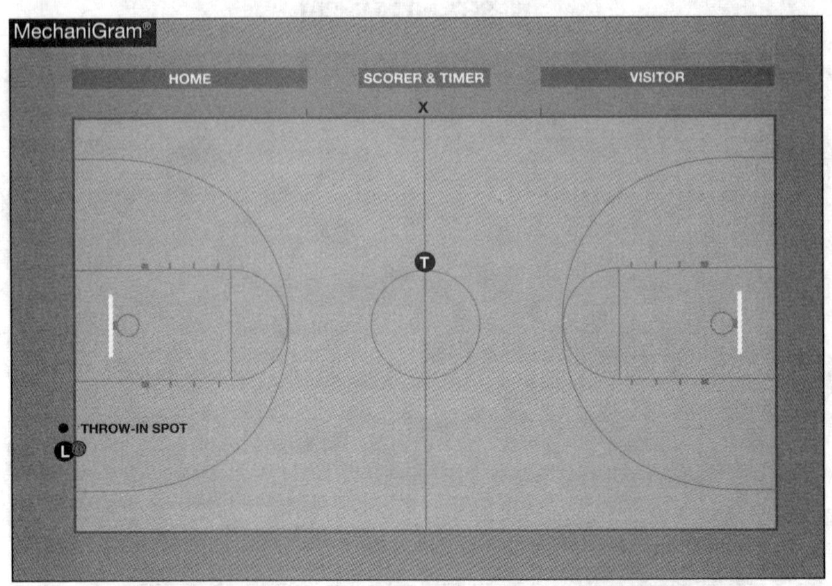

During a 30-second time-out, officials will use the same mechanics as a 60-second time-out with the following differences:

• The non-administering official shall be on the division line on the circle closest to the team benches.

• By rule, players shall remain standing for the duration of and no on-court entertainment shall occur during a 30-second time-out.

4.2 Jump Ball

AFTER INTRODUCTIONS, BEFORE JUMP BALL

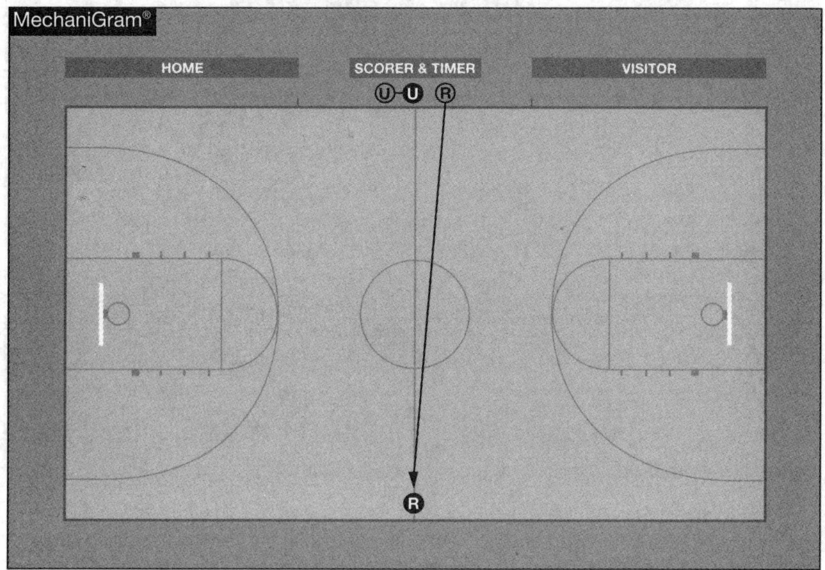

After the National Anthem and the introductions of the players, the players are usually getting last words of instruction before going out onto the court. At that time, the officials should leave their positions at the scorer's table and go to specific locations on the court. The R (or the official designated to throw the jump ball) takes the ball and moves to a spot near the far sideline, facing the scorer's table.

The U shall take a position on the table side sideline, at the division line, facing the R.

Note: The R can toss the jump ball or designate the U. Within this manual, the official tossing the ball will always be referred to as the R. Even though the R may designate a tosser, the R will handle all ensuing throw-ins to start the remaining periods.

POSITIONING

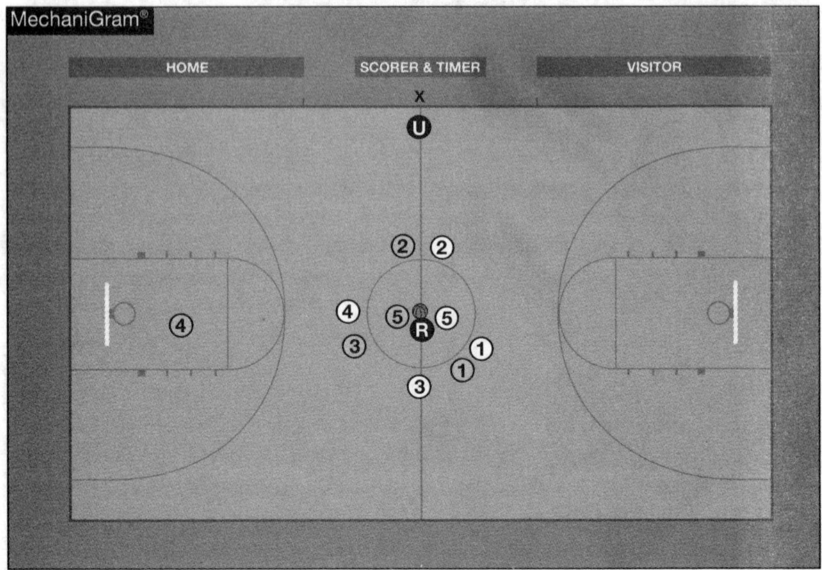

The U (or non-tosser) is positioned near the intersection of the sideline and the division line facing the R directly in front of the table. Before entering the Center restraining circle, the R makes eye contact with the U, who signals to the R that table personnel and the U are ready to go. Both officials make sure the teams are facing the correct direction, count the number of players of both teams and ensure the game clock is properly set.

While still outside the circle, the R notifies both team captains that play is about to begin. The R then verbally states the jersey color of each team and indicates the direction of its goal for the first half. The R blows the whistle with a sharp blast before entering the circle, then removes the whistle from the mouth prior to tossing the ball.

Before the toss, the U uses the "stop clock" signal (Signal 2). The R tosses the ball high enough so the jumpers tap the ball on its downward flight. The U starts the clock when the ball is legally touched. If the toss is poor, either official should immediately sound the whistle, signal the game clock should not start and re-administer the jump ball.

The U must maintain a wide field of vision while the R administers the toss. The U is primarily responsible for the position and action of the eight non-jumpers. The R is primarily responsible for the position and action of the two jumpers.

JUMP BALL GOES TO R'S LEFT

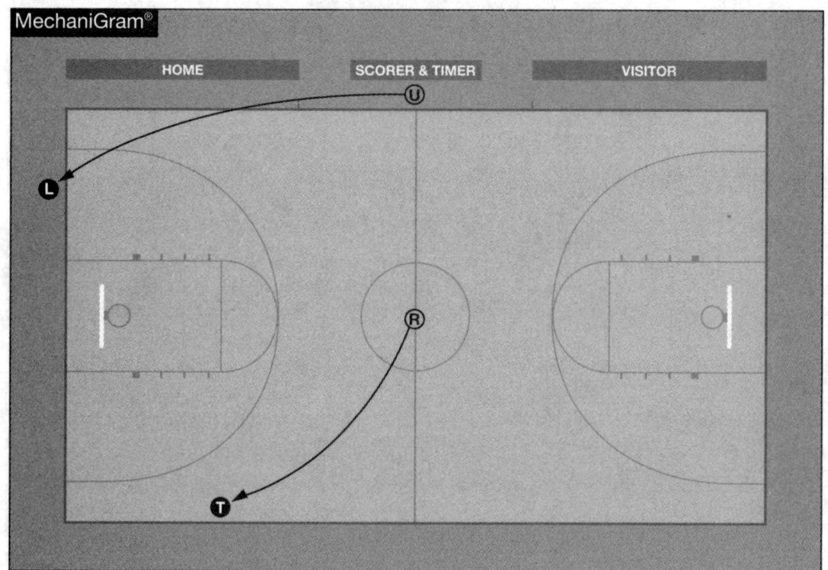

If the ball goes to the R's left, the U will move to U's right and become the Lead. The Lead should be prepared to rule on a quick three-point attempt from anywhere on the court until the R has cleared the players and begun to move into position.

The R will hold momentarily to allow players to clear and then will move to the Trail enabling coverage of the sideline opposite the Lead.

After the ball is possessed, the Trail should glance at the alternating-possession arrow to make sure it is pointing in the right direction. If incorrect, the crew will wait for the first dead ball and correct it.

Note: If possession is gained in the backcourt, the U may need to move with the ball to become the Trail. If that happens, the R would then move to the Lead position.

JUMP BALL GOES TO R'S RIGHT

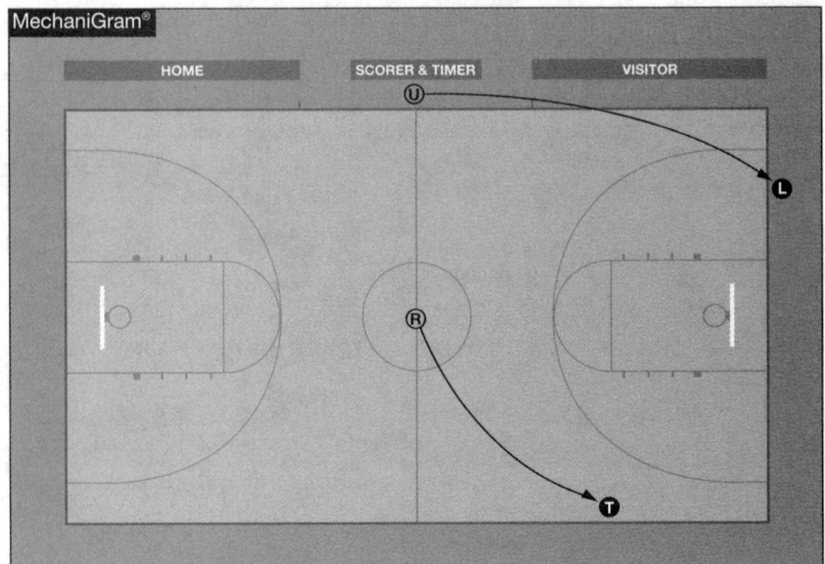

If the ball goes to the R's right, U will move to the left and become the Lead. The Lead should be prepared to rule on a quick three-point attempt anywhere on the court until the R has cleared the players and begun to move into position.

The R will hold momentarily to allow players to clear and then will move to the Trail enabling coverage of the sideline opposite the Lead. After the ball is possessed, the Trail should glance at the alternating-possession arrow to make sure it is pointing in the right direction. If incorrect, wait for the first dead ball and correct it.

Note: If possession is gained in the backcourt, the U may need to move with the ball to become the Trail. If that happens, the R would then move to the Lead position.

4.3 Court Coverage

BASIC FRONTCOURT COVERAGE

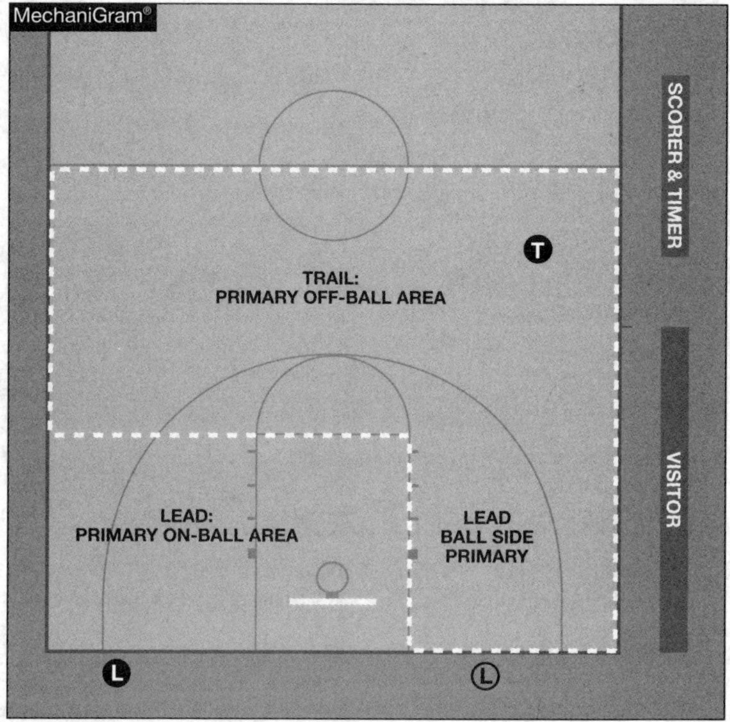

In the frontcourt, PCAs shift depending on which official is on-ball. In general, the officials will work to keep all players "boxed in."

In the MechaniGram, the Lead's on-ball responsibilities include the area below the free-throw line extended to the far edge of the free-throw lane line (away from the Lead) when the Lead is opposite the Trail. If the Lead is ball side, the Lead's area of responsibility grows. It includes the area below the free-throw line extended to the three-point arc.

When the Lead is on-ball, the Trail's off-ball responsibilities include the area above the free-throw line extended to the division line and the lane area from the free-throw lane line (nearest the Trail) to the sideline nearest the Trail. The Trail's off-ball area of responsibility decreases when the Lead is on-ball, ball side. It is the area above the free-throw line extended and outside the three-point arc.

Five-Second Closely-Guarded Count: Officials are responsible for a silent and visible five-second closely-guarded (within 6 feet) count (Signal 9) within their PCA. During this count, if the ball moves out of an official's PCA, that official shall maintain the count until the count is appropriately ended. Anytime a count restarts (going directly from a holding to a dribbling count or a dribbling to a holding count), the official shall switch hands/arms.

HALFCOURT BOUNDARY LINE

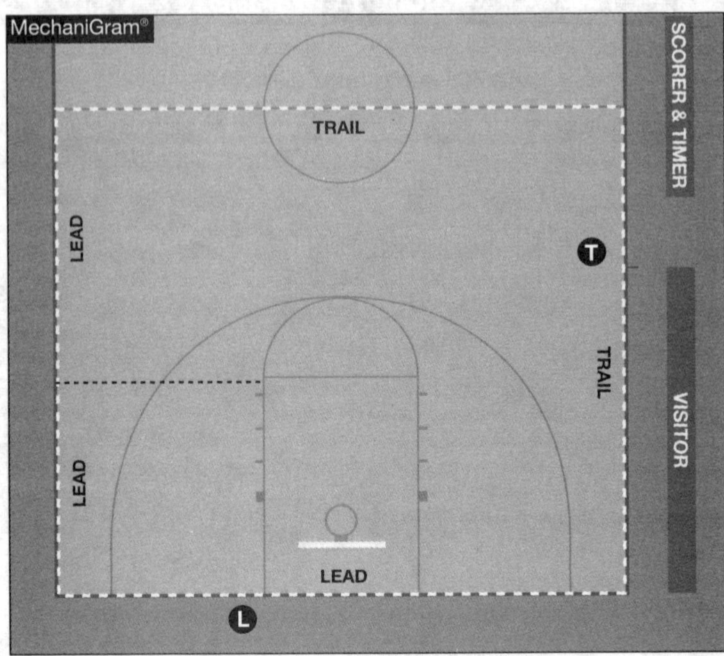

Covering boundary lines is among the most difficult tasks using a crew of two officials. In emphasizing off-ball coverage for the Lead, it can become difficult for the Lead to officiate the Lead's sideline.

The Lead is primarily responsible for the nearer frontcourt end line and and nearer sideline as shown above. The Trail is primarily responsible for the nearer sideline and is responsible for ruling on all possible backcourt violations at the division line. In addition, in the event of a quick transition, the Trail is also responsible for the end line at the other end.

If the ball goes out of bounds and the covering official needs help, that official should first stop the clock (Signal 2) and look in the direction of the other official and verbalize "help." If the non-ruling official has definite knowledge, that official will verbally and visually signal the appropriate ruling (no conference between officials). The primary official will then mirror this information.

If the non-ruling official has definite information regarding an out-of-bounds ruling that has been made by a partner, the non-ruling official goes to the ruling official and provides the additional information. If the ruling official makes the decision to change the ruling, the ruling official is the one to sound the whistle and signal the change.

One particular item of note is when the ball goes out of bounds above the free-throw line extended on the Lead's sideline. While the Lead has primary responsibility of this area, the Trail must be aware of the situation and be ready to provide assistance, if needed. Officials should pregame the situations in which a non-responsible official should approach the ruling official.

THREE-POINT RESPONSIBILITIES

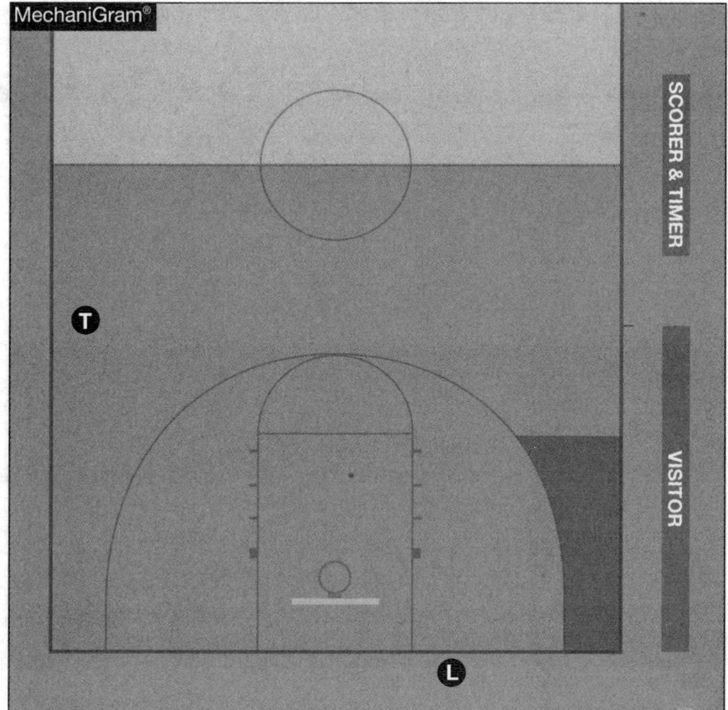

In the frontcourt, the Trail is responsible for the majority of the three-point arc. The Trail's coverage of a three-point try extends to the free-throw line extended opposite of the Trail's current position. The Lead is responsible for any attempt below the free-throw line extended on the Lead's PCA of the court.

On three-point attempts, only the covering official should indicate the attempt (Signal 18). The indication should be made with the arm closest to the center of the court so the table personnel can see it better. The covering official should also signal if the attempt is successful (Signal 18).

If the Trail signals a successful three-point attempt, the Lead shall not mirror the successful signal. If the Lead signals an attempt, which is successful, the Trail mirrors the successful signal. There is no need to mirror an attempt signal. This is imperative since the covering official signaling the attempt is also primarily responsible for monitoring the airborne shooting player's return to the floor.

The Lead should be ready to assist the Trail on a three-point attempt in transition.

HANDLING DOUBLE WHISTLES

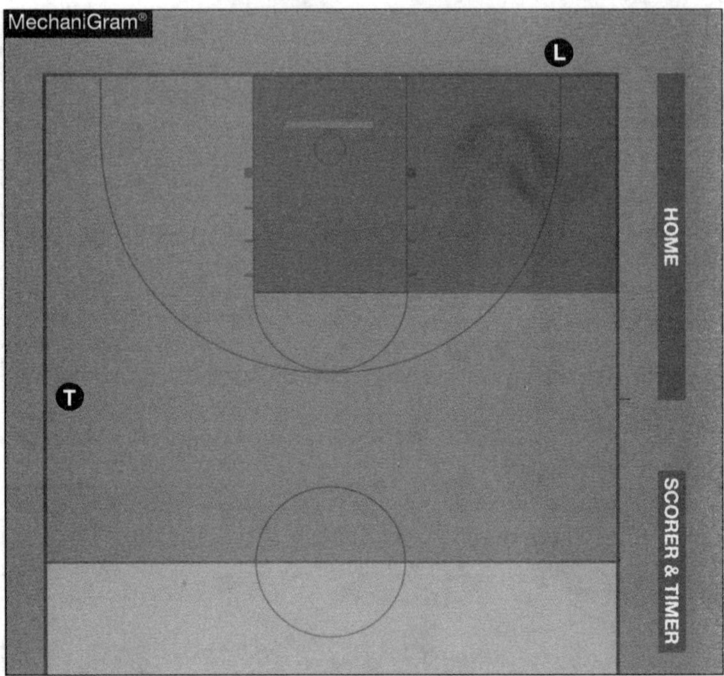

While coverage areas for all officials are well-defined, there can be areas on the court that occasionally are watched by more than one official — typically where PCAs intersect. Generally, the official who has primary coverage at the time of the whistles should make the ruling.

If the secondary official has a ruling that occurred before the primary official's ruling or has information that should be discussed with the primary official, the secondary official should close into the play quickly toward the primary official.

Only if necessary should the officials come together to discuss the play. Generally, the decision on the final ruling should be left to the primary area official.

Keys to managing double-whistles:

1. Give the "stop clock" signal (Signal 2) and refrain from giving an immediate preliminary signal.
2. Make good eye contact with each other.
3. Understand where the play originated.
4. Understand each position's PCA.

PASS/CRASH IN LANE

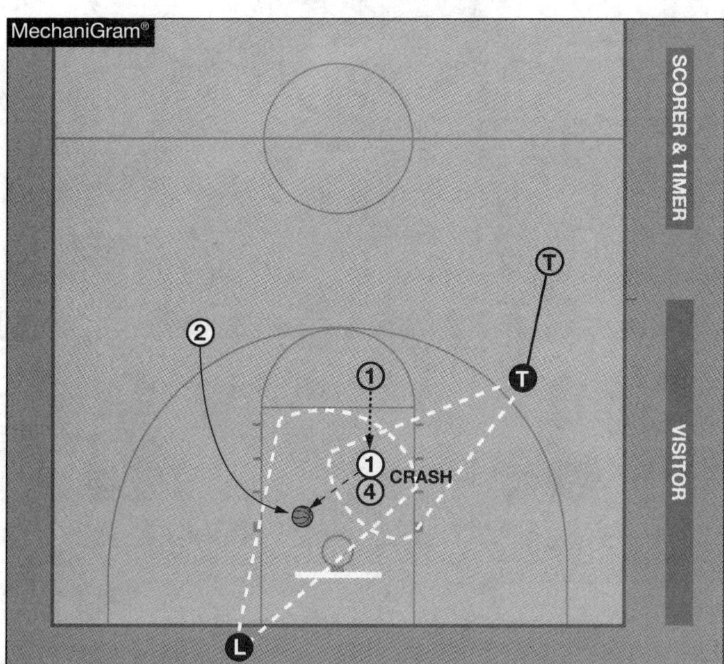

Drives to the basket when the ball handler passes the ball to a teammate then crashes into a defender below the free throw line are known as "pass and crash" situations.

In general, when a player is driving to the basket with the ball from an official's PCA, that official has primarily responsibility for that player and the ball all the way to the basket – even if the drive moves into the other official's primary area.

In addition, on drives to the basket initiated on the Trail side of the court, if the ball handler makes a pass, the Trail stays with the "crash" and Lead takes the "pass."

The official with primary responsibility of the play must be given the opportunity to make an initial ruling first. This does not preclude the non-covering official from make a ruling, but a delayed response is warranted.

REBOUNDING AREAS

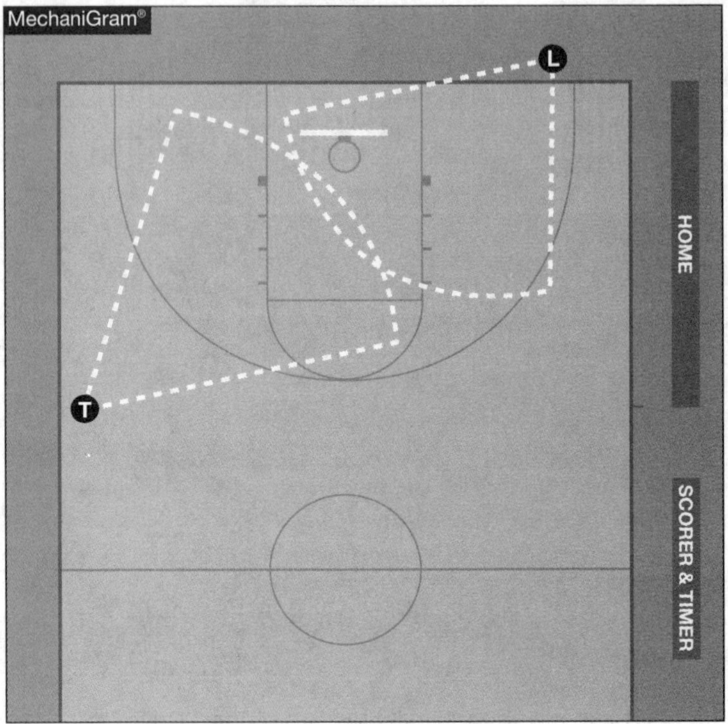

Rebounding coverages are divided and fall into primary and secondary coverage areas. If a try is attempted in the Trail's PCA, the Trail is primarily responsible for following the airborne shooter's return to the floor. After clearing the shooter's return, the Trail is primarily responsible for basket interference/goaltending and perimeter rebound coverage.

The Lead is primarily responsible for all other rebounding action. Both officials maintain secondary responsibility for rebound outside of their primary responsibility and should be prepared to rule as such.

OFFICIATING THE DELAY OFFENSE

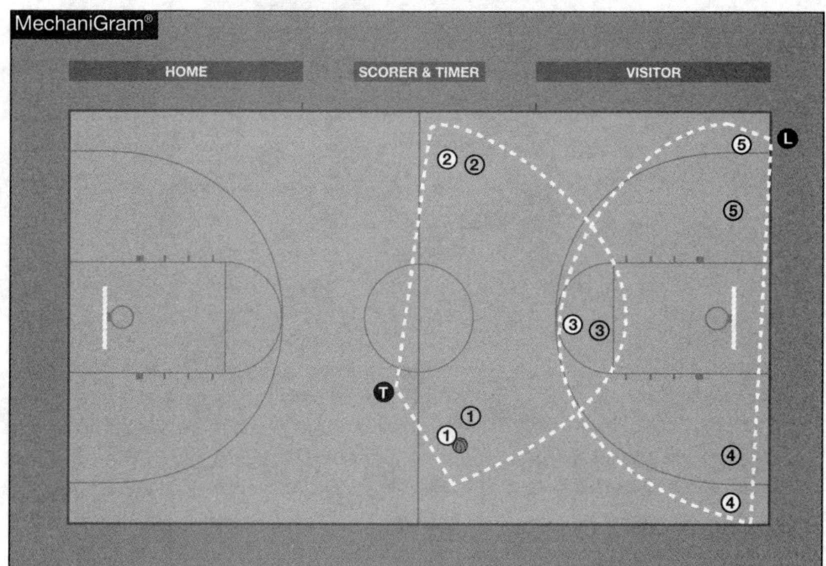

The delay offense, sometimes referred to as the "spread" or "four-corner" offense requires officials to change their basic positions. The delay offense spreads players out to all corners of the frontcourt and is designed to run the clock down while avoiding double teams.

The Trail must be behind the offense. The Lead must move around the corner to monitor lateral movement. The Lead can move across the corner to monitor the action near the basket.

LAST-SECOND SHOT

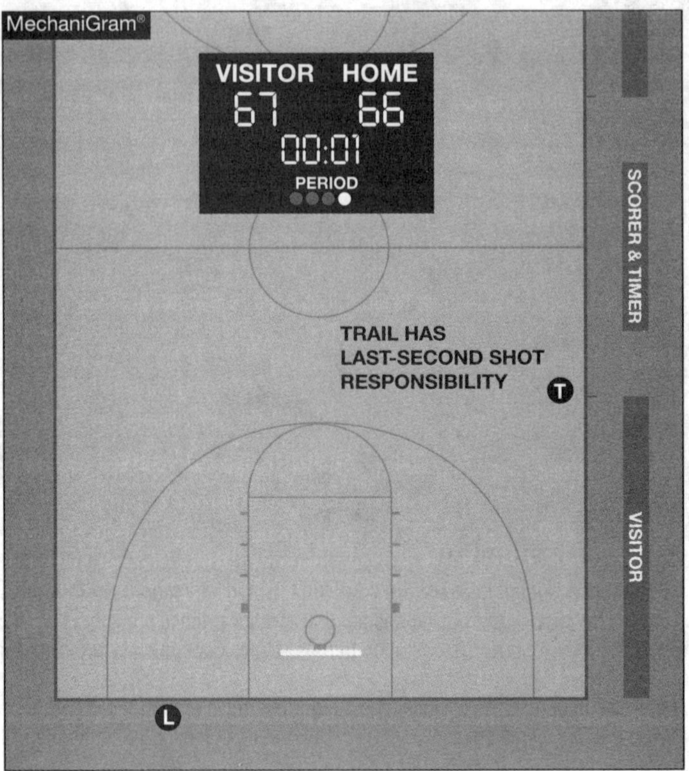

With less than one minute remaining on the game clock in each quarter/period, both officials should communicate this by raising one arm straight above the head and extending one finger in the air.

Regardless of the end of the court, the Trail official is responsible for making the ruling on any last-second shot and should communicate this to the Lead by signaling with a hand-on-chest signal when the game clock is near 15 seconds. This signal should be repeated when the responsibility changes between officials on any change of possession.

When there is a throw-in from the backcourt a long pass is expected, the Lead should be prepared to assist, especially if the shot attempt is near the three-point line. If the Lead (non-ruling official) has information regarding the allowing or disallowing of a goal, the Lead should go directly to the Trail (ruling official) for a brief discussion. Ultimately, the R will make the final decision in case of disagreement, or in rare instances, the table officials may be consulted in the event the horn did not sound or could not be heard.

When play is resumed with a throw-in or free throw and three-tenths of a second or less remains on the game clock, no field goal may be scored by a try for goal. Only a tap may score. This does not apply if the game clock does not display tenths of a second.

4.4 The Lead Position

GENERAL POSITIONING

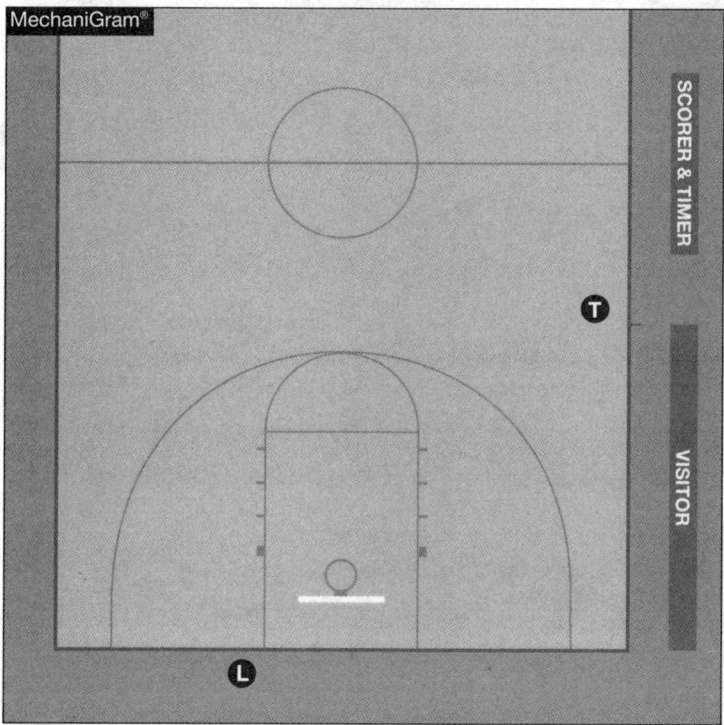

The Lead's base position is approximately four feet off the end line. Officials may need to adjust their depth as the Lead based on their own comfort level.

In general, the Lead should always remain off the end line and should not be wider than the three-point line and will move along the end line based on the movement and location of players.

As the ball crosses to the Trail's side of the court, the Lead should close down to be located just outside the lane line extended.

BALL-SIDE MECHANICS

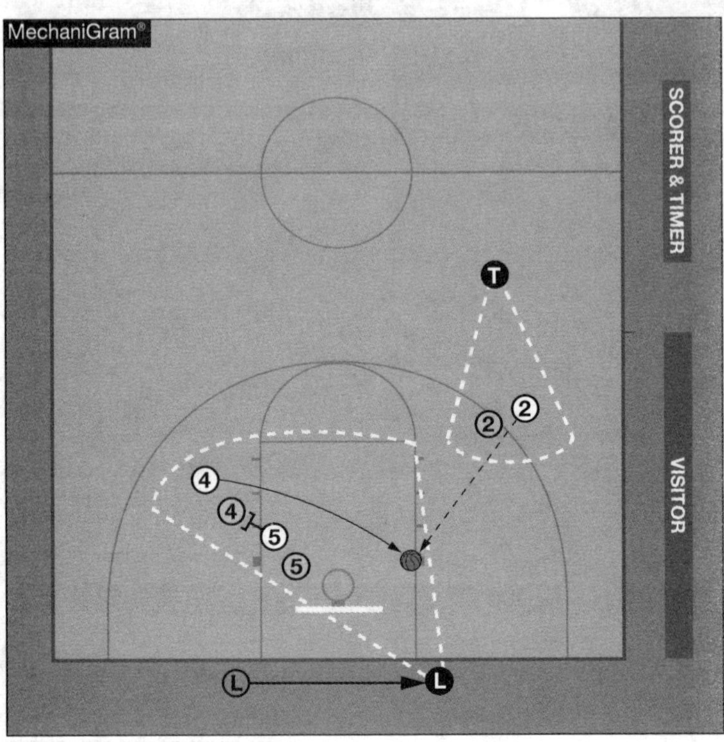

The use of ball-side mechanics are dependent upon the location of players and the ball. When the majority of players and the ball are on the Trail's side, below the free-throw line extended, the Lead should close-down toward the near lane line.

Moving across the lane is a similar rotation used in a crew of three. If the Lead reads a possible play below the free-throw line extended on the Lead's side of the court (quick try or drive excluded), this dictates the need for the Lead to rotate over. Movement by the Lead across the lane should be brisk and with purpose. Even when moving across the lane, the Lead must continue to officiate players in the post. The Lead should work to not be caught under the basket as play moves there.

This temporary rotation is to assist the Trail in covering the bottom of the Trail's PCA. When action moves outside of this area or if a turnover occurs, the Lead should return across the lane.

BALL-SIDE MECHANIC: MOVEMENT AFTER SUCCESSFUL GOAL

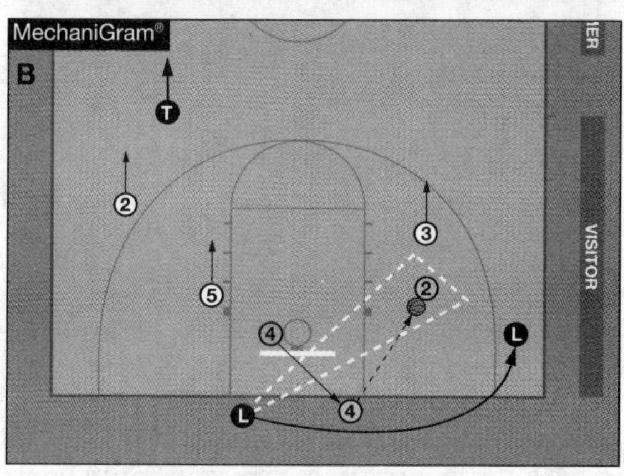

When the Lead is ball side watching action in the post and a goal is scored, there is no need to rush back to the lane line opposite the Trail and balance the floor. If the Lead can immediately balance the floor after the successful goal without interfering with the ensuing throw-in, the Lead should do so. However, in most situations, there is not enough time to balance the floor without interfering and missing action.

The Lead should watch for players interfering with the ball after the successful goal. The Lead watches the player collect the ball and move out-of-bounds for the throw-in. Finally, the Lead watches the thrower, the throw-in and action on the court. It is acceptable to do this from the Trail side of the court before transitioning back to the far sideline.

In MechaniGram A, the Lead is ball side watching the post players when Team A makes a jump shot. Team B grabs the ball and moves out-of-bounds for a throw-in. The Lead does not have enough time to balance the floor before the throw-in. In MechaniGram B, Team B is out-of-bounds and throws a quick inbounds pass. The Lead, still on the opposite side, watches the thrower and throw-in, then quickly swings behind the thrower to balance the floor.

MOVEMENT TOWARD SIDELINE

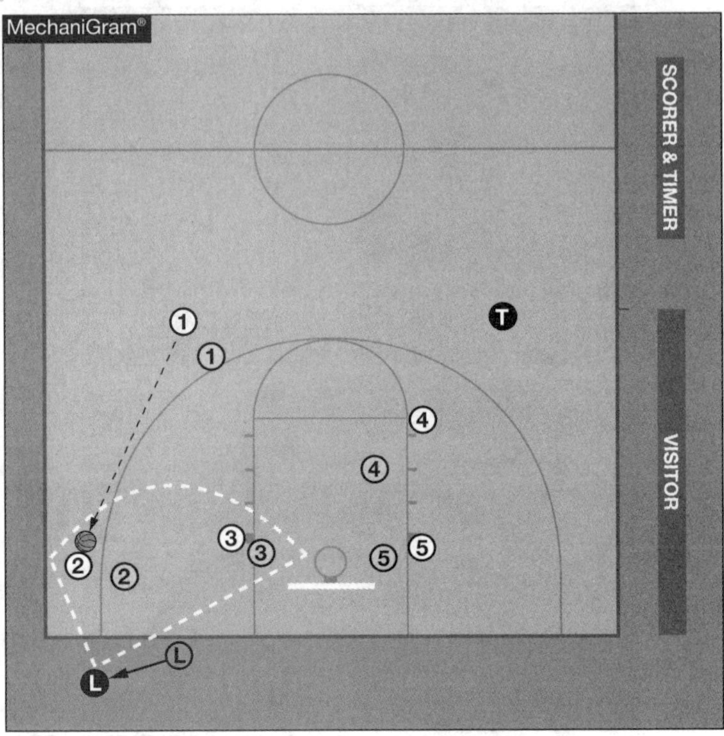

When the ball drops below the free-throw line extended on the Lead's side of the court, the Lead has two responsibilities: Watch the post players on the near low block and watch the perimeter player with the ball.

To best cover this area, the Lead should back off the end line and move toward the sideline. The Lead's shoulders should not be parallel to the end line and angle them slightly; that movement increases the Lead's field of vision and gives the Lead a chance to see both areas.

Primary coverage is on-ball; secondary coverage is off-ball. With that improved position, the Lead has a chance to see both in this field of view.

4.5 The Trail Position

GENERAL POSITIONING

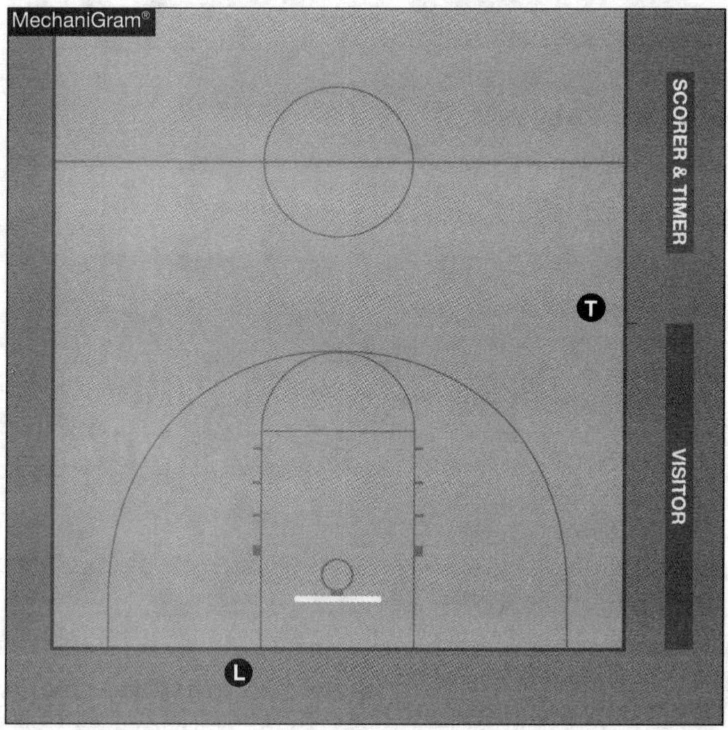

The Trail's home position is at or above the top of the semi-circle (three-point line) and along, or just inside, the sideline.

The Trail should be prepared to "officiate the arc" to obtain better angles on play, but must be mindful of passing lanes. The Trail may move down toward the end line to obtain a better angle, as needed.

INSIDE-OUT LOOK

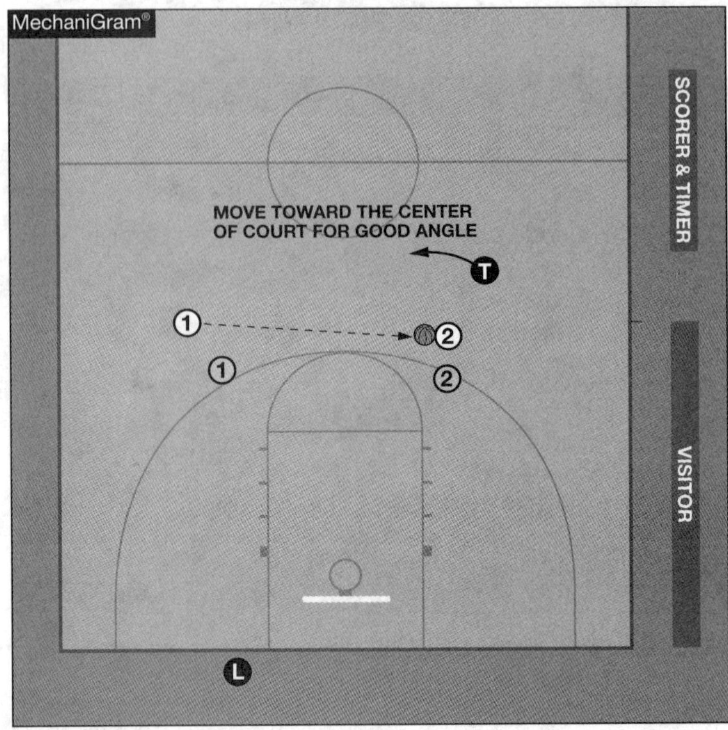

With a crew of two officials, the Trail official often has to get off the sideline and move toward the center of the court to officiate action on the far side of the floor. When that happens, the Trail can get caught in the middle on a swing pass from one side of the court to the other. Adjustments must be made.

When a swing pass moves from the sideline opposite the Trail across the top of the semi-circle (three-point line) to the near-side wing, the Trail can get straightlined because of the position off the sideline.

By using a "move to improve" approach, a simple one- or two-step adjustment toward the Center of the court gives the Trail the proper angle. The Trail must fight the urge to run around the entire play toward the sideline, using countless and inefficient steps.

MOVEMENT OFF SIDELINE

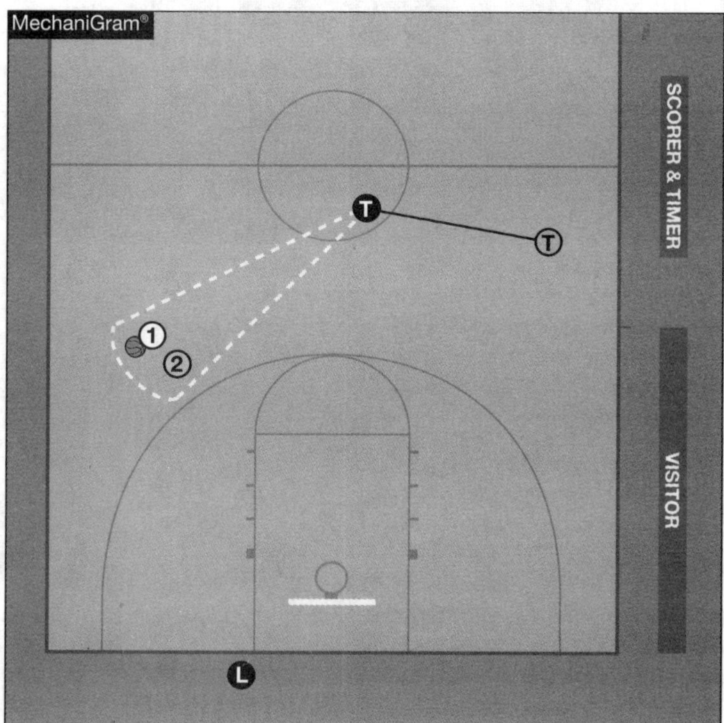

Effective court coverage requires significant movement by the Trail.

When an offensive player has the ball on the side of the floor opposite the Trail, the Trail must move away from the near sideline and get proper angles. By staying too close to the near sideline, the Trail cannot effectively see action near the ball and must make judgments from a distance — way too far away to convince anyone the Trail saw the play correctly.

In the MechaniGram, the player with the ball is far away from the Trail official — though the player is still the Trail's responsibility — and there is defensive pressure. To see the play well, the Trail must move off the near sideline and work to get a good angle.

Avoid moving straight toward the play: Officials could interfere with the play by stepping into a passing lane. Take an angle toward the division line to decrease the chances of interfering with the play. In extreme cases, officials may even position themselves in the backcourt.

By moving off the sideline and angling toward the backcourt, officials are in a much better position to see the play.

MOVEMENT ON JUMP SHOT

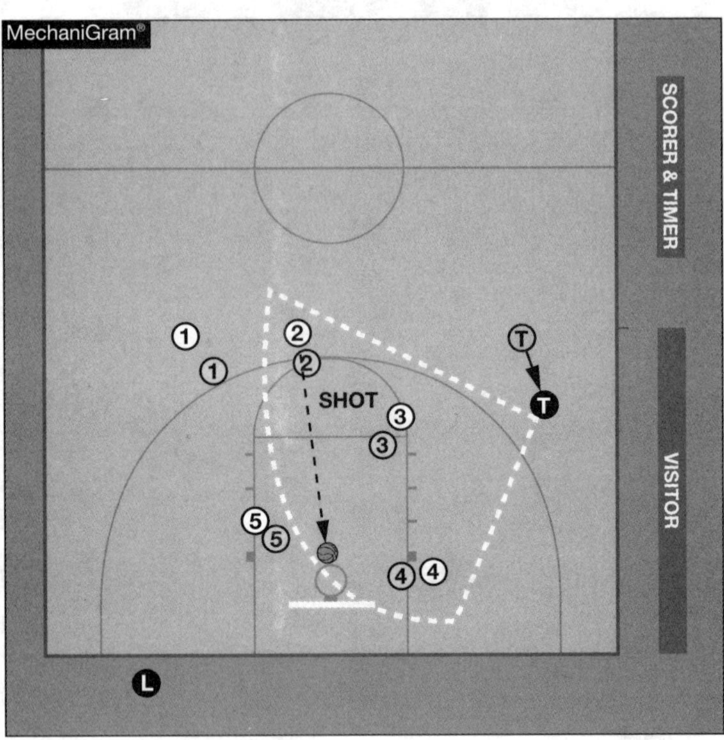

The Trail has more responsibilities than simply watching the shooter. Too often, a shot goes up and the Trail's first thought is to start moving to the other end of the floor to avoid getting beat down court. When the Trail leaves, the Lead is left with offensive players crashing the boards and defensive players doing all they can to grab the rebound.

The Trail must help with rebounding action. When a player takes a jump shot within the Trail's coverage area, the first responsibility is to watch the airborne shooter all the way back to the floor to ensure there are no offensive or defensive fouls. While watching that action, the Trail should be moving a couple of steps toward the end line.

Once everything is okay with the shooter and surrounding action, the steps toward the end line allow the Trail to help the Lead by watching rebounding action. A step or two to improve an official's angle is all that is necessary to successfully watch rebounding action. The Trail is likely to see an offensive player pushing (or crashing into) a defensive player from behind — something that is difficult for the Lead to see from the end line. The Trail should avoid going below the free-throw line extended.

Resist the urge to sprint to the other end of the floor when the shot goes up. Move toward the end line to get rebounding angles.

TRAIL PICKS UP SHOOTER

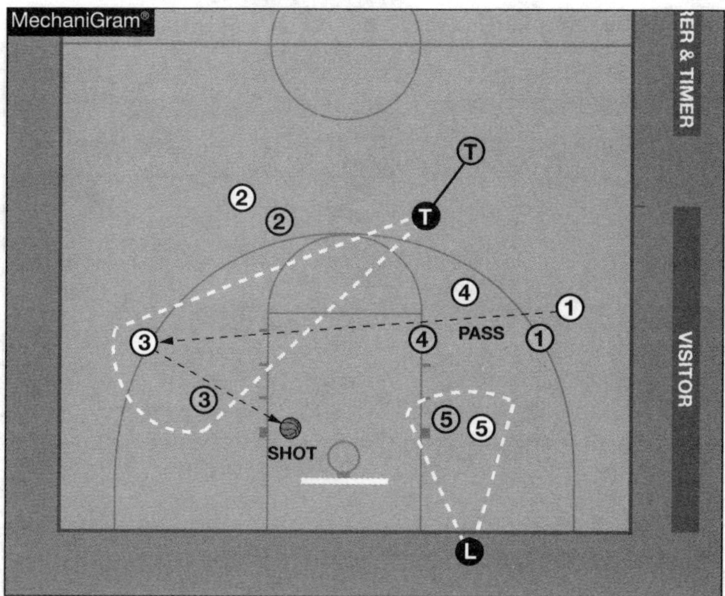

In two-person mechanics, the Lead official should move to the ball side of the lane when the player with the ball is below the free-throw line extended and a potential post pass is evident.

Though ball-side mechanics are effective for controlling post play, one weakness is coverage of a skip pass to the opposite wing player for a quick shot. A skip pass is a quick pass from one side of the floor to the other, designed to take advantage of a sagging defense.

Though the opposite wing player is primarily observed by the Lead official (even though the Lead moved ball side), when a skip pass occurs the Trail should adjust a step or two toward the wing player (to the center of the floor) and get a good angle to rule on three-point attempts, fouls and possibly obvious out-of-bounds infractions. Though a long-distance look, that is better than having the Lead guess because the Lead's looking through lane traffic or sprinting head-down to the other side of the court and missing the banging going on in the post.

If there is no quick shot and the Lead can adjust back to the other side of the court without haste, the Lead then picks up the ball (assuming it is below the free-throw line extended) and the Trail moves back toward the sideline, getting good angles to watch off-ball. The Lead must continue to watch off-ball in the lane area while moving until completely across the lane and in a good position to pick up the player with the ball.

In the MechaniGram, the Lead has moved ball side when a skip pass is thrown and that player immediately shoots. Since the Lead is ball side and does not have enough time to balance the floor, the Trail picks up the shot, even though the attempt is below the free-throw line extended. The Trail should close down toward the play to improve the angle.

TRAIL WORKS BACKSIDE

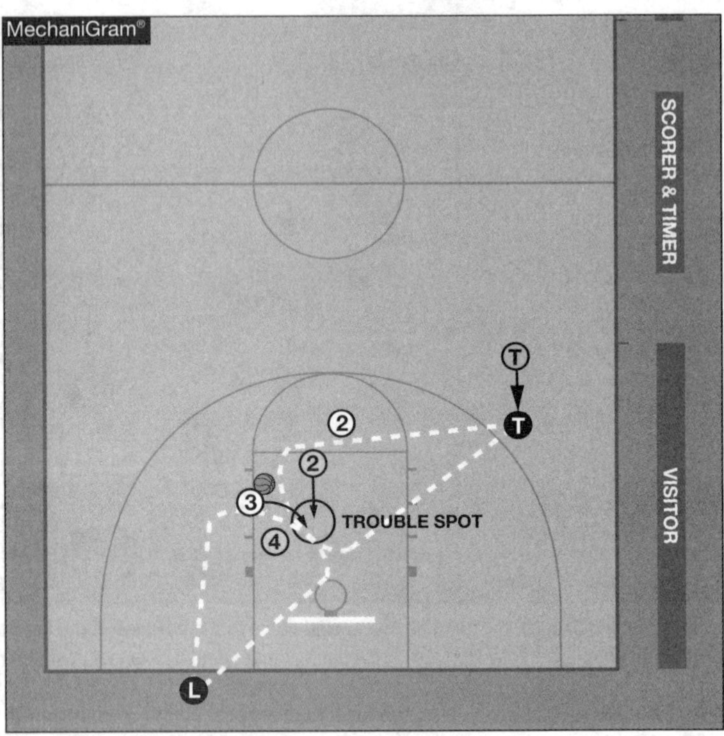

A trouble spot for the Lead develops when a player with the ball on the low block spins toward the middle of the lane away from the Lead. The quick spin move often leaves the Lead straightlined and without a good look on the play.

Many times, a defender near the free-throw line will drop down into the lane and challenge the move toward the basket. That is when an official will commonly see that defender slap at the offensive player, trying to poke the ball away. That steal attempt is sometimes a foul — one that goes unseen by the now-straightlined Lead.

The Trail must help out and watch the area in the lane when a post player spins away from the Lead. Commonly referred to as the Lead's "backside," the Trail has a much better look at the play after penetrating toward the end line for an improved angle.

In the MechaniGram, the post player has the ball on the low block in front of the Lead. That player spins toward the middle of the lane and drives toward the basket. The defender drops down and attempts the steal. The Lead watches the post-up action and the initial spin move. The Trail should close down toward the end line, gets a good angle and watches the perimeter defender on the play. The Lead's backside is protected.

If the Trail sees a foul, the Trail should come in with a strong ruling. This is done by moving toward the action to cut down the distance on the play.

TRAIL LOOKS WEAKSIDE

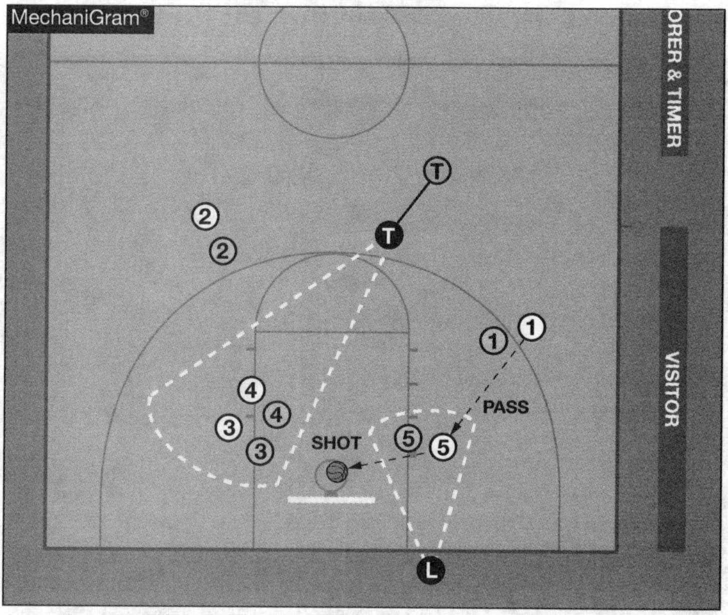

MechaniGram®

ORER & TIMER

VISITOR

PASS

SHOT

There are many benefits of the Lead moving ball side for post action. One potential problem, however, is weak-side rebounding action. With the Lead on the same side of the floor as the Trail, the lane area opposite both officials can present problems.

With the Lead ball side and already watching post play near the closest lane line, it is difficult for the Lead to watch players away from that area in the lane. First, primary concentration is — and should be — on the post play. Second, it is difficult for the Lead to see the opposite side of the lane because the Lead is looking through lane congestion and is easily straightlined.

When the Lead moves ball side, it is the Trail's responsibility to observe weak-side rebounding action. Though somewhat of a long-distance look, with the proper close down toward the end line to get a good angle the Trail can effectively watch weak-side rebounding action.

In the MechaniGram, the Trail watches the perimeter player deliver a drop pass to the post player, who has effectively posted up on the low block. The Lead already moved ball side anticipating the play. The post player seals off the defender and pivots strongly to the basket. The Lead watches the post-up action.

Anticipating the play, the Trail adjusts for a good angle and looks opposite. From that spot, the Trail can look through the lane and watch the players battle on the weakside for rebounding positioning.

If the Trail sees a foul on the weakside, the Trail should come in with a strong ruling. This is done by moving toward the action to cut down the distance on the play.

4.6 Transitions

BUMP AND RUN

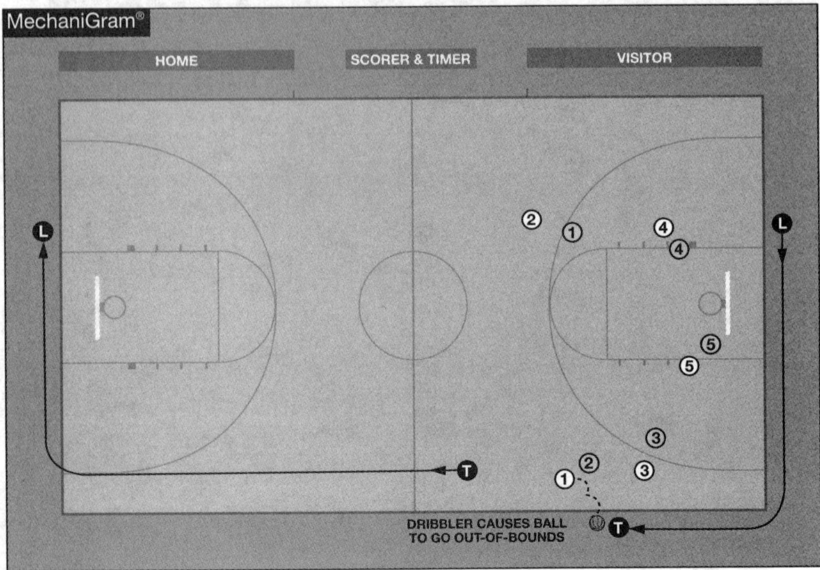

The bump-and-run is a mechanic used by two-person crews to move swiftly from the frontcourt after a violation.

When an offensive violation occurs in the Trail's coverage area, the Trail stops the clock, signals the violation and the direction of play, then points to the designated spot for the throw-in. Next – after checking that there are no problems – the Trail hustles down court while viewing the action behind and become the new Lead.

After seeing the Trail's signals, the Lead will move toward the designated spot for the throw-in. The Lead becomes the new Trail. The Lead "bumps" the Trail down court and the Trail moving to Lead "runs" the floor.

In the MechaniGram, Team A causes the ball to go out-of-bounds. The Trail correctly stops the clock, signals a violation and the direction, then communicates the throw-in spot to the Lead. The Trail then moves down court and becomes the new Lead.

The bump-and-run serves two main purposes: The Trail official has a better chance of avoiding problems near the violation and the officials move into place quicker and get the ball live faster.

THE MOVEMENT OFF SIDELINE

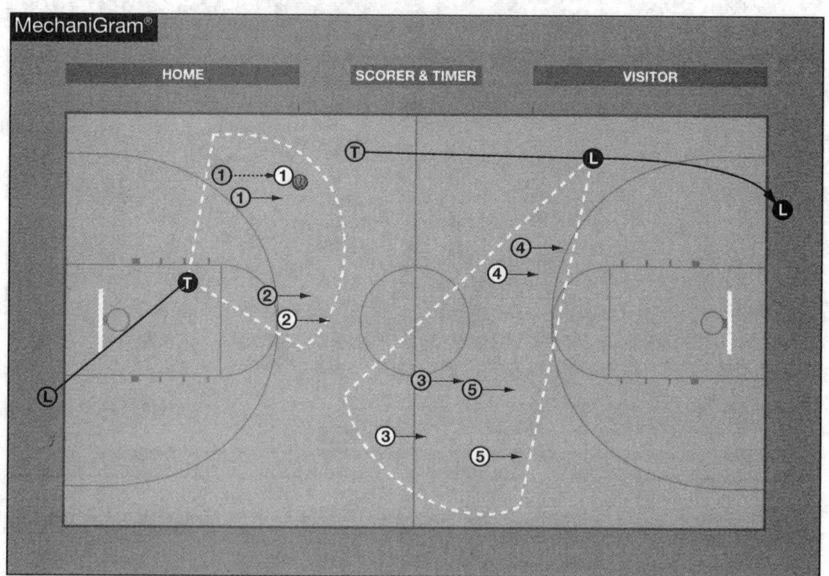

Effective two-person court coverage requires significant movement by the Trail off the sideline. The same philosophies are true in the transition game when play is moving from the backcourt to the frontcourt.

When an offensive player has the ball on the side of the floor opposite the Trail, the Trail must move away from the near sideline and get proper angles. By staying too close to the near sideline, the Trail cannot effectively see action near the ball and must make judgments from a distance — way too far to convince anyone the Trail saw the play correctly.

In the MechaniGram, the offense dribbles the ball upcourt opposite the new Trail as defensive pressure is applied. The rest of the players are advancing to the frontcourt as the new Lead watches off-ball. To see the play well, the new Trail must move far off the near sideline and work to get a good angle.

The new Trail should maintain distance and avoid moving straight toward the play as to not interfere with the play by stepping into a passing lane.

By moving off the sideline and angling toward the play, the official is in a much better position to see the play.

LEAD HELPS IN BACKCOURT

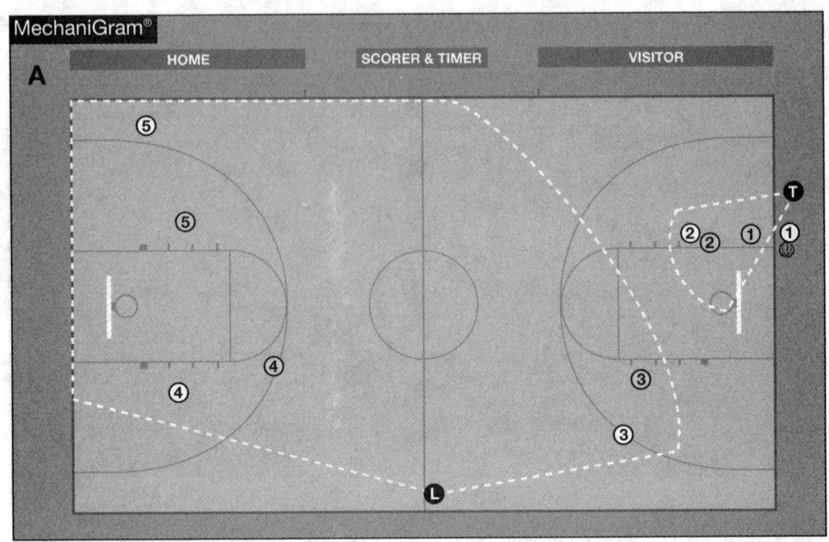

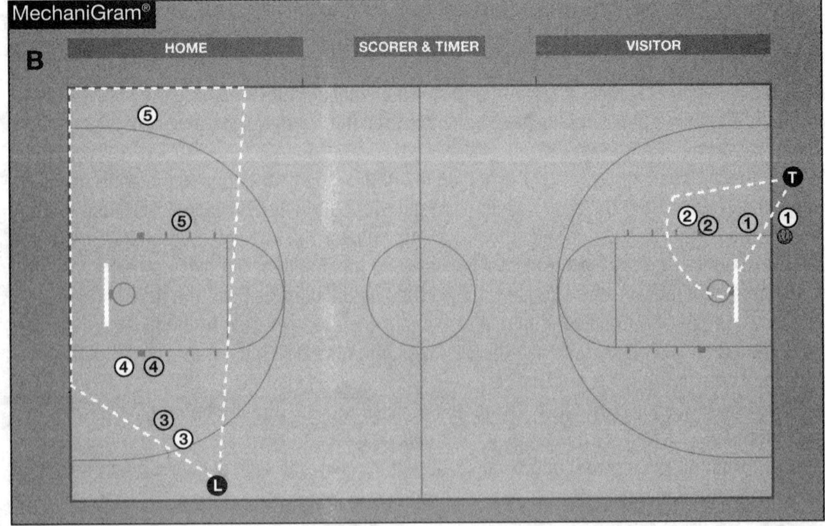

In MechaniGram A, there are six players in the backcourt. The Lead is positioned near the division line to help with backcourt players away from the Trail. The Lead must also watch players in the frontcourt.

In MechaniGram B, there are four players in the backcourt. The Trail is responsible for all of those players. The Lead moves into the frontcourt and watches all players there, eventually moving to the frontcourt end line.

PASS/CRASH IN TRANSITION

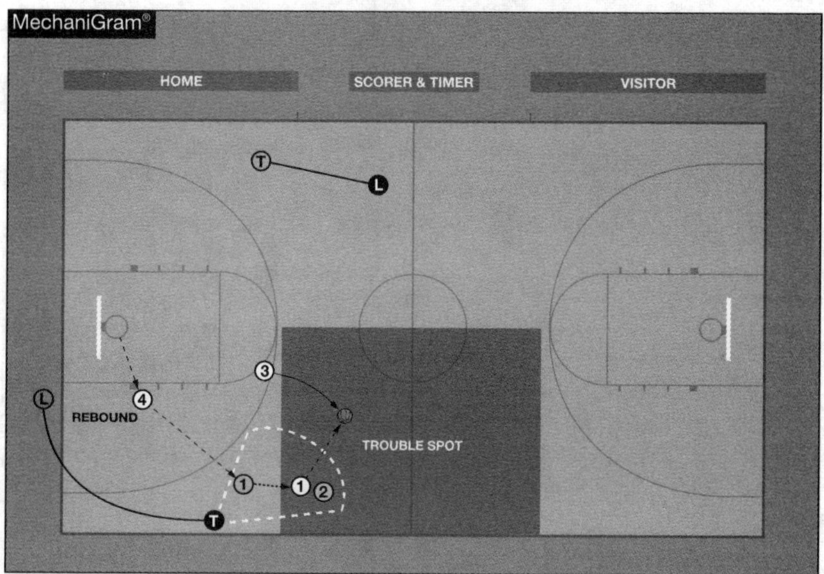

The same pass/crash principles that apply in the lane area apply all over the court. One trouble spot for officials is the pass/crash when a team in transition starts a break up the court. Many times players will leave their feet to make a pass then crash into defenders.

In the MechaniGram, the rebounder throws an outlet pass to a streaking teammate. That player catches the pass and dribbles up court trying to start a fastbreak.

The defender steps in to stop the offensive player from advancing into the frontcourt. As the offensive player leaps into the air and passes to a teammate, a crash ensues.

The Lead must quickly read the fastbreak and move toward the sideline to become the new Trail. The new Trail has a good look at the offensive player leaping, passing and crashing.

The Trail who becomes the new Lead must also quickly read the fastbreak and move into the frontcourt. The new Lead's primary responsibility is the player catching the pass. In rare circumstances, if the new Trail did not get out on the break fast enough to see the crash, the new Lead's secondary coverage area is the crash. That is more likely, however, when the pass/crash occurs in the center of the court.

LEAD HELPS ON THREE-POINTER

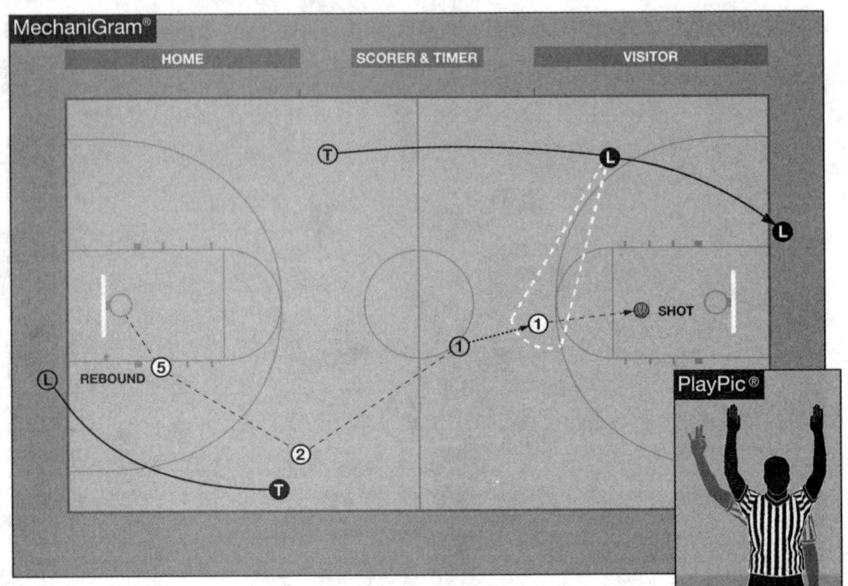

The transition game is difficult to cover with a crew of two officials. It is especially tough when quick outlet passes Lead to quick shots at the other end of the court.

When quick, long passes advance the ball upcourt, the new Lead must be prepared to help the Trail determine whether or not a shot is a three-point try. The help occurs even though the shot attempt is in an area not normally covered by the Lead.

When there is a quick outlet pass that leads to another quick, long pass, the new Trail usually does not have enough time to get into the frontcourt and get a good angle on a shot. Because of the distance and poor angle between the Trail and the shot, the Trail is left guessing. The new Lead must recognize the quick transition play and help the new Trail by judging the shot.

In the MechaniGram, the rebounder throws a quick, long outlet pass to a teammate, who throws another quick, long pass to another teammate. That player catches the pass near the center restraining circle, dribbles to the top of the key and shoots. The Lead moving to new Trail does not have enough time to get a good look at the shot. The Trail moving to new Lead recognizes that and makes the judgment on the shot, even though a shot attempt at the top of the three-point arc is normally covered by the Trail.

When that type of transition play occurs near the end of a period, the new Lead judges whether or not the shot was a three-pointer, but the Trail still judges whether the shot was released in time.

THE BUTTON HOOK

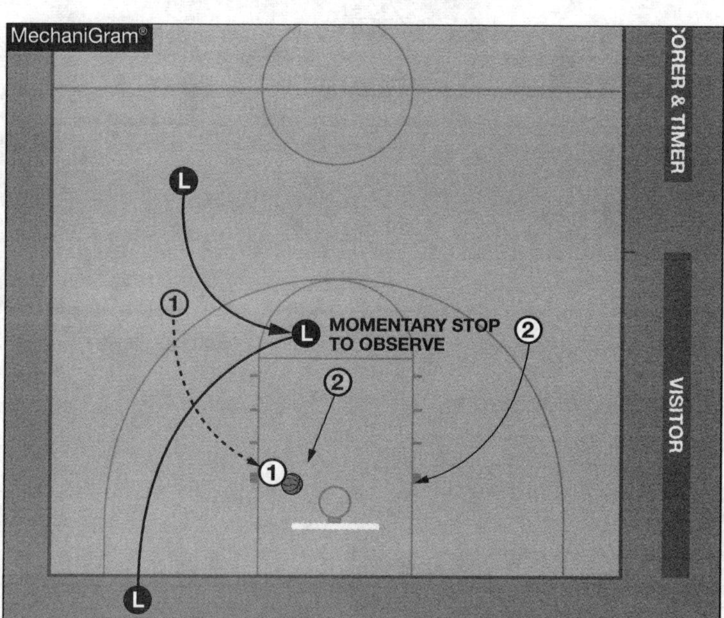

There are times when officials get beat downcourt on fastbreaks – especially in a Crew of Two. While not ideal, the transitioning Lead can utilize a “button-hook” to get the best possible angle to officiate the play.

Before transitioning from Trail to Lead, the official must be certain the play is moving to the other end. Leaving an official to officiate much of the play alone is not a good practice.

While in transition, the new Lead should restrain from sprinting as fast as possible (out-of-control) to stay ahead of players. Rather, it may become needed to allow players to pass, observe and pause the initial play at the goal.

The position shown in the MechaniGram above is merely temporarily and allows the covering official the best possible angle to make a ruling before moving to the Lead’s base position.

When in this temporary position, the official must be alert to other players on the court and work to create as little disturbance as possible to the play.

BACKCOURT WITH PRESSURE

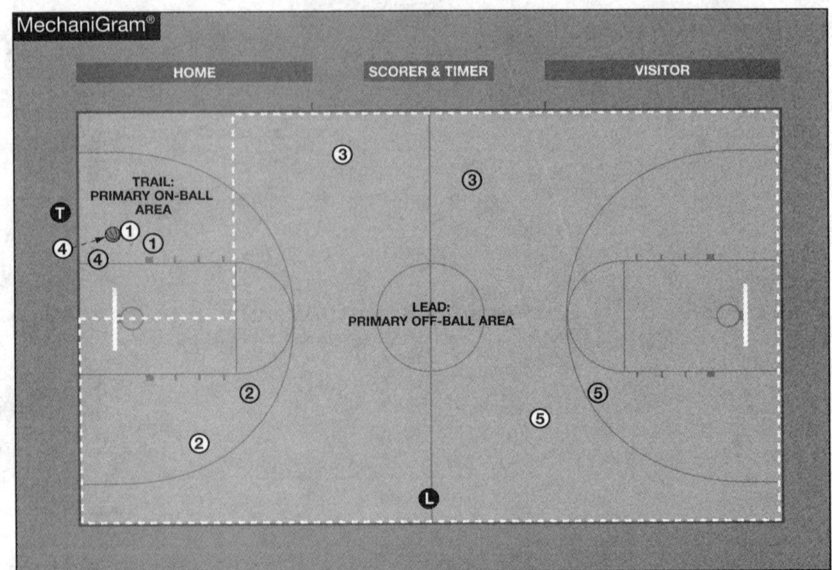

When play moves from one end line toward the other, the Trail has primary responsibility in the backcourt. However, when there is defensive pressure in the backcourt, sometimes the Lead must help.

When there are four or fewer players in the backcourt, the Trail should work that area alone. If there are more than four players in the backcourt, the Lead should work to assist the Trail.

When there is more than four players in the backcourt, the Lead is positioned near the division line. If all the players are in the backcourt, the Lead may move closer to the backcourt end line for better angles. If some players are in the frontcourt, however, the division-line area is the best position.

When near the division line, the Lead must stay wide and constantly glance from backcourt to frontcourt. That "swivel" glance allows the Lead to help the Trail with backcourt traffic plus watch players in the frontcourt.

The Lead should be ready to help on long passes and possible infractions involving the division line. The Lead will also cover quick breaks and long passes, keeping the players boxed in.

BACKCOURT NO PRESSURE

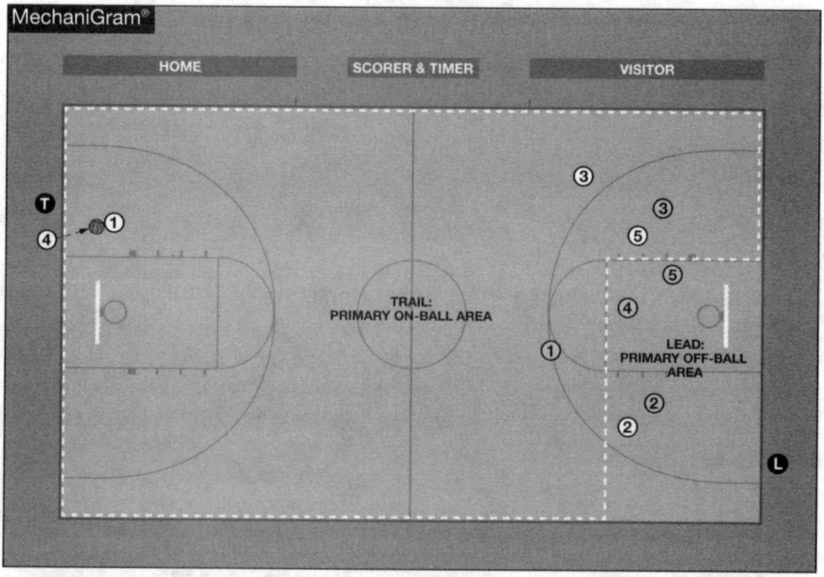

MechaniGram®

HOME | SCORER & TIMER | VISITOR

TRAIL: PRIMARY ON-BALL AREA

LEAD: PRIMARY OFF-BALL AREA

When play moves from one end line toward the other, the Trail has primary responsibility in the backcourt. For example, after a successful goal, the Trail is responsible for the throw-in and watches the players move to the other end of the court.

In any transition, effective coverage means significant movement by the Trail. Similar to halfcourt coverage, the Trail must move off the sideline. The Trail must stay behind the players as the ball is being brought up the court.

4.7 Throw-ins

BOXING IN: LEAD ADMINISTERS

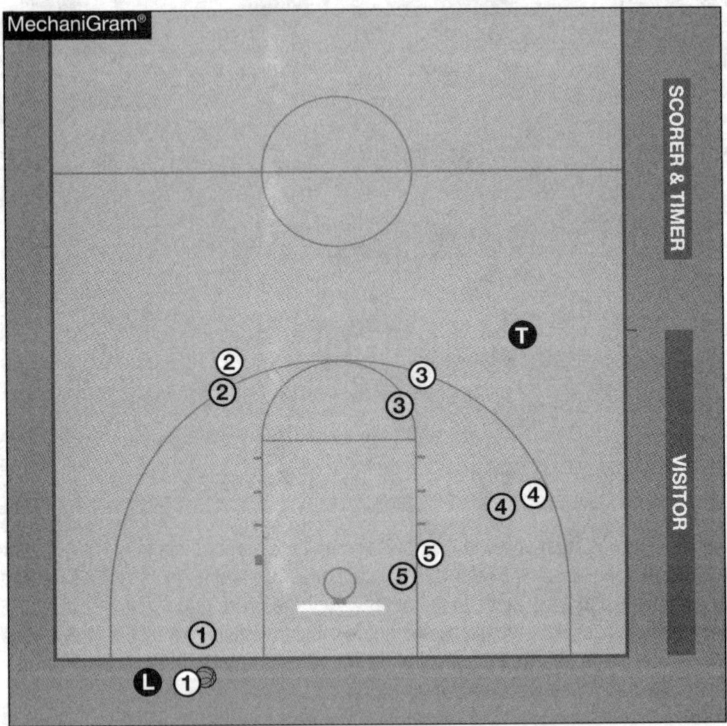

The Lead administers all throw-ins on the frontcourt end line.

For throw-ins in the frontcourt inside the three-point line, the Lead shall be on the outside between the thrower and the sideline. For throw-ins in the frontcourt outside the three-point line, the Lead shall be on the inside between the thrower and the basket. The Trail is positioned between the free-throw line extended and the division line, opposite the Lead, to ensure both sidelines, both end lines and the division line are covered. The Trail is also responsible for mirroring the “start clock” signal (Signal 1) of the Lead.

The Lead should always hand the ball to the thrower when remaining in the frontcourt.

BOXING IN: TRAIL ADMINISTERS

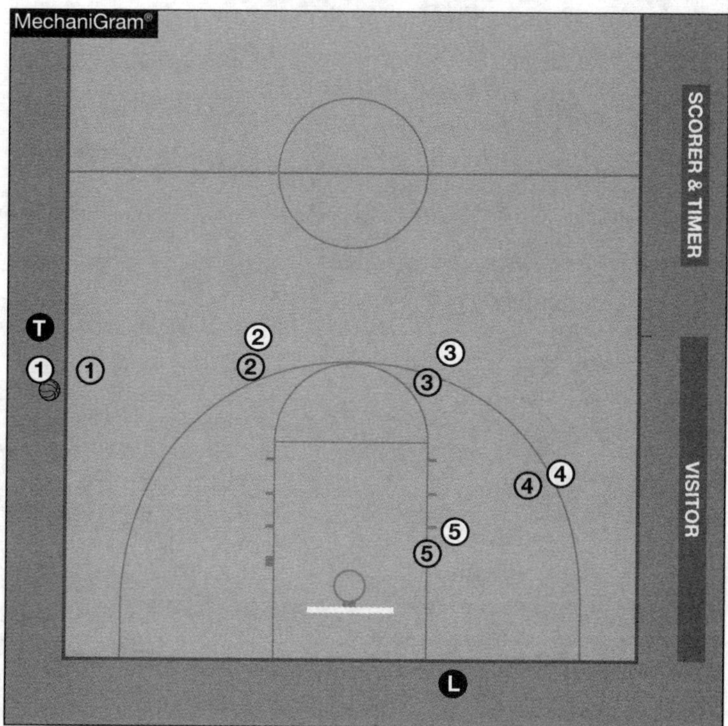

When the Trail administers the throw-in, the thrower is always between the Trail and the frontcourt basket. Unless otherwise dictated by an anticipated play, the Lead is positioned on the end line opposite the Trail to ensure both sidelines, the frontcourt end line and the division line are covered.

There are two ways the officials might have wound up in the positions shown in the MechaniGram. The old Lead would have been responsible for out-of-bounds calls along the sideline where the ball went out. Since the ball is being taken out above the free-throw line extended, the Lead would move up the sideline to new Trail, while the Trail would move to new Lead.

LEAD BALL SIDE

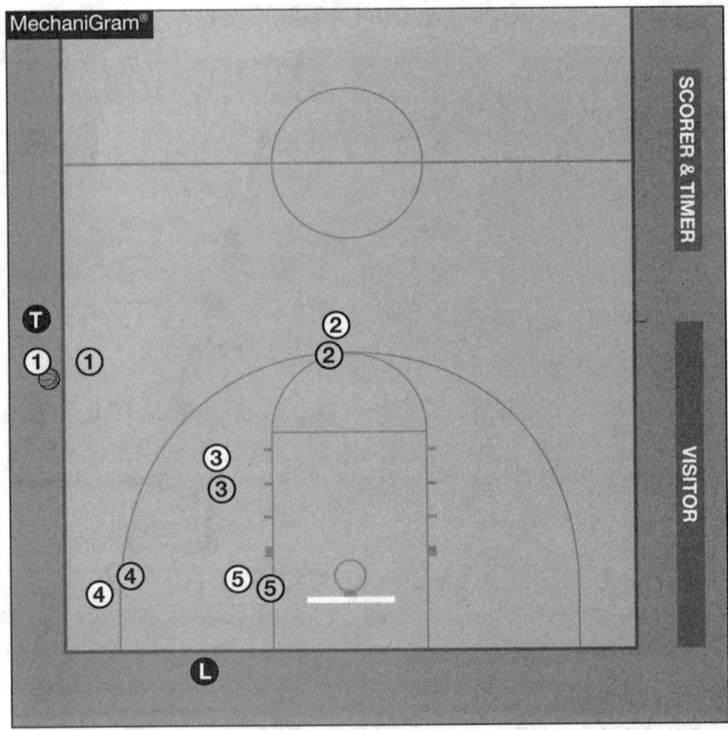

When the Trail administers the throw-in, the thrower is always between the Trail and the frontcourt basket. Normally, the Lead is opposite the Trail, however the players' location on the court now dictates the Lead to be ball side for the throw-in, while taking a position on the end line.

Even though the Lead is ball side, the Lead is still responsible for two boundary lines: the end line and sideline opposite the Trail.

BOXING IN: TRAIL IN BACKCOURT

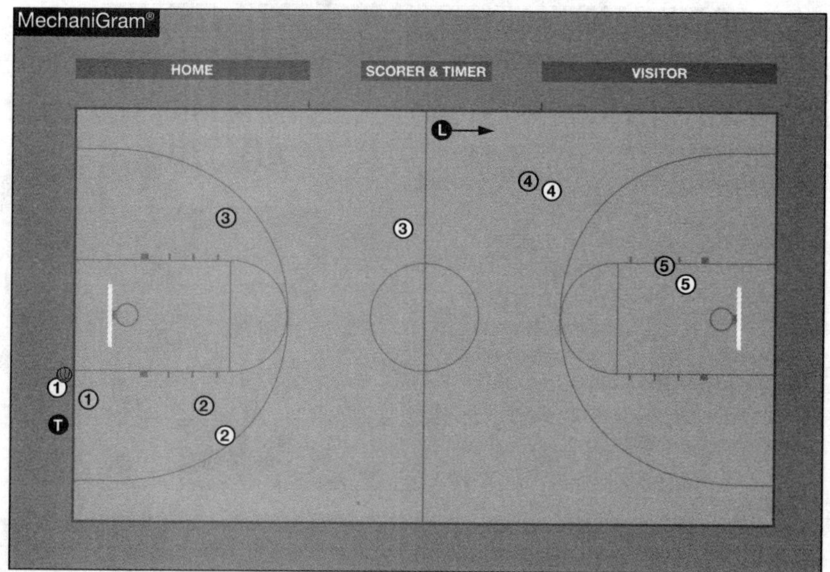

The Trail administers all throw-ins in the backcourt. The thrower is always between the Trail and the thrower's goal. Depending on backcourt pressure, the Lead is positioned near the division line on the sideline opposite the Trail, to ensure both sidelines and both end lines are covered.

The Trail should bounce the ball to the thrower in the backcourt, unless there is defensive pressure, in which the Trail should hand the ball to the thrower.

If play is resumed after a stoppage (charged time-out, injury, etc.) with a throw-in along the end line after a successful goal, the administering official should use Signal 8 to indicate the thrower may move along the end line since the throw-in is not a designated spot throw-in.

THROW-IN ABOVE FREE THROW LINE

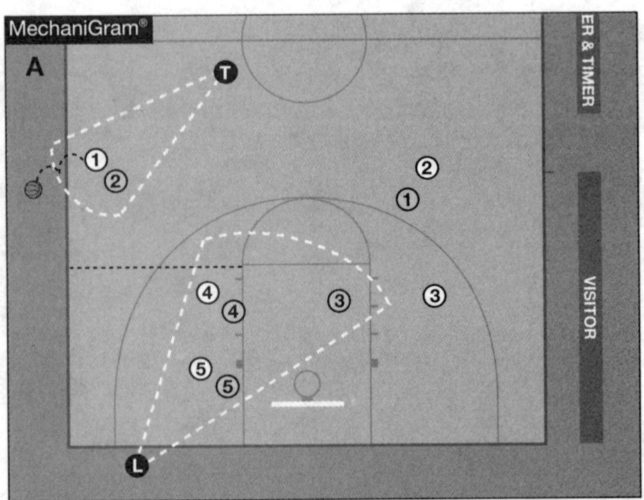

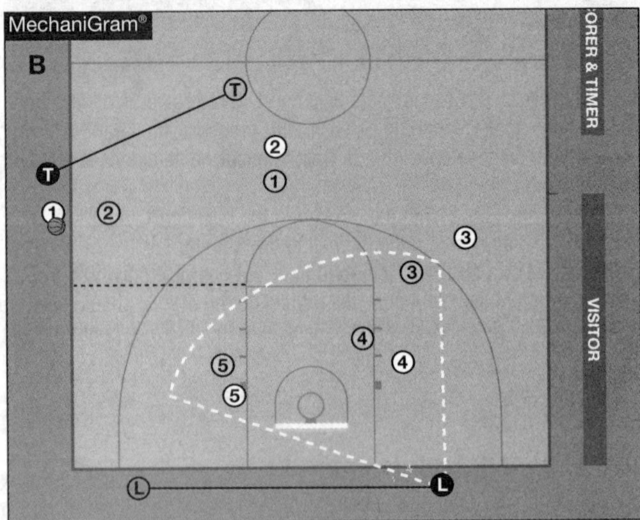

The throw-in is administered by the official responsible for the boundary line. The Trail administers all throw-ins that occur above the free-throw line extended on either side of the floor so the Lead can watch off-ball.

In MechaniGram A, the ball is knocked out of bounds by the defender along the Trail's sideline and PCA.

In MechaniGram B, the Trail administers the throw-in above the free-throw line extended and assumes all responsibility for starting the clock. The Trail can bounce the ball to the thrower and back up as necessary. The Lead will be responsible for off-ball coverage. Both officials should be alert for time-out requests.

THROW-IN BELOW FREE THROW LINE

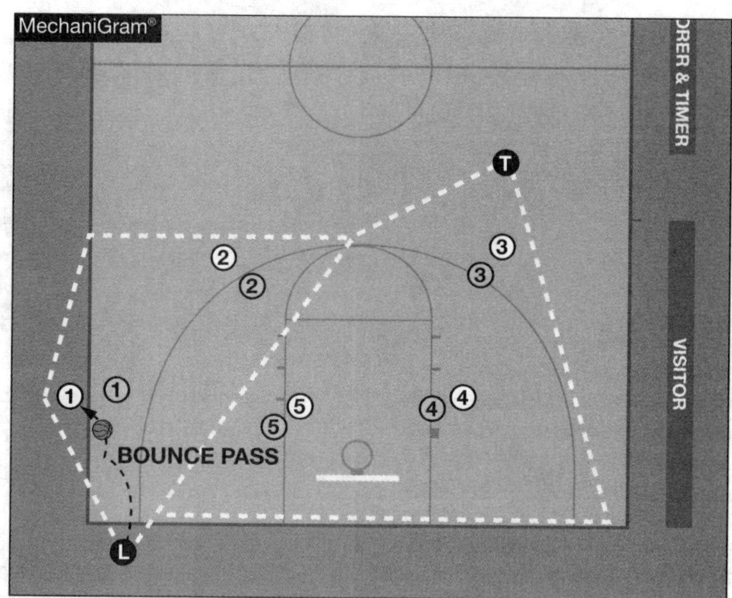

The Lead has primary on-ball coverage when the ball is below the free-throw line extended opposite the Trail. When a throw-in occurs on the sideline opposite the Trail below the free-throw line extended, the Lead administers the throw-in using the boxing-in method by bouncing the ball to the thrower. This means the Lead and Trail will not have to switch or move across the court to administer a throw-in below the free-throw line extended.

In order for the Lead to administer the sideline throw-in, significant coverage adjustments must be made. The Lead must move closer toward the sideline before bouncing the ball to the thrower to ensure a proper visual field that includes the thrower and throw-in plane. The Lead should also get deep (move back away from the end line) to increase the field of vision and see secondary coverage of post play on the low block (MechaniGram).

With the Lead focused nearer the throw-in, the Trail must move off the opposite sideline and onto the court to officiate all off-ball action, including action in the lane area. The Trail must be aggressive if an off-ball foul in the lane is detected, moving toward the foul to close the distance. The Trail is also responsible for mirroring the "start clock" (Signal 1) of the Lead.

As with all throw-ins, the Lead and Trail should make eye contact before the Lead bounces the ball to the thrower.

Keep in mind the Lead administers throw-ins below the free-throw line extended when the ball goes out of bounds on the Lead's side of the court. If the ball goes out of bounds below the free-throw line extended on the Trail's side of the court (opposite the Lead), the Trail administers that throw-in. There is no need for the Lead to come across the court to administer that throw-in because the Trail would also have to cross the court to apply boxing-in principles.

AFTER BACKCOURT VIOLATION

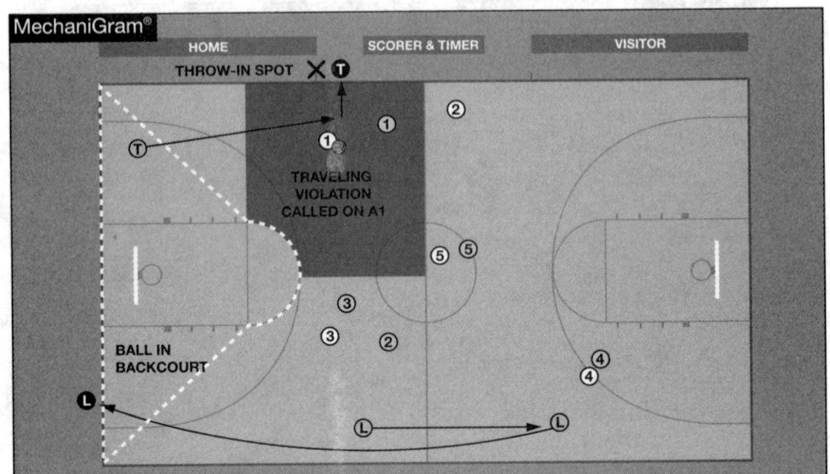

If a violation or out-of-bounds situation occurs in a team's backcourt and reverses the direction of play so that the throw-in team is in the frontcourt, the ball will be inbounded by the official responsible for that boundary line. The change will take place only if the violation or out-of-bounds situation occurs on the Trail's half of the court in the area above the dotted line and the division line as shown.

In the MechaniGram, a traveling violation has been whistled on A1 in Team A's backcourt above the dotted line and below the division line. The Trail official will stay and put the ball in play in Team B's frontcourt at the nearest of the four designated spots (28-foot mark near the home team's bench in this case) going the opposite direction for Team B, becoming the "new Trail." The previous Lead will swing down the court and become the "new Lead" in Team B's frontcourt.

DESIGNATED THROW-IN SPOTS IN THE FRONTCOURT

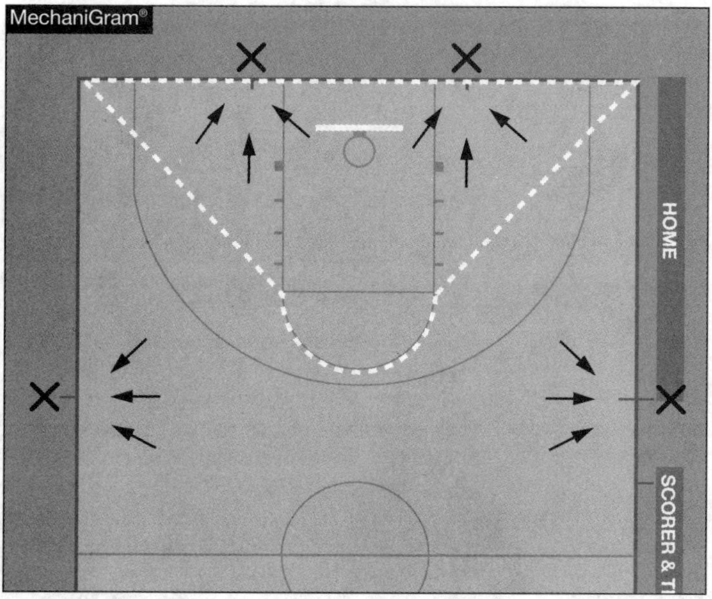

MechaniGram®

HOME

SCORER & TI

If there is a designated-spot frontcourt throw-in caused by a foul, a violation or a stoppage (i.e. an inadvertent whistle or a time-out), the throw-in spot will be the nearest of the four designated spots shown in the MechaniGram: either the 28-foot line along either sideline or the three-foot spot outside the lane along the end line.

4.8 Reporting Fouls and Switching

FOUL REPORTING AREA

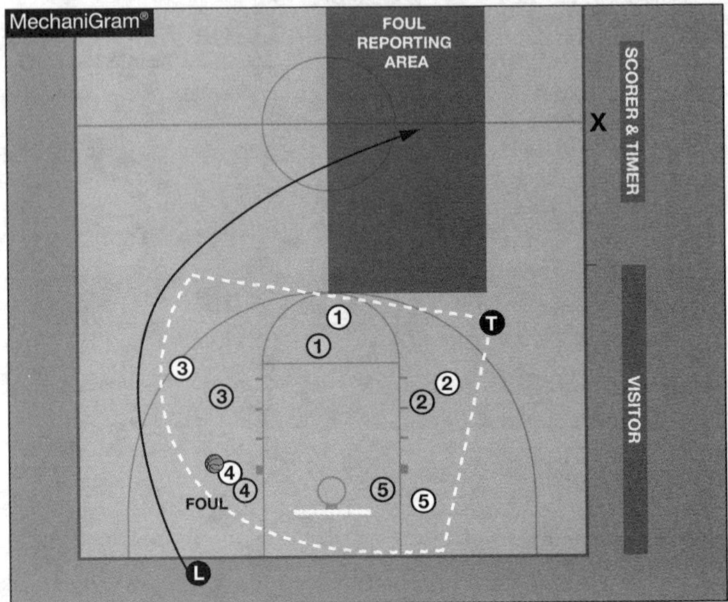

In the MechaniGram, the Lead official has called a foul on the defender in the low post. At that time, the Lead must do a number of things:

1. Delay momentarily after signaling the foul at the spot to ensure there is no continuing action or trash-talk among the players.
2. Do not worry about the basketball. Many times the ball will bounce away from the area. It is not the responsibility of the official to chase it. Going after the ball leaves players unattended.
3. Once the immediate area appears calm, the Lead clears all the players by running around them toward the reporting area. Officials should not run through a crowd and lose sight of the players.
4. Stop and square up to the scorer's table in the reporting area. Make eye contact with the scorer before communicating and do not get too close to the table.
5. Give clear, crisp signals.

The non-ruling official also has specific duties during the dead ball:

1. Keep all players in view. Close down toward the crowd of players slightly — maybe just a step or two depending on where the players are. During that dead-ball time, the non-ruling official can prevent many extracurricular illegal activities from brewing into bigger problems. The non-ruling official should use their voice to let players know they are there; the mere presence of an official can help prevent a problem from occurring.
2. If the players appear calm, begin moving toward the throw-in spot or begin preparing players for free throws. The non-ruling official should move slowly, with their head up, watching the players as they move. Officials should have the players ready for the next play, so that the ball will get back in play quickly and smoothly.

SWITCHING ON FOULS: NO FREE THROWS

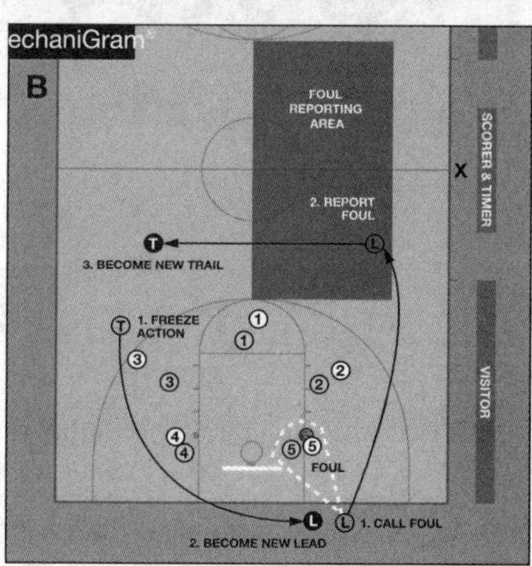

Officials switch positions on all non-shooting fouls, regardless of backcourt or frontcourt.

For shooting fouls, the calling official reports the foul to the table, then remains table side at Trail. The calling official has the option of going to Lead (opposite table) to avoid a confrontational situation with a coach/bench after a technical foul or disqualifying foul.

In MechaniGram A, the Lead opposite the table has called a foul in the post that will result in an out-of-bounds throw-in. The Lead will report the foul and switch with the Trail table side. The table side Trail will move to become the new Lead opposite the table and handle the ensuing throw-in. The non-calling official should force the switch just prior to the ball being brought back into play and get the players lined up for the throw-in.

In MechaniGram B, the Lead table side has called a foul in the post. The Lead will move to the foul reporting area to report the foul and then proceed to the Trail position opposite the table. The old Trail will move to the table side Lead position and handle the ensuing throw-in.

SWITCHING ON FOULS: LEAD CALL WITH FREE THROWS

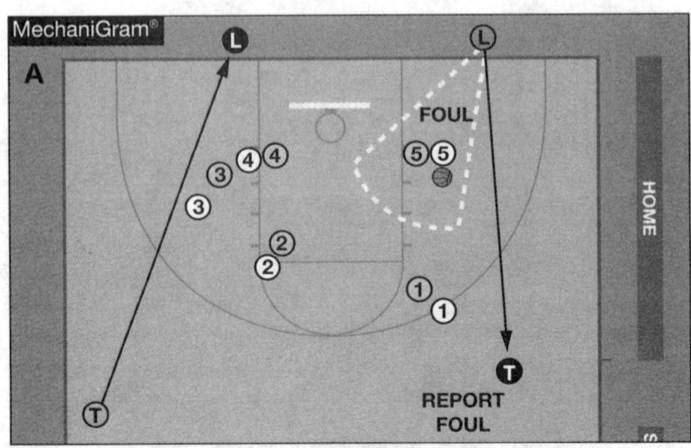

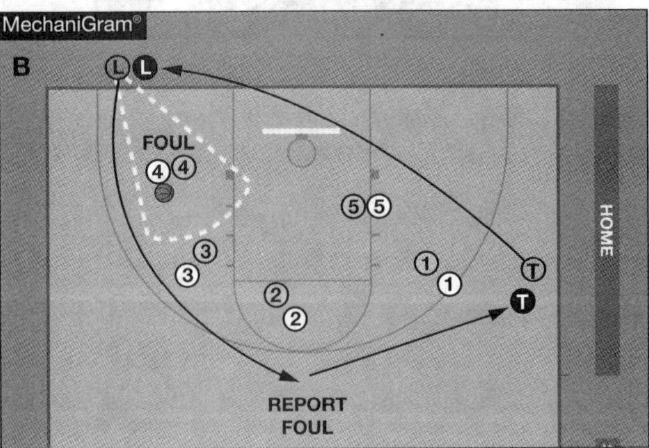

In free-throw situations (shooting or bonus), the rotations will vary depending upon the official's spot on the court. The calling official will always assume the table side Trail position for all free throws.

In MechaniGram A, the table side Lead official calls a foul on the low block that will result in free throws. The Lead will report the foul and then assume the new table side Trail position. While the Lead has switched positions, the Lead will stay on the same side of the court. The Trail opposite the table will freeze and then move to the Lead position opposite the table to administer the free throws. The new Lead will get the players lined up while the new Trail reports the foul. The new Lead then confirms the number of attempts with the new Trail prior to bouncing the ball to the shooter.

In MechaniGram B, the Lead official opposite the table has whistled a shooting foul. The Lead will move to report the foul and then assume the table side Trail position. The old table side Trail will move to the new Lead position opposite the table to administer the free throws. That scenario will be the most comfortable to most officials because it is the same switch as if it were a non-shooting foul.

SWITCHING ON FOULS: TRAIL CALLS WITH FREE THROWS

MechaniGram®
A
FOUL
REPORT
FOUL
HOME

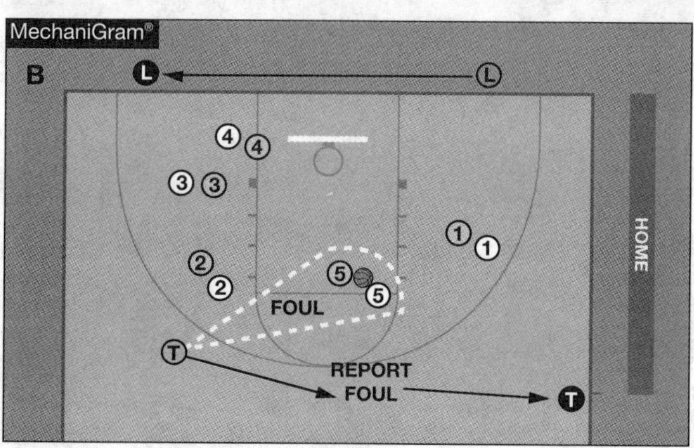

In MechaniGram A, the table side Trail has called a foul that will result in bonus free throws being attempted. The Trail will turn to report the foul and then stay in the table side Trail position. The Lead will freeze and then proceed to get the players lined up for the ensuing free-throw attempts. The Lead should visually confirm the number of attempts and glance at the table for late arriving substitutes before bouncing the ball to the free-throw shooter.

In MechaniGram B, the Trail opposite the table has whistled a shooting foul. The Trail will move across the court to the reporting area, report the foul and then proceed to the table side Trail position. The Lead will move from a table side position across the line to the Lead position opposite the table to administer the free-throw attempts. While the officials will move across the court, they technically will not switch positions.

SWITCHING ON FOULS: NO FREE THROWS

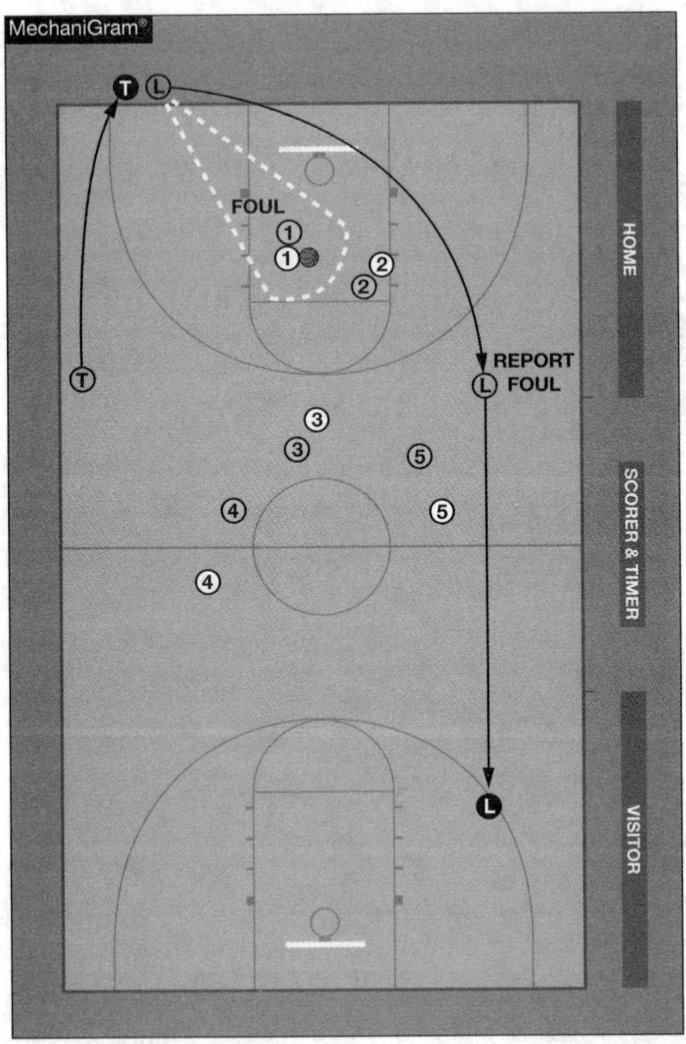

In the MechaniGram, the Lead has whistled a rebounding foul in the lane that will not result in free throws. The ball will be inbounded and move down the court. Although it is considered a long-switch situation, the Lead and Trail will switch positions. The Lead will move into the reporting area to report the foul and then proceed downcourt to become the new Lead. The Trail will move to the new Trail position and inbound the ball for the ensuing throw-in.

4.9 Free Throws

COVERAGE

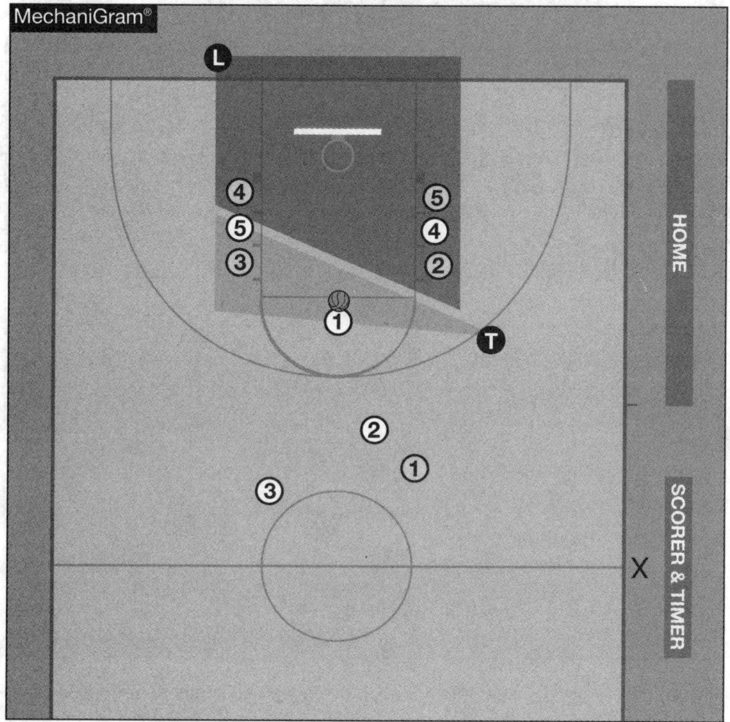

The Lead watches players on the opposite lane line (closer to the Trail) for potential violations, etc. The Lead also watches the lane space nearest the end line on the lane line nearest the Lead.

The Trail watches players on the opposite lane line (closer to the Lead) except the opposite low block area. The Trail also watches the free thrower.

As shown in the MechaniGram, the Trail will face away from the table. The Lead should be aware of such and watch for late-breaking substitutions toward the table or time-out requests, prior to administering the free throw.

LEAD MOVEMENT

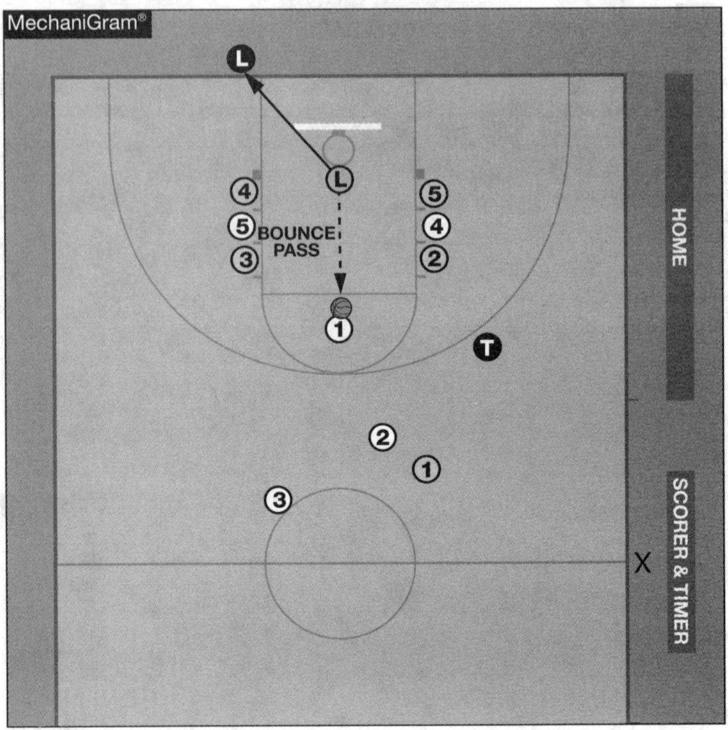

Before administering the free throw, the Lead has the ball and is positioned in the lane under the basket. The Lead should look for late-arriving substitutes at the scorer's table and beckon them in, if appropriate. Signal the number of remaining free throws to the players in the lane and the free thrower. Simultaneously verbalize the number of free throws. Before bouncing the ball to the free thrower, make sure there are no players moving into or leaving lane spaces.

When the free thrower is ready to catch the ball, bounce the ball to the free thrower.

The Lead is positioned approximately four feet from the nearer lane line well off the end line. That position is maintained regardless of the number of free throws.

After the shot is airborne, the Lead should adjust position along the end line a step or two to get a good angle on strong-side rebounding.

TRAIL MOVEMENT

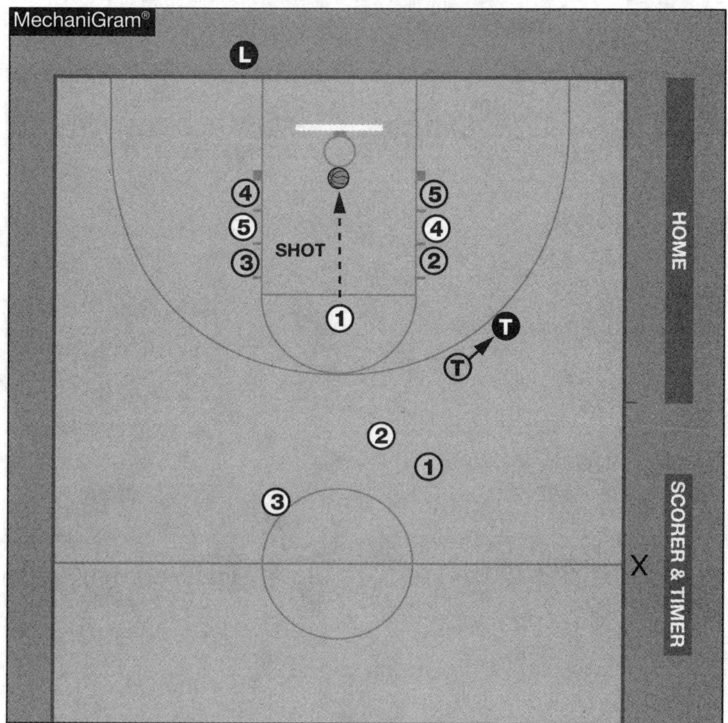

The Trail administers a silent and visible 10-second count with the arm farthest from the basket. Using the outside arm ensures the wrist flick does not distract the shooter and shows the count clearly to bench personnel, etc. When showing a visible count as a Trail during a free-throw attempt, the count should be less demonstrative than a normal visible count so as to not distract the shooter and draw unnecessary attention to the official.

On the last free throw, use the "stop clock" signal (Signal 2) with open hand raised directly above the head immediately after the shooter releases the shot. Use the same arm (farthest from the basket) to ensure the timer clearly sees the signal. During the flight of the try and with the arm still raised, close down slightly toward the end line. That movement ensures good angles on rebounding action. If the shot is good, lower the arm. If the shot is no good and the ball is to remain live, use the "start clock" signal (Signal 1) as soon as the ball is touched by or touches a player.

There is no need to signal a successful free throw.

TECHNICAL FOUL ADMINISTRATION

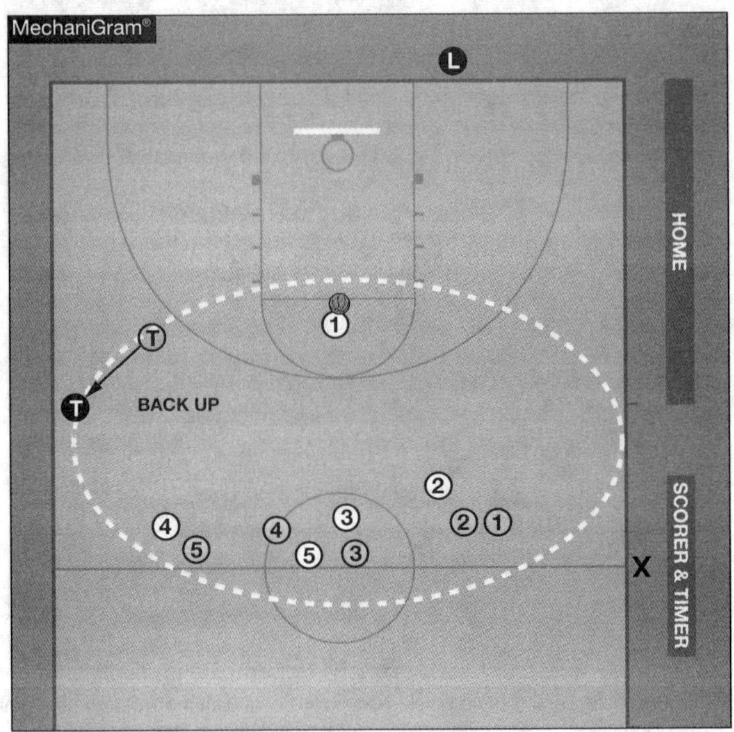

The calling official will assume the Trail position near the table. If a confrontational situation is apparent, the calling official may go opposite to assume the Lead position and administer the free throws.

When the Trail remains near the free-throw line, back up farther toward the sideline than normal positioning to ensure all players near the division line can be seen. There is no need to be in tight like during a normal free throw because there are no players along the lane line. The Trail's primary responsibility is the remaining nine players and the benches; secondary responsibility is the free thrower.

After a technical foul, the throw-in shall be administered at the division line opposite the scorer's table.

Note: Non-shooting players do not have to be behind the division line.

4.10 Substitutions

HANDLING SUBTITUTIONS: HALFCOURT

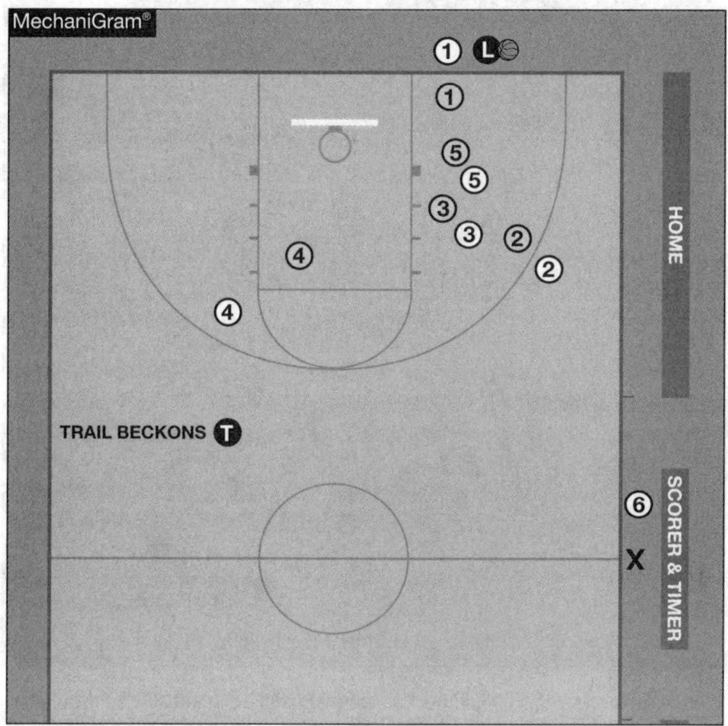

The official near the table, typically the Trail, will acknowledge and beckon substitutes onto the court.

Both officials count all players before putting the ball back in play.

On a foul, report the foul before beckoning substitutes. Hold the substitutes at the table until the calling official has completed the reporting procedure. The new nearer official should either beckon the subs or hold them at the table if there will be multiple free throws.

The official acknowledging the substitution is also to blow the whistle to initial the substitution process.

HANDLING SUBSTITUTIONS: TRANSITION

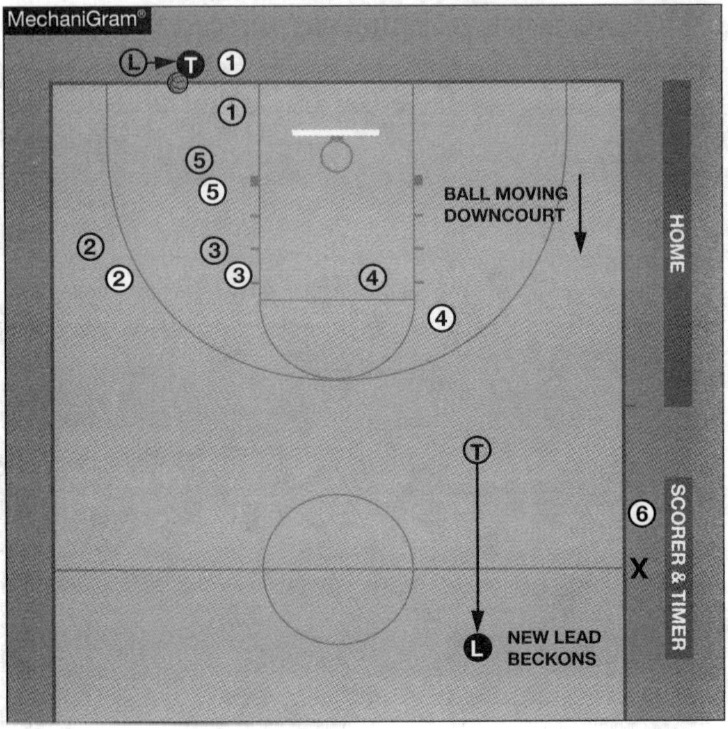

The official near the table should beckon in the substitute. In the MechaniGram, the old Trail is moving to the new Lead position down the court. While passing the table, the horn sounds and the new Lead should stop and beckon in the substitutes (Signal 10). Even though a horn will sound, blow the whistle so that the new Trail is aware that a substitution is still in progress. Keep a hand up and be visible until both teams have the appropriate five players on the court. Then put the hand down and proceed to the new Lead position (assuming it is not a press situation).

Game Procedures for a Crew of Three Officials

Game Procedures – Crew of Three

The three-official system is designed to provide better coverage by all three officials. This coverage gives more emphasis on primary areas of responsibility, thus eliminating the possible trend of over or under officiating. Always having an official in position acts as a deterrent to fouling and therefore promotes better basketball. The advantages of having the Lead and Trail officials on-ball and the Center official with off-ball responsibly:

1. Enhances the ability of three officials to be in the proper position to monitor play and all players.
2. Provides improved court coverage, in both front and backcourt.
3. Treats both sides of the court the same in regard to areas of coverage.
4. More clearly defines specific areas of coverage and responsibility.
5. Enhances the officiating procedures of wide triangle coverage.
6. Demands total concentration of the officiating crew.
7. Allows the officiating crew to do a better job of officiating contact situations.
8. Provides more effective coverage in pressing and full-court situations.
9. Ensures PCAs are the same for both sides of the court.
10. Advocates a stronger teamwork approach to officiating and requires that officials put trust and confidence in their partners.
11. Increases the technique of ball side officiating by allowing the Lead and Trail to officiate the ball and the players who are between them.
12. Increases proper off-ball coverage because the Center official has the responsibility for off-ball screens, backside coverage and weak-side rebounding.
13. Ensures the officials adjust their positions to the ball and the players on the court.
14. Increases the opportunity for all three officials in the crew to become more involved and participate in officiating the game.

5.1 Pregame, Intermissions, Time-outs

PREGAME

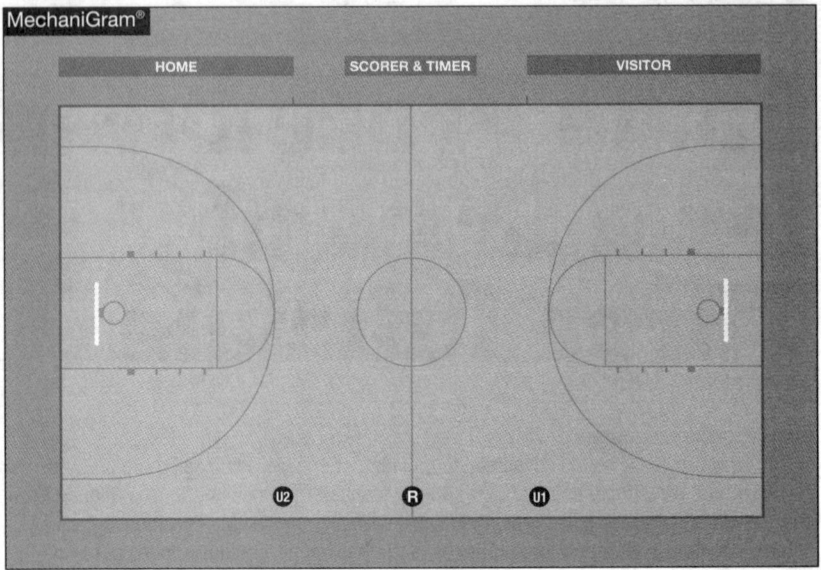

Officials shall arrive on the court at least 15 minutes prior to game time and be positioned on the side of the court opposite the scorer's table. The R will stand at the division line. U1 and U2 should be approximately 28 feet from the nearest end line closest to the team they are observing. U2 observes the visiting team while U1 observes the home team. All three officials perform duties as prescribed in 1.5.

HALFTIME

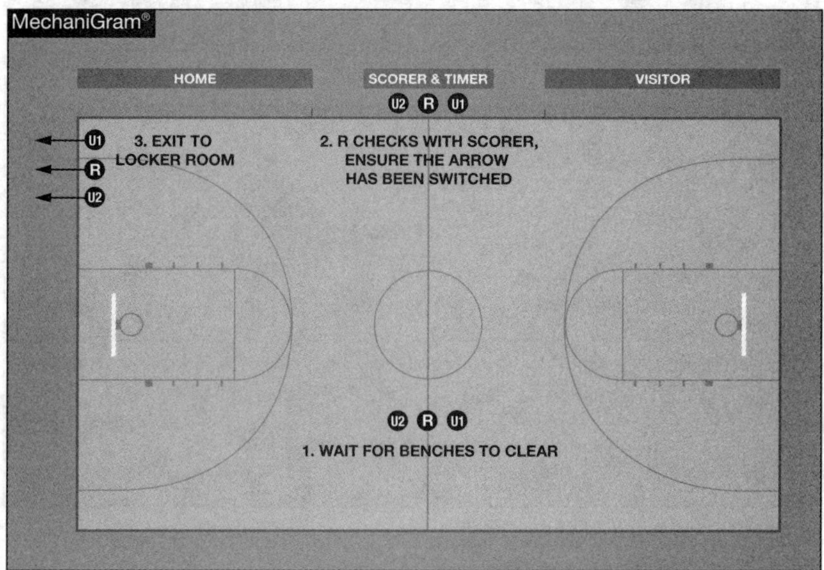

At the conclusion of play for the first half, the officials are now positioned halfway between the farthest point of the center circle and the sideline opposite the scorer's table (#1 in MechaniGram). After both teams have left their benches and gone to their respective locker rooms, all three officials walk over to the scorer's table and the R takes care of specified duties (#2 in MechaniGram). After the R confirms the possession arrow is pointed in the proper direction to begin play in the third quarter, the officials leave together for their locker room (#3 in MechaniGram)

The officials should ensure both teams are notified three minutes prior to the start of the second half. During the halftime intermission, the officials shall return to the court for the second half, the officials will stand across the court (U1 observes the home team and U2 observes the visiting team) until the one-minute mark. At that time, the U2 will secure the ball and bounce it to the R. The R will take a position with the ball at the division line on the sideline opposite the table indicating the direction of play with the placement of the ball. The U1 and U2 assume their 60-second time-out positions until first horn sounds.

BETWEEN QUARTERS

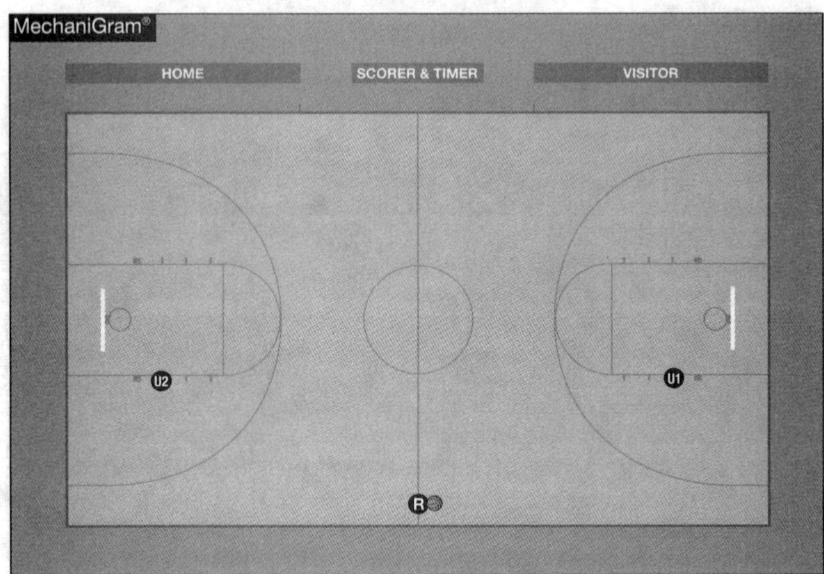

During the intermission between quarters and any extra periods, the R stands with the ball at the division line on the sideline opposite the table.

The umpires stand on the blocks on the lane line opposite the table facing the benches. It does not matter which end the U1 and U2 are on, just as long there is one official on each block.

There should be no visiting with coaches or players unless it is to confer about a game situation. The officials are then responsible to count the players when the teams return to the court to begin play. Use preventive officiating to make sure there are five players on the court per team.

The throw-in to start the second, third and fourth quarters shall be administered by the R at the division line opposite the table. The R indicates jersey color and direction, designates the throw-in spot, sounds the whistle to alert players that play is about to begin and places the ball at the thrower's disposal.

TIME-OUTS PROVISIONS:

1. If a player or head coach requests a time-out while the ball is live, ignore it if the ball is in control of an opponent, not in control of an opponent or not in control of either team.
2. If the request is during a dead ball or during a live ball that is in control of the requesting player or a teammate, it shall be granted.
3. No time-out may be granted during an interrupted dribble.
4. The opponents may not be granted a time-out once the ball is at the disposal of the thrower for a throw-in or the ball is at the free-thrower's disposal.
5. Do not grant a time-out after a foul until the necessary information has been reported to the scorer.
6. Do not grant a time-out until an injured, disqualified or player directed to leave the game has been replaced.
7. After the free thrower has the ball or the ball is at the disposal of the thrower on a throw-in, the thrower or a teammate may request and be granted a time-out, but the opponent may not.
8. After a successful free throw or field goal, any player or head coach may request a time-out, until the non-scoring team secures the ball for the throw-in. Once the official begins the 5-second count, the scoring team cannot be granted a time-out.
9. If an official erroneously grants a time-out request, it is not a team infraction. The time-out will be granted and charged but there is no other penalty assessed.
10. A request for an excess time-out shall be granted, but it is penalized with a team technical foul.
11. If opponents simultaneously request a time-out during a dead ball, charge a time-out to each team (or better, hear or see one request before the other).
12. The official may suspend play to permit a player to correct or replace displaced eyeglasses or contact lens without charging a time-out.

REPORTING PROCEDURES:

1. Sound the whistle while giving the stop the clock signal.
2. While moving to the reporting area, look for verification from the head coach as to what type of time-out is to be charged. Communicate the type of time-out using the proper signal.
3. A non-ruling official should ensure that the non-ruling team is aware of the type of time-out being granted.
4. Within the reporting area, then signal the type of time-out being granted, Signal 11 for a 60-second time-out and Signal 12 for a 30-second time-out. Verbally indicate the team color, verbally and visually give the player number or head coach (indicate by forming the shape of a "C" with the hand) making the request. Allow players reasonable time to get to their time-out areas, then point to the timer and verbally instruct the timer to begin the time-out period.
5. Notify a coach when that team has used its allotted time-outs.

INJURY/BLOOD:

1. If a player is injured, an officials' time-out shall be declared when necessary. When appropriate, bench personnel should be beckoned at the first opportunity. If bench personnel enters the court (beckoned or not), the injured player must leave the game

until the next opportunity to re-enter by rule (game clock properly starts) unless a time-out is requested and granted by that player's team.

2. Officials should not touch an injured player.
3. Any player who exhibits signs, symptoms or behaviors consistent with a concussion (such as loss of consciousness, headache, dizziness, confusion or balance problems) shall be immediately removed from the game by the officials and shall not return to play until cleared by an appropriate health care professional.
4. If a player is apparently bleeding, has an open wound, an excessive amount of blood on the uniform or has blood on their person, that player shall be directed to leave the game and may not re-enter until the bleeding/blood has been taken care of. The same re-entry procedures as above apply.

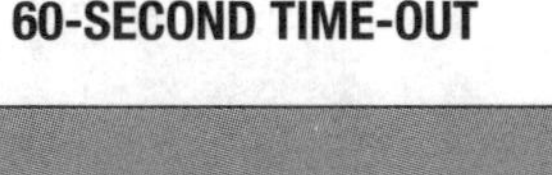

60-SECOND TIME-OUT

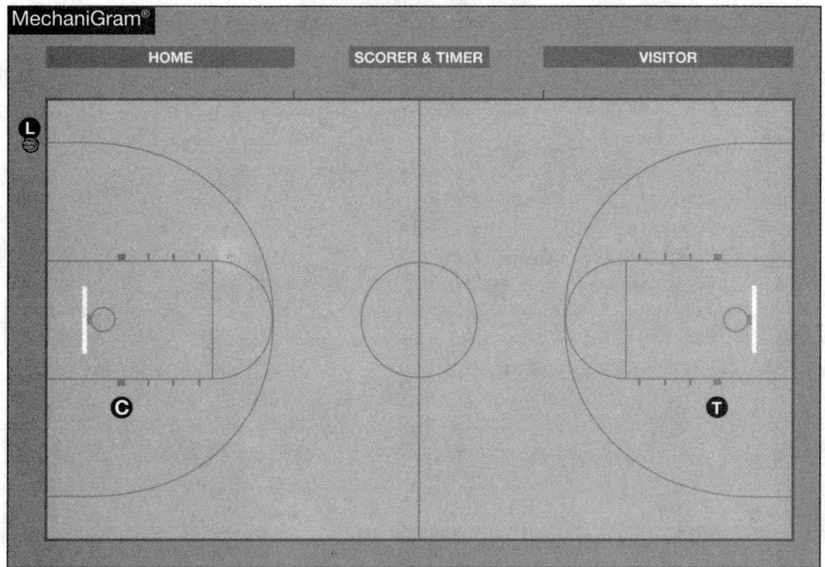

During any time-out, the administering official should take the ball to where it will be put in play. If that official needs to leave the administering spot, that official should have the partner hold the ball at the throw-in spot where play will resume. If play is to be resumed near the scorer's table or team benches, move straight out onto the floor in line with the other officials. If play is to be resumed with a free throw, take a position on the free-throw line, in line with the other officials.

During a 60-second time-out, the non-administering officials shall be on the blocks farthest from the team benches. Those officials are responsible for beckoning substitutes into the game and should be prepared to give the scorer or timer any necessary information. During any time-out, the officials should remain in good posture and be alert.

If activity on the court makes it necessary to move, the officials should move to a safe location and move back to the designated spots at the conclusion of the activity.

At the first horn (15 seconds remaining), the non-administering officials will step toward the nearest team huddle and notify that team by raising an index finger and saying "first horn."

30-SECOND TIME-OUT

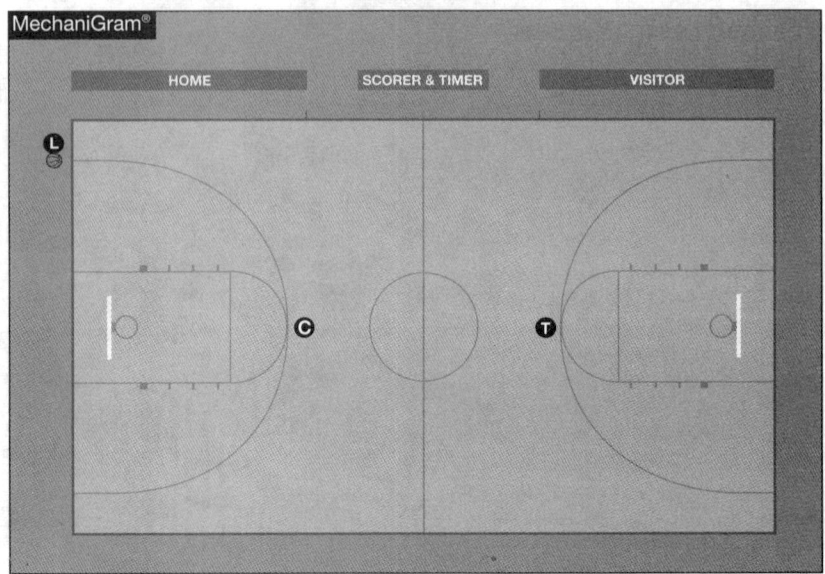

During a 30-second time-out, officials will use the same mechanics as a 60-second time-out with the following differences:

- The non-administering officials shall stand at the top of the three-point arc, on both sides of the court.
- By rule, players shall remain standing for the duration of and no on-court entertainment shall occur during a 30-second time-out.

5.2 Jump Ball

AFTER INTRODUCTION, BEFORE JUMP BALL

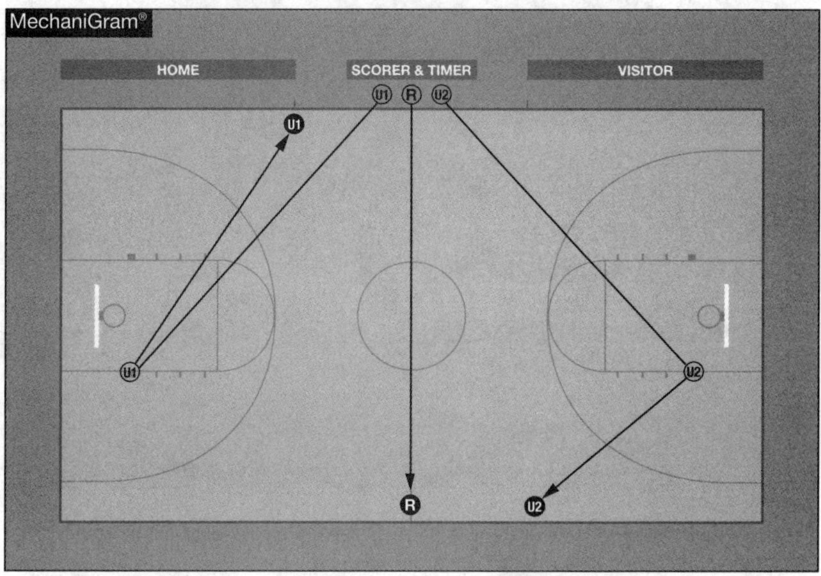

After the National Anthem and the introductions of the players, the players are usually getting last words of instruction before going out onto the court. At that time, the officials should leave their positions at the scorer's table and go to specific locations on the court. The R (or the official designated to throw the jump ball) takes the ball and moves to a spot near the far sideline, facing the scorer's table. U1 and U2 go to the blocks opposite the team benches. Hold those positions until both teams start to come onto the court. As both teams are coming onto the court, U1 and U2 can move to the proper jump ball locations and the R can prepare for the game's opening jump ball.

Note: The R can toss the jump ball or designate one of the umpires to toss if that official throws a better jump ball. Within this manual, the official tossing the ball will always be referred to as the R. Even though the R may designate a tosser, the R will handle all ensuing throw-ins to start the remaining periods.

POSITIONING

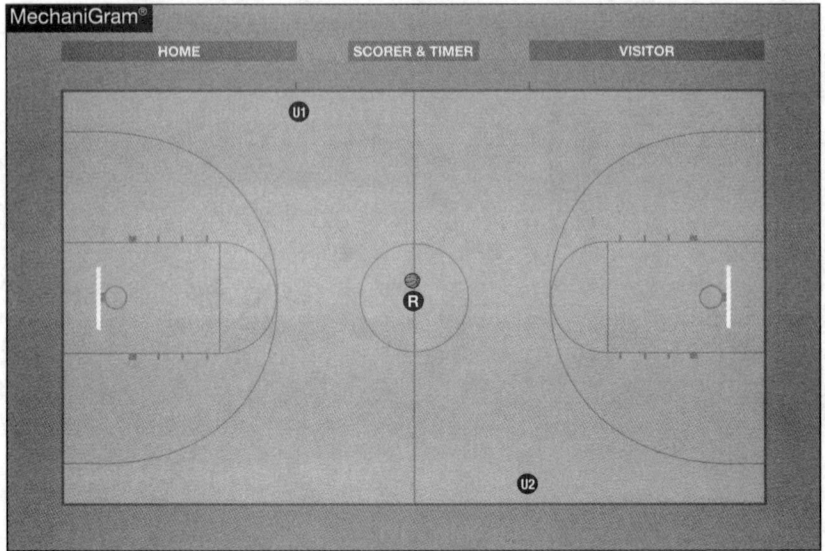

U1 takes a position on the table side sideline, approximately 28 feet from the end line to the left of the R. U1 is primarily responsible for calling back a poor toss, signaling the clock to start when the tossed ball is legally touched and counting the home team players. U1 also watches both jumpers.

U2 takes a position on the sideline opposite the table, approximately 28 feet from the end line and on the opposite half of the court U1 is on. U2 is responsible for the position and action of the nonjumpers and counting the visiting team players.

The R should allow ample time for the players to get settled into their spots around the center restraining circle. While that occurs, U1 checks with the table personnel to ensure they are ready. Before entering the center restraining circle, the R makes eye contact with U2 first, then U1. By checking with U2 first and U1 last, if there is a problem at the table that needs immediate attention, the R will be facing U1, making it easier for U1 to get the attention of the R. U1 signals to the R that table personnel and U1 are ready to go. All officials make sure the teams are facing the correct direction.

While still outside the circle, the R notifies both team captains that play is about to begin. The R then verbally states the jersey color of each team and indicates the direction of its goal for the first half. The R blows the whistle with a sharp blast before entering the circle, then removes the whistle from the mouth prior to tossing the ball.

Before the toss, U1 uses the "stop clock" signal (Signal 2). The R tosses the ball high enough so the players tap the ball on its downward flight. The U1 starts the clock when the ball is legally touched. If the toss is poor, any official should immediately sound the whistle, signal the game clock should not start and re-administer the jump ball.

U1 and U2 must maintain a wide field of vision while the R administers the toss. The U2 is primarily responsible for the position and action of the eight non-jumpers. The R is primarily responsible for the position and action of the two jumpers.

JUMP BALL GOES TO R'S LEFT

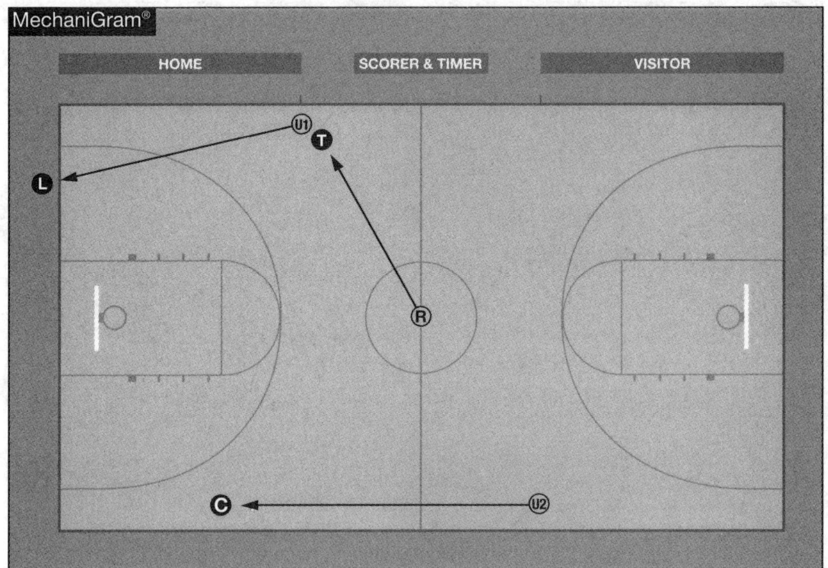

If the ball goes to the R's left, U1 will move to U1's right and become the Lead. U2 will move to U2's left and become the Center. The R will hold momentarily and then will move to the Trail enabling coverage of the sideline opposite U2. U1 and U2 must be alert to move in either direction should a quick turnover occur, before the R becomes free to move. The R will assume sideline responsibility that U1 had during the jump ball.

After the ball is possessed, the Trail should glance at the alternating-possession arrow to make sure it is pointing in the right direction. If incorrect, the crew will wait for the first dead ball and correct it.

JUMP BALL GOES TO R'S RIGHT

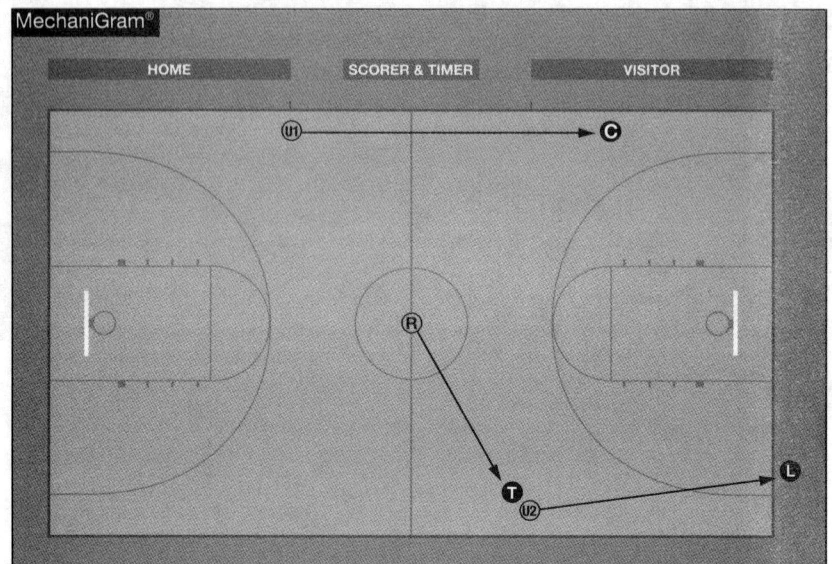

If the ball goes to the R's right, U2 will move to U2's right and become the Lead. U1 will move to U1's left and become the Center. The R will hold until players clear and then move to become the Trail. The R will assume sideline responsibility that U2 had during the jump ball.

After the ball is possessed, the Trail should glance at the alternating-possession arrow to make sure it is pointing in the right direction. If incorrect, the crew will wait for the first dead ball and correct it.

5.3 Court Coverage

BASIC FRONTCOURT COVERAGE

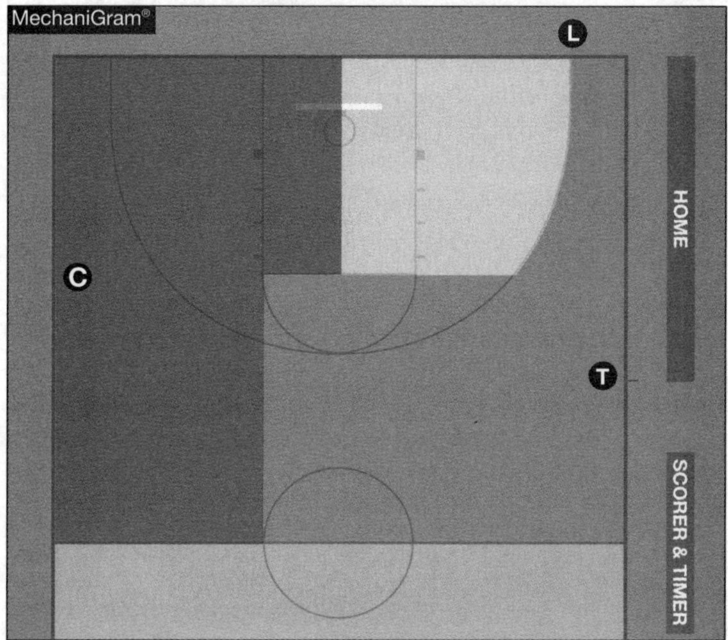

In the frontcourt, each official has a particular area of responsibility. Those areas of coverage do not change regardless if the official is on the ball or off the ball. When the ball comes into an official's particular area, that official is on ball. When the ball leaves a particular officials' area, that official is off ball.

- The Trail's responsibilities include the area to the far free-throw lane line extended, above the free-throw line, to the division line and the sideline nearest the Trail. The Trail also has three-point coverage on 60 percent of the court. The Trail has primary three-second responsibility when officiating off-ball.
- The Center's responsibilities include the area from the near free-throw lane line extended to the division line, the sideline nearest the Center and half of the lane itself. The Center also has three-point coverage on 40 percent of the court. The Center has primary three-second responsibility when officiating off-ball.
- The Lead's responsibilities include half of the lane, free-throw line extended to the three-point arc down the to end line on the Lead's side of the court. The Lead has primary three-second responsibility on offensive players in the lane when the ball is above the free-throw line extended.

Five-Second Closely-Guarded Count: Officials are responsible for a silent and visible five-second closely-guarded (within 6 feet) count (Signal 9) within their PCA. During this count, if the ball moves out of an official's PCA, that official shall maintain the count until the count is appropriately ended. Anytime a count restarts (going directly from a holding to a dribbling count or a dribbling to a holding count), the official shall switch hands/arms.

HALFCOURT BOUNDARY LINE

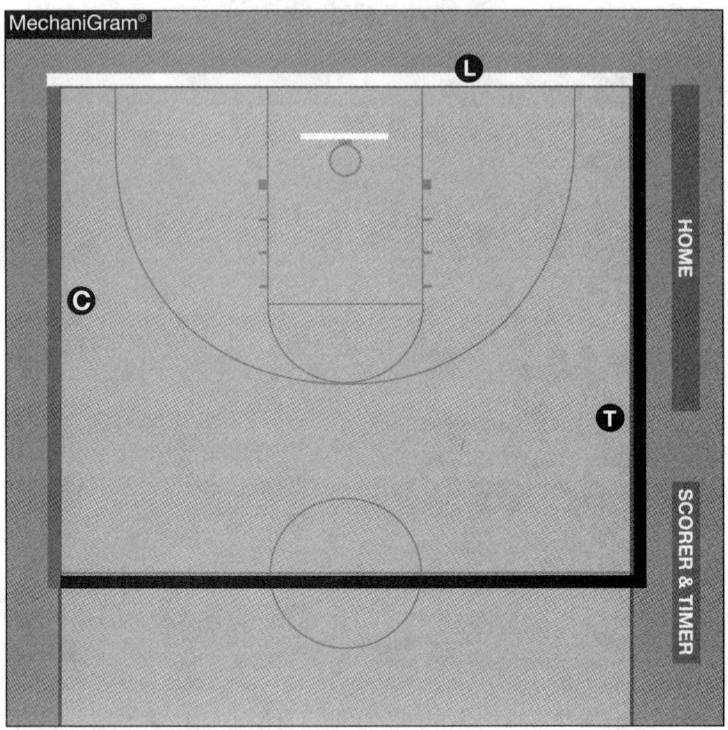

Every official on the court is responsible for particular boundary lines in a halfcourt setting. The Lead and Center are responsible for only one line, while the Trail is responsible for two.

- The Lead is responsible for the frontcourt end line.
- The Center is responsible for the sideline nearest the Center.
- The Trail is responsible for the sideline nearest the Trail and the division line.

If the ball goes out of bounds and the covering official needs help, that official should first stop the clock (Signal 2) and look in the direction of the nearest official likely to have an angle and verbalize "help." If the non-ruling official has definite knowledge, that official will verbally and visually signal the appropriate ruling (no conference between officials). The primary official will then mirror this information.

If a non-ruling official has definite information regarding an out-of-bounds ruling that has been made by a crewmate, that non-ruling official goes to the ruling official and provides the additional information. If the ruling official makes the decision to change the ruling, the ruling official is the one to sound the whistle and signal the change.

THREE-POINT RESPONSIBILITIES

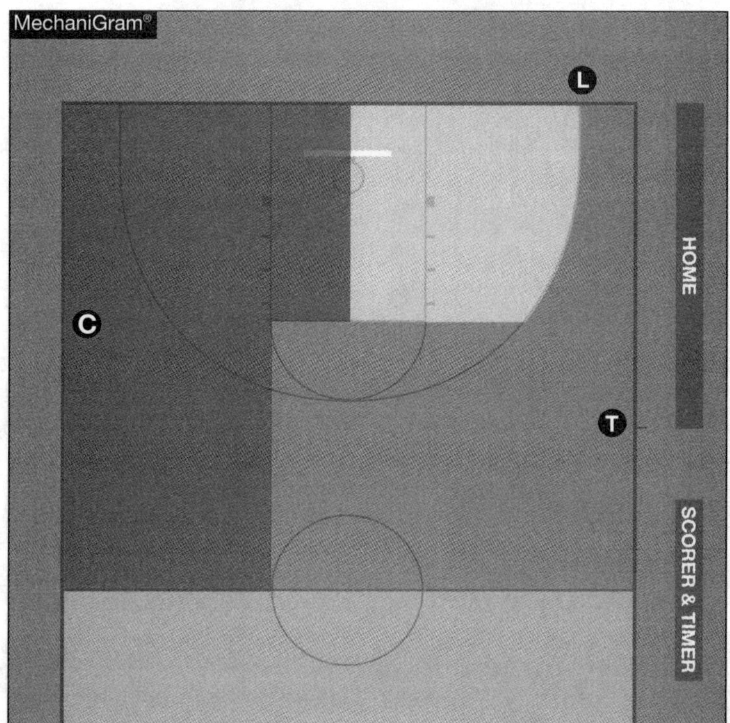

In the frontcourt, the Trail is responsible for 60 percent of the three-point arc, up to the far lane line and down to the end line. The Center is responsible for the three-point arc from the near lane line down to the end line. The Lead does not have three-point arc responsibility except when helping in transition.

On three-point attempts, only the covering official should indicate the attempt (Signal 18). The indication should be made with the arm closest to the center of the court so the table personnel can see it better. The covering official should also signal if the attempt is successful.

If the Trail signals a successful three-point attempt, the Center mirrors the successful signal. If the Center signals a successful three-point attempt, the Trail mirrors the signal. There is no need to mirror an attempt signal.

HANDLING DOUBLE WHISTLES

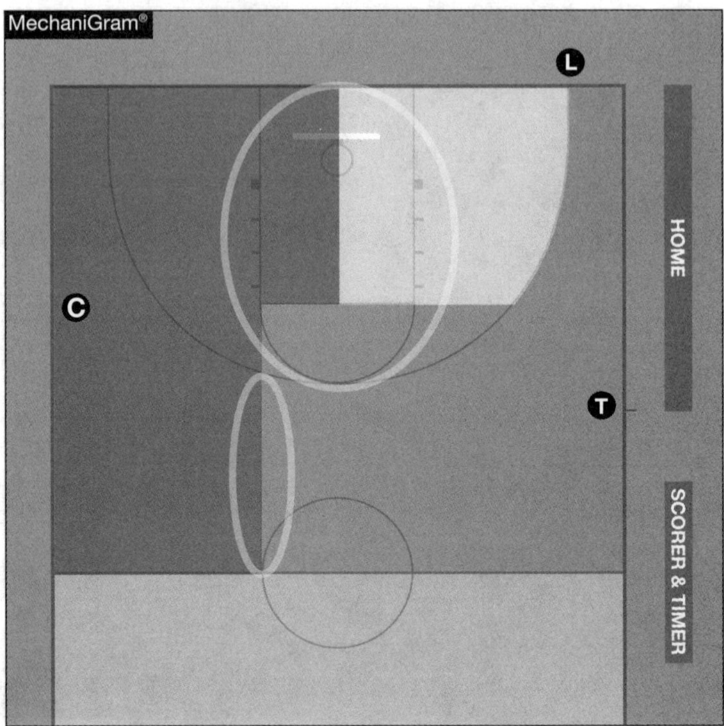

Double whistles are more likely to occur in areas where coverage intersects, such as in the lane, near the free-throw line and near the free-throw line extended.

Generally, the official who has primary coverage at the time of the whistle should make the ruling.

If the secondary official has a ruling that occurred before the primary official's ruling or has information that should be discussed with the primary official, the secondary official should close into the play quickly toward the primary official. The outside officials (Trail and Center) should be patient with signals on plays to the basket.

Keys to managing double-whistles:

1. Give the "stop clock" signal (Signal 2) and refrain from giving an immediate preliminary signal.
2. Make good eye contact with each other.
3. Understand where the play originated.
4. Understand each position's PCA.

PASS/CRASH IN LANE

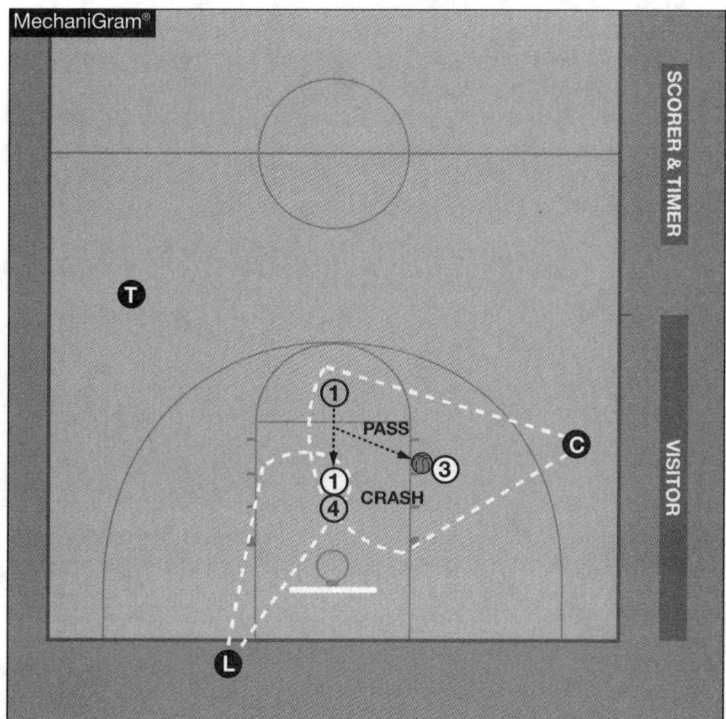

Drives to the basket when the ball handler passes the ball to a teammate then crashes into a defender below the free throw line are known as "pass and crash" situations.

If the passer sends the ball out toward the Trail, the Trail will follow the ball and the Center and Lead will stay with the crash. If the ball is passed toward the Center's side of the floor, the Center will follow the ball while the Trail and Lead momentarily stay with the crash.

The Center or Trail official should close down toward the end line to get a better view of the play, but should be aware of the kickout pass and should make sure they are not too close to an ensuing three-point attempt.

Once the Lead official determines that a drive down the lane is imminent, the Lead should move toward the close-down position along the lane line (as shown in the MechaniGram) to get a better view of the activity in the lane.

REBOUNDING AREAS

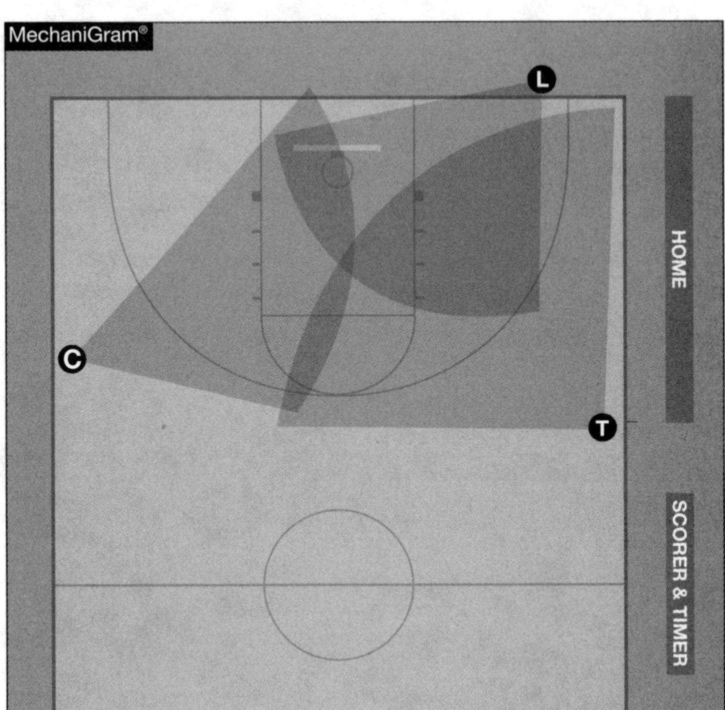

Rebound coverage in a three-person crew has the same basic principles of a two-person crew. A shot taken from an official's PCA dictates that official stays with the shooter then focuses on rebounding action. When a shot is taken from outside an official's coverage area, that official should immediately pay attention to the rebounding action.

The third official on the court simply adds another set of eyes for rebounds. That extra set has a specific area to focus on. Those areas are very similar to basic frontcourt responsibilities, with one main difference: overlaps in coverage.

As the MechaniGram shows, there are areas on the court where two officials have the same rebounding coverage area.

While any official can call a foul during rebounding action, the Trail and Center officials are primary on pushing fouls when offensive players crash the boards. The Lead should not call those fouls as the Lead does not have the proper perspective the Center and Trail officials have. The Lead, however, can have a foul such as illegal contact or holding that is better seen from the end line.

If the shot attempts originates from the Trail's coverage area, the Center official becomes primary on goaltending and basket interference. Likewise, if the shot originates from the Center's area of coverage, the Trail then becomes primary for goaltending or basket interference.

REBOUNDING STRONGSIDE

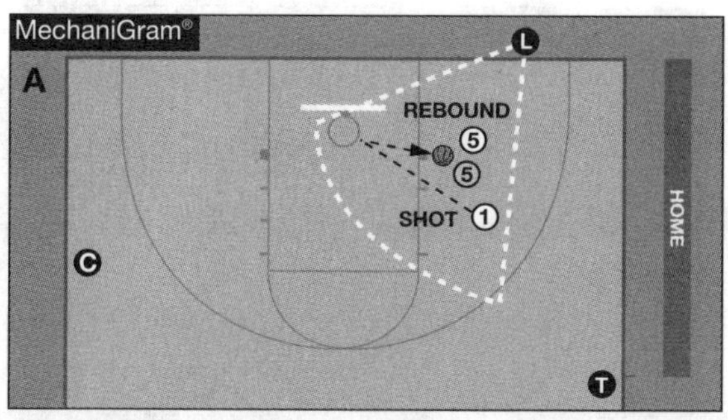

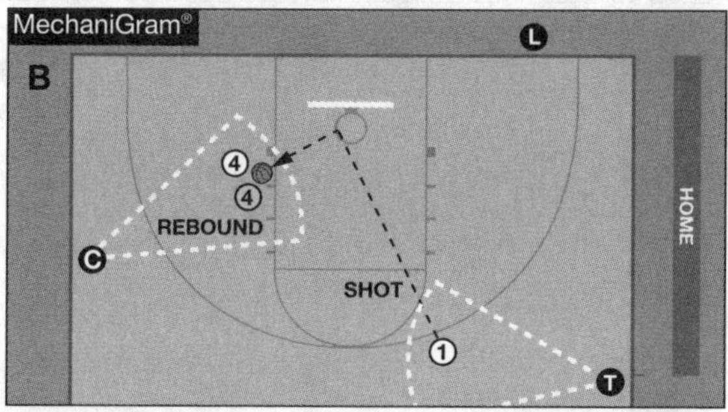

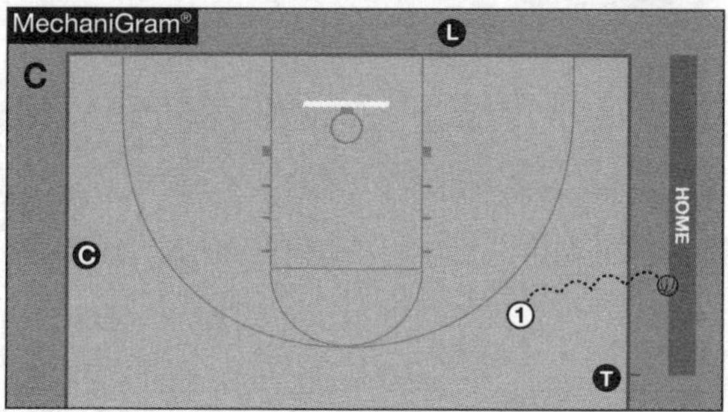

When shots are taken from the strongside, each official has certain responsibilities.

In MechaniGram A, the shot is taken from the Lead's coverage area. The Lead is responsible for the shooter and strong-side rebounding. The Trail should also help with strong-side rebounding. The Center is responsible for weak-side rebounding action and should work to get a proper angle.

In MechaniGram B, the Trail is responsible for the shooter. The Center is first responsible for basket interference and goaltending, followed by observing weak-side rebounding action.

In MechaniGram C, the Trail is first responsible for the shooter, followed by observing perimeter rebounding. The Center is responsible for basket interference and goaltending. The Center can also help with perimeter rebounding.

REBOUNDING WEAKSIDE

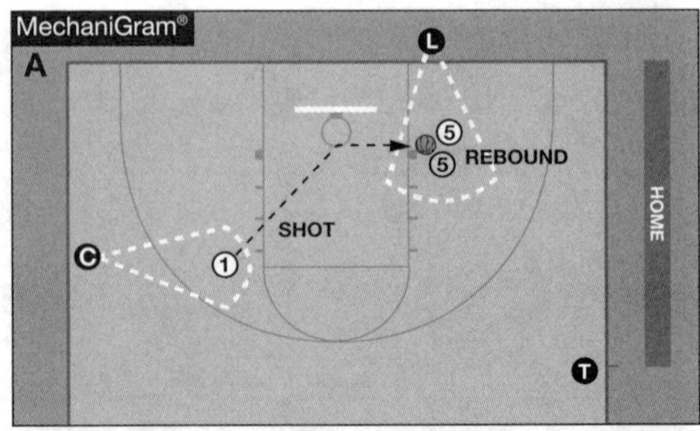

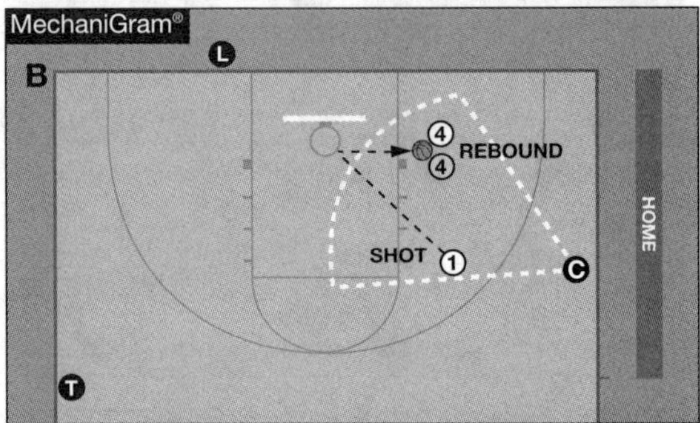

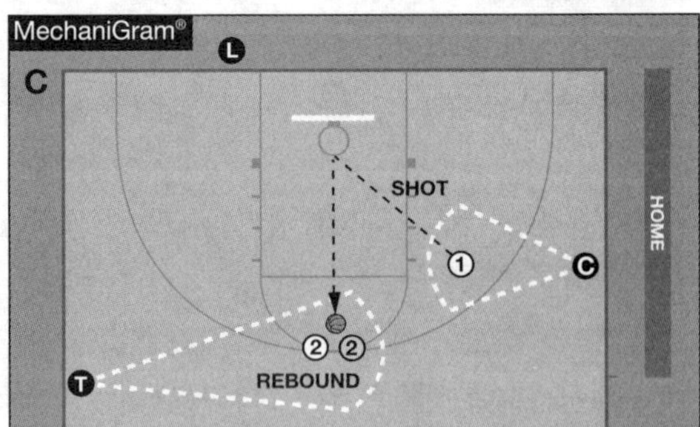

When shots are taken from the weakside, the Center is responsible for staying with the shooter. The Lead is responsible for strong-side rebounding, as seen in MechaniGram A.

The Center, after staying with the shooter, also has weak-side rebounding, as seen in MechaniGram B. The Trail is primary on basket interference and goaltending and should help with perimeter and strong-side rebounding.

In MechaniGram C, after checking for basket interference or goaltending, the Trail is then responsible for perimeter rebounding action.

STAY NEAR SIDELINE

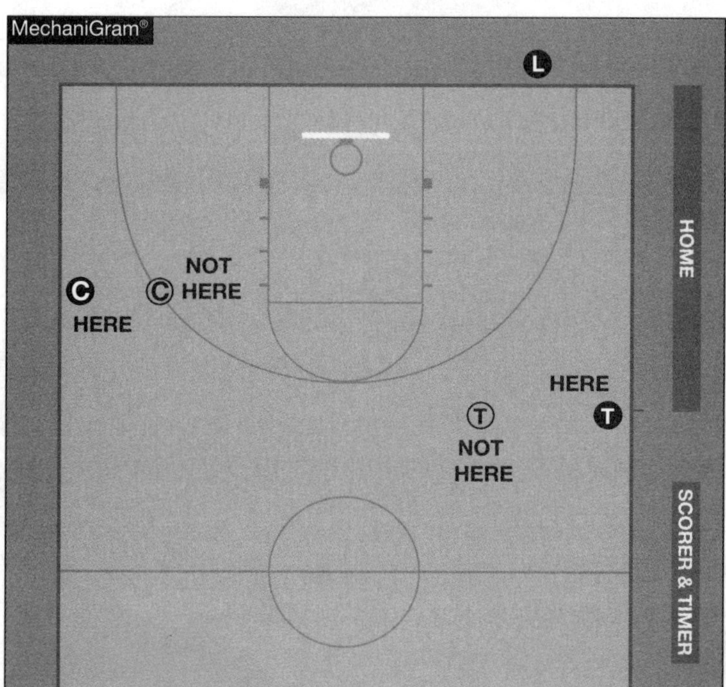

A three-person crew has an official on both sidelines. Having both sidelines covered allows the Trail and Center to stay near the sideline, as seen in the MechaniGram. Staying near the sideline not only takes away the possibility of getting caught in the play, but also opens the angle of the entire court allowing for better coverage.

There may be times in which a temporary one- or two-step adjustment onto the court or along the sideline is necessary to avoid straightlining or feeling "pinched" along the sideline (when players are too close) or when all of the action is far away from the wing official.

DO NOT BAIL OUT ON TRY

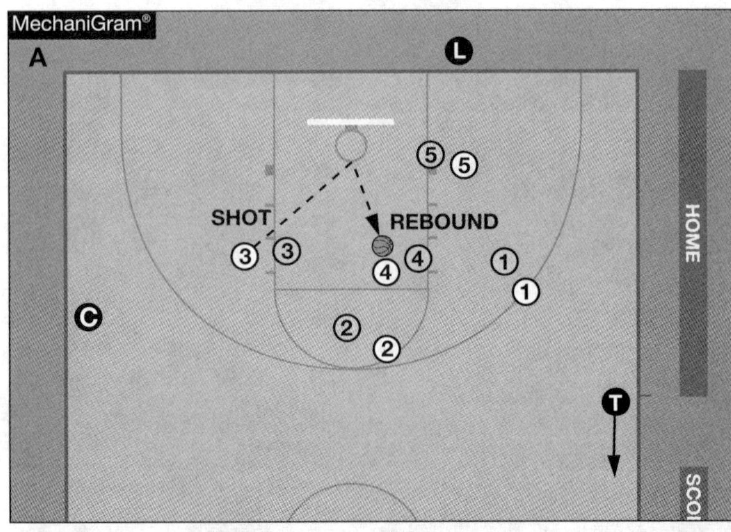

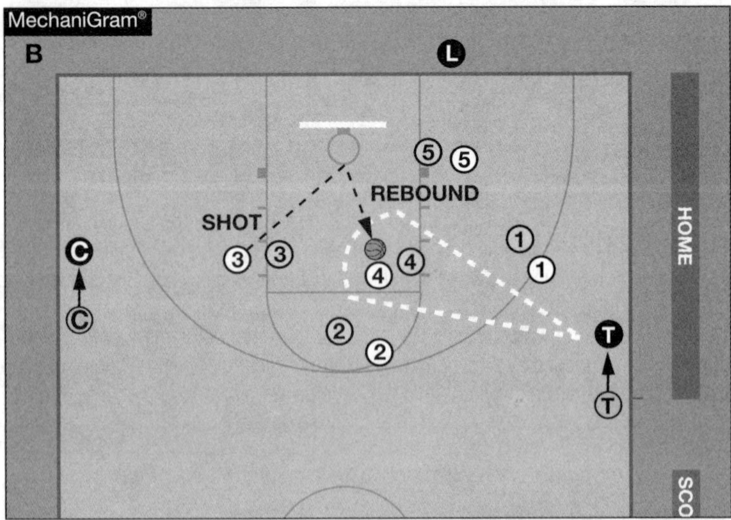

On trys, the Trail and Center should close down and not bail out. When bailing out, as the Trail does in MechaniGram A, the Trail puts pressure on the rest of the crew to officiate rebounding. Instead, the Trail and Center should step down toward the end line when trys are attempted. That helps the crew better officiate rebounding action as seen in MechaniGram B. Closing down can help officials avoid bailing out on plays.

OFFICIATING THE DELAY OFFENSE

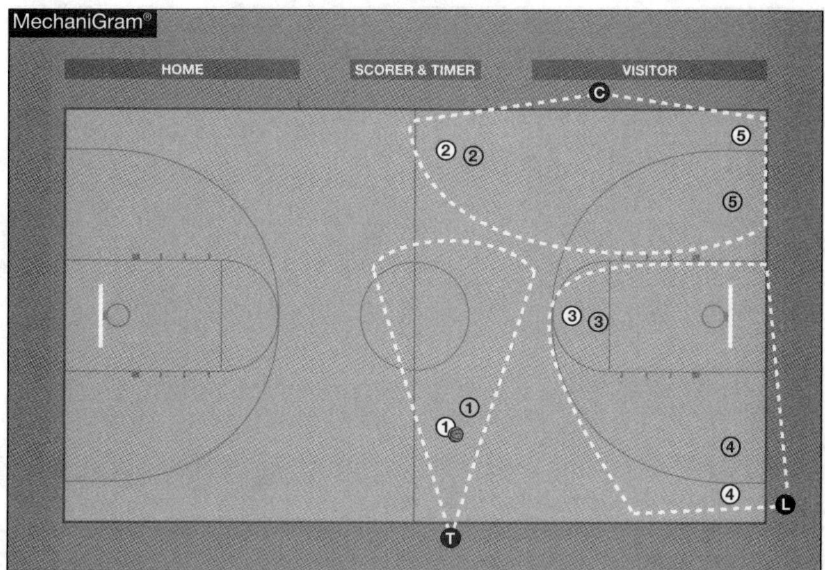

The delay offense, sometimes referred to as the "spread" or "four-corner" offense, requires officials to change their basic positions. The delay offense spreads players out to all corners of the frontcourt and is designed to run the clock down while avoiding double teams.

When a team goes into a delay offense, the wing officials may have to officiate from outside the court, as seen in the MechaniGram, to keep wide triangle coverage. That way, the players have enough room to maneuver without using an official as a screen. It also keeps officials out of the passing lanes.

BACKCOURT BOUNDARY

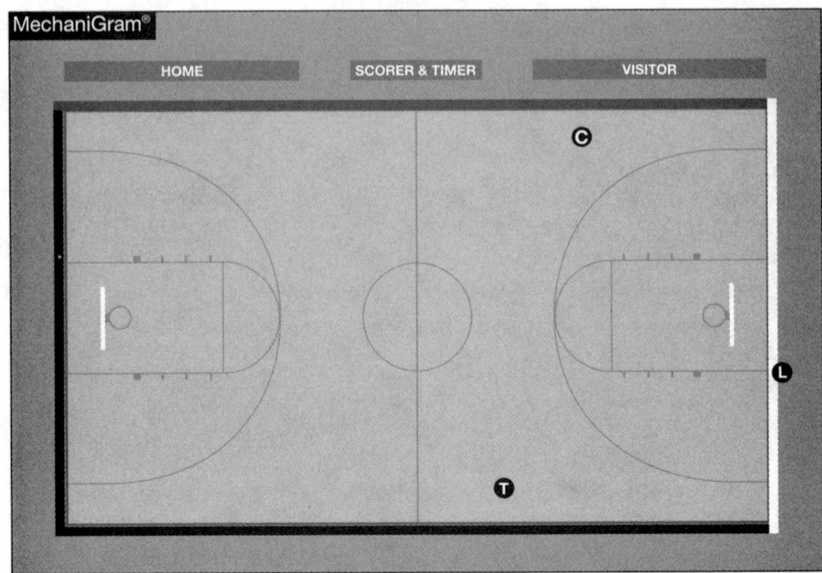

In the backcourt, the new Trail is responsible for the backcourt end line and the sideline on that side of the court. The Center is responsible for the sideline on the Center's side of the court. The Lead is responsible for the frontcourt end line.

In a pressing situation, the Center should also be prepared to help out the Trail on any activity involving the division line. Many times, a quick pass to a teammate near the division line will not give the Trail enough time to get up the court and get a proper angle on the play. The Center is close enough to rule on any such action and penalize any backcourt violations that might occur.

BACKCOURT NO PRESSURE

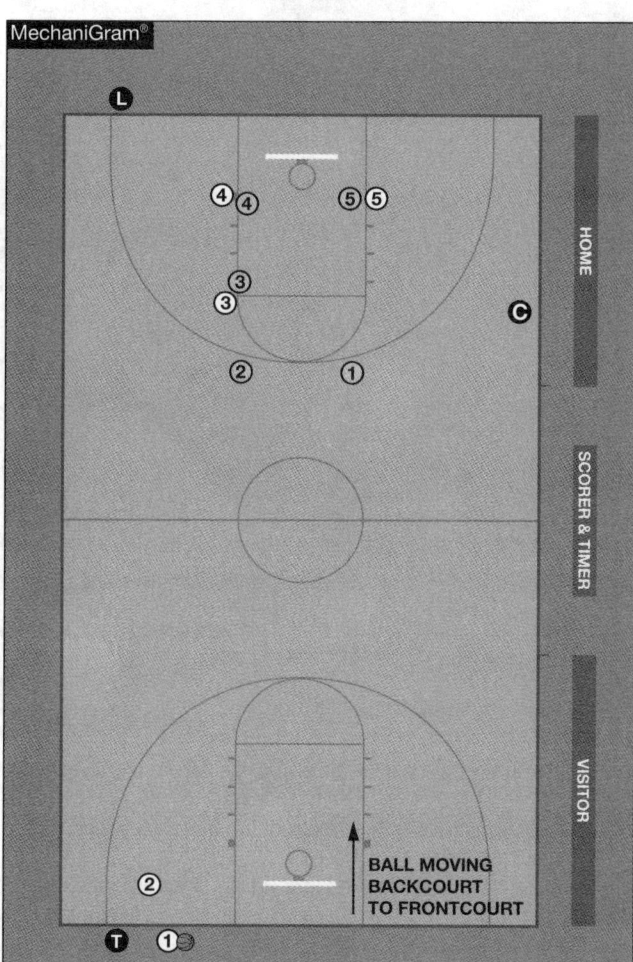

When play moves from one end line toward the other, the Trail has primary responsibility in the backcourt. For example, when there is no defensive pressure, after a made basket, the Trail is responsible for the throw-in and watches the players move until they get to the division line. Once all players are in the frontcourt, normal frontcourt coverage areas apply.

The Trail should remain behind the players at all times, even if there is no defensive pressure.

BACKCOURT WITH PRESSURE

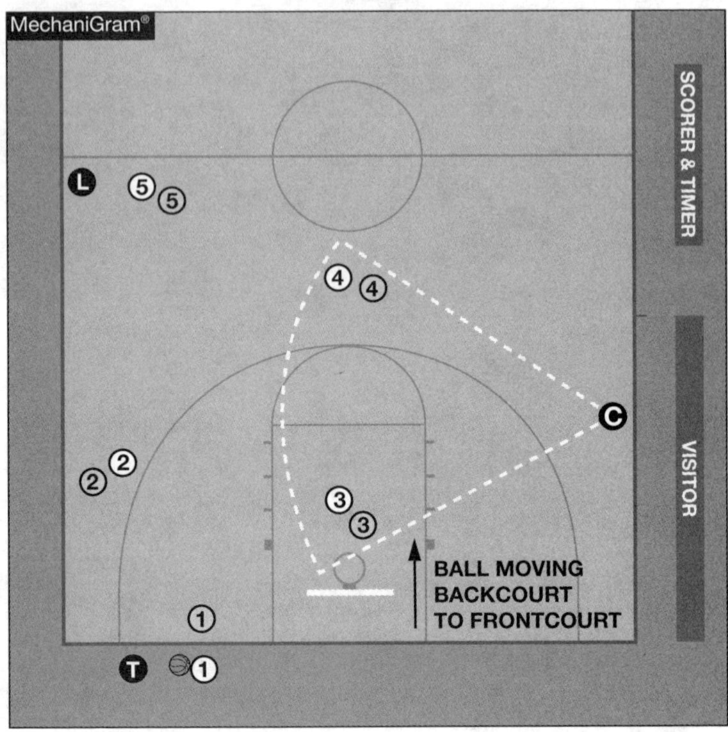

When there is defensive pressure in the backcourt, the Center, and sometimes the Lead, must help.

If there are four or fewer players in the backcourt, the Trail works alone. If there are more than four players, the Center helps.

When there are more than four players in the backcourt, the Center's starting position is near the free-throw line extended. If the Center stays in place after a made basket, the Center is in perfect position to help. The free-throw line extended position can vary depending on the location of the players. The Center must move to a spot along the sideline that gives the Center the best angle to officiate. The Center is responsible for the action of players in the backcourt, such as illegal screens or holding.

The Center should stay in position after a successful goal just long enough to observe there will not be any problems the new Trail cannot handle with ease. Then the Center can move down the court at the same rate as the players. The Lead is positioned a bit beyond the last offensive player on the court.

LAST-SECOND SHOT

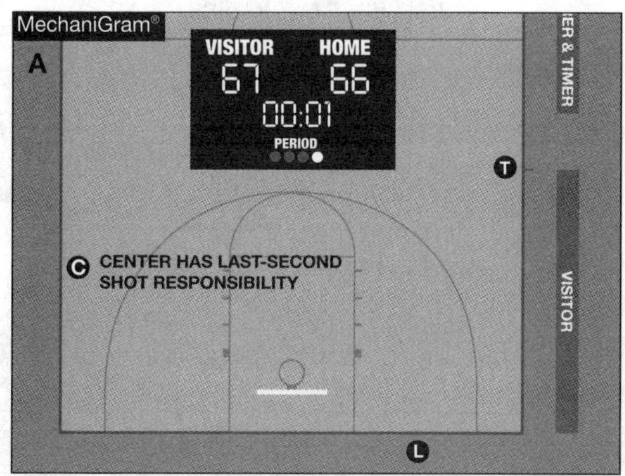

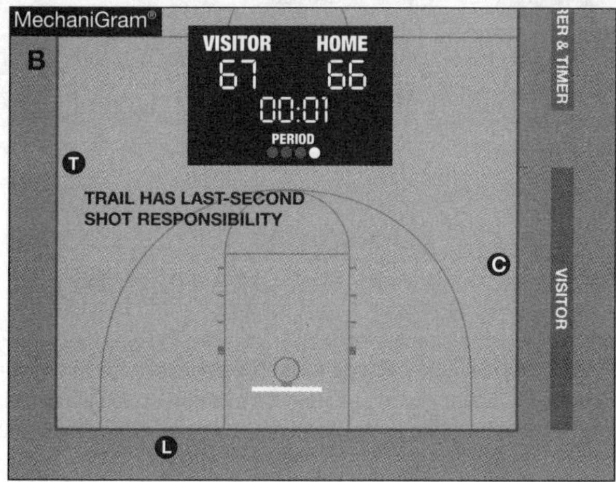

The official opposite the table, Trail or Center, has last-second responsibilities as seen in the MechaniGrams. That official should communicate that message and responsibility to both partners by signaling with a hand-on-chest signal when the game clock is near 15 seconds. Such communication should be repeated on any change of possession.

If the non-ruling official has information regarding the allowing or disallowing of a basket to share with the calling official, that official should go directly to the responsible official for a brief discussion. The R will make the final decision in the case of disagreement or if it is necessary to consult the timer.

When play is resumed with a throw-in or free throw and three-tenths of a second or less remains on the game clock, no field goal may be scored by a try for goal. Only a tap may score. This does not apply if the game clock does not display tenths of a second.

5.4 The Lead Position

BALL-SIDE MECHANICS

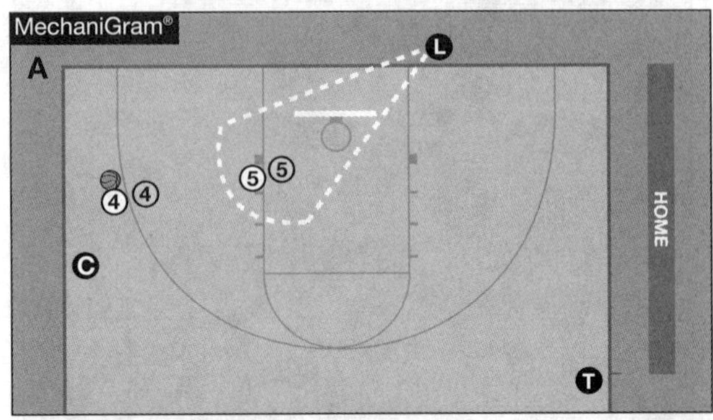

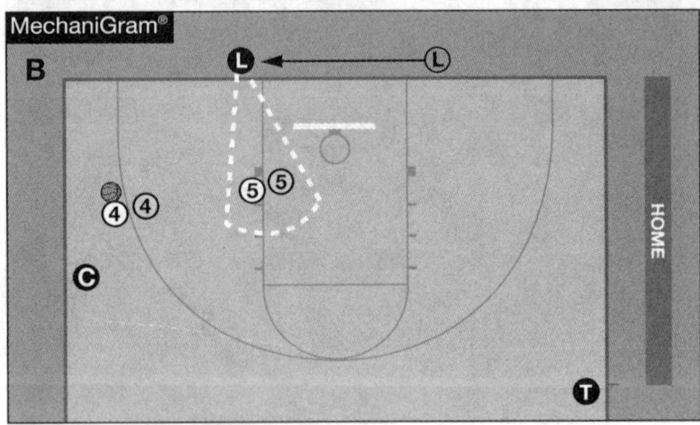

In three-person crews, the strong side would ideally be ball side at all times. While that is not possible, the Lead can move along the end line and make the strongside the ball side. The Lead must anticipate a drop pass into the low post on the opposite lane line when the ball is near the free-throw line extended. In MechaniGram A, the Lead is near the lane line opposite the play and does not have a good angle.

In MechaniGram B, the Lead has rotated by moving across the end line to the lane line on the Center's side of the court to clearly see the post play.

Officials should keep their head and shoulders turned toward the players in the lane when moving. Remember, officials still have responsibilities for watching screens and other action in their PCAs. Officials should move with purpose, but under control and with eyes on the primary off-ball area.

The Lead moves for two reasons: The Lead is in a better position to see the play clearly (if the Lead stayed on the off-ball side, the Lead would be looking through bodies and guessing) and the Lead is closer to the play.

If a trap occurs near the division line on the Center's side of the court, the Center should move toward the division line to immediately officiate the play and the Lead should initiate a rotation. If the Lead does not rotate, the Center should go back to a normal Center position when play permits. The Trail or Center can facilitate a rotation, but only the Lead initiates a rotations.

AVOID POSITIONING UNDER THE BASKET

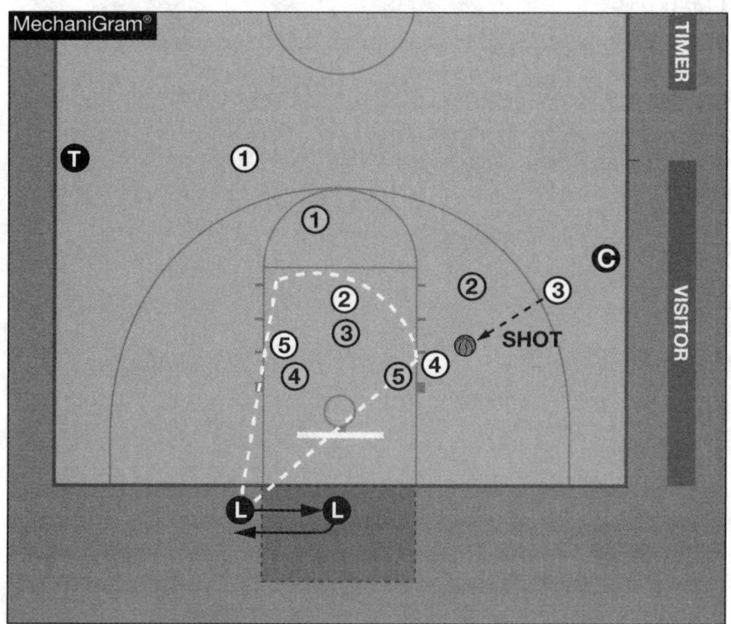

Positioning under the basket is a danger area for the Lead. An official should never be positioned directly under the basket because nothing can be seen or officiated from there.

The Lead can get caught under the basket when initiating a rotation and moving ball side as a player takes a shot. For example, the Lead moves ball side anticipating a drop pass into the post. Instead, a shot is quickly taken while the Lead is moving ball side. Now, the Lead must get out from under the basket and establish good rebounding angles.

When caught under the basket, the Lead must go back where the Lead came from because the rotation was not completed before the shot was attempted. If the Lead continues with the rotation during the try, partners might not catch a rotation occurred and end up in the wrong positions.

In the MechaniGram, the Lead begins the rotation and moves ball side to watch low post action. When the Lead is halfway through the lane, a shot is taken. Instead, after the shot, the Lead should back out from under the basket until the Lead is again in good position to watch rebounding action.

To know when a shot is being attempted, the Lead can read off-ball players' movements and should avoid watching the shooter. Off-ball players in the lane area will begin to obtain rebound positioning when a shot is airborne.

WIDE ANGLE/CLOSE DOWN

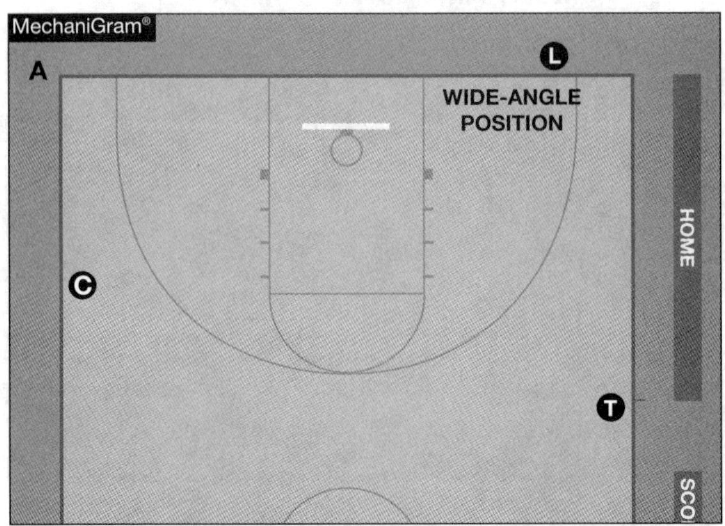

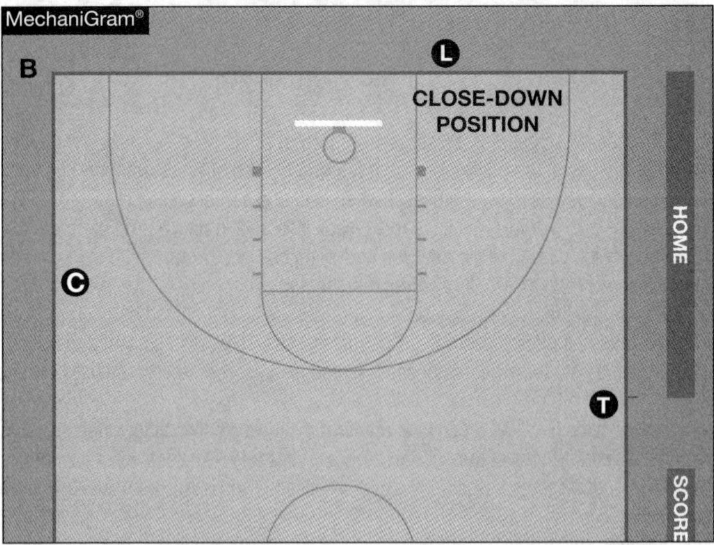

There are two basic starting positions for the Lead on the end line. When the ball is on the Lead's side of the court, the Lead establishes a wide-angle position, which is two to three steps inside the three-point arc line extended off the court as seen in MechaniGram A. When the ball is in the middle of the court or on the Center side of the court, the Lead establishes a close-down position which is one step outside the free-throw lane line extended off the court, as seen in MechaniGram B. The close-down position makes it easier for the Lead to rotate.

MOVEMENT TOWARD SIDELINE

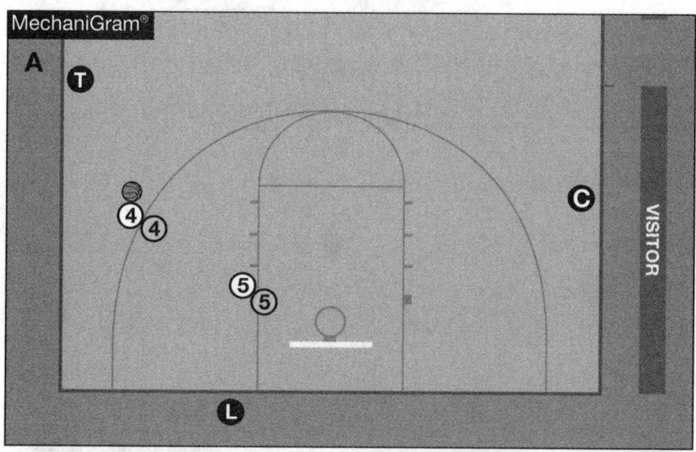

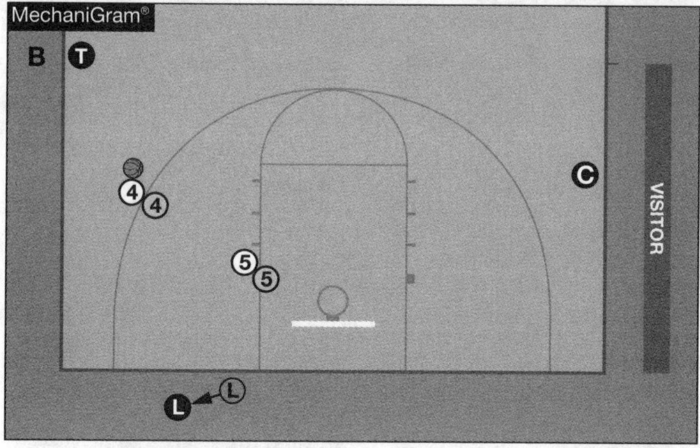

When the ball drops below the free-throw line extended on the Lead side of the court, the Lead's main responsibility is to watch the post players on the near low block. Officials too close to the low block do not have a wide angle and may not have the proper perspective.

For a wide angle and better perspective, officials should back off the end line and move toward the sideline. Shoulders should not be parallel to the end line; they should be angled slightly. That movement increases the field of vision and provides an opportunity to see both areas.

In MechaniGram A, the Lead is too close to the play and is not close enough to the sideline.

In MechaniGram B, the Lead is in better position after moving off the end line, moving closer to the sideline and angling the shoulders. With that improved position, the Lead has a better perspective on low block action and is not on top of the play, which makes officiating the low-block area easier.

LEAD HELP ON THREE-POINT TRY

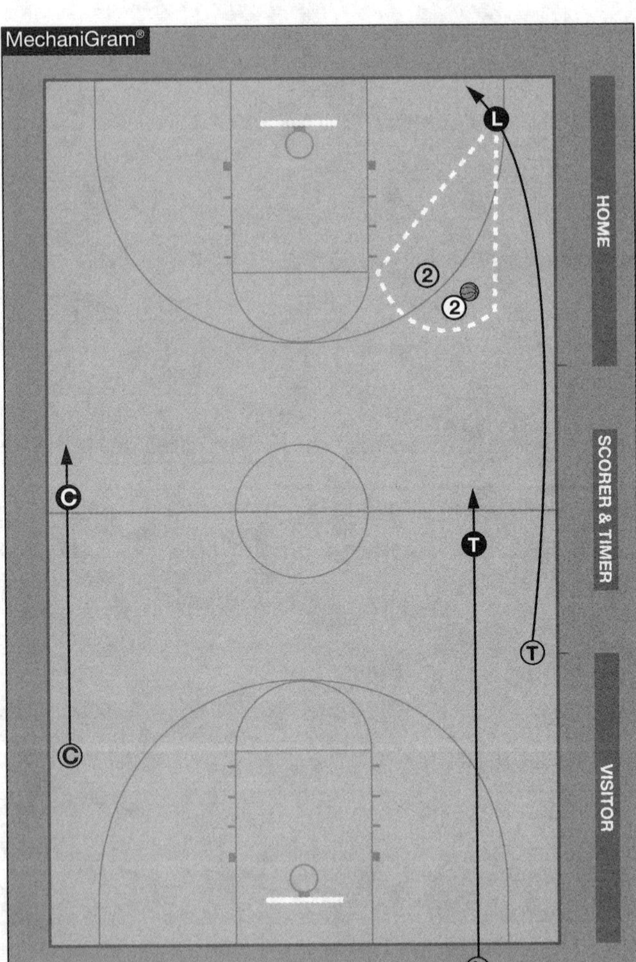

In a halfcourt setting, the Lead does not signal a three-point try or successful attempt. However, in transition that is not always the case. If a quick transition puts the ball in the frontcourt followed by a quick three-point attempt, the Center and Trail may not be in position to properly rule on a three-point try. In such cases, the Lead can rule whether or not the try is attempted from behind the three-point arc, as seen in the MechaniGram.

5.5 The Center Position

RANGE OF MOVEMENT

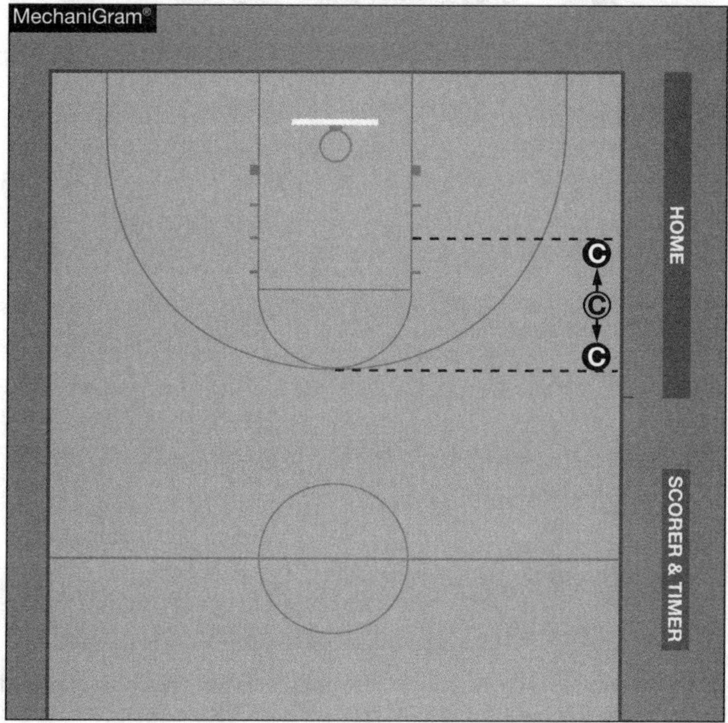

The normal starting point for the Center in a halfcourt setting is free-throw line extended. That is just a starting point though and it is not the only location the Center can be. The Center can move comfortably up and down the sideline from the top of the key extended to the second lane space mark extended, as seen in the MechaniGram.

Movement within that range allows for the Center to open angles and does not alter the positions or responsibilities of the Lead and Trail. It is the accepted range of motion for the Center.

The majority of the Center officials will move out toward the division line at any opportunity. Officials should stay lower and possibly step down toward the end line instead of up toward the division line. Angles will open up on off-ball coverage and will be far better from that spot on the court.

MOVE ONTO COURT

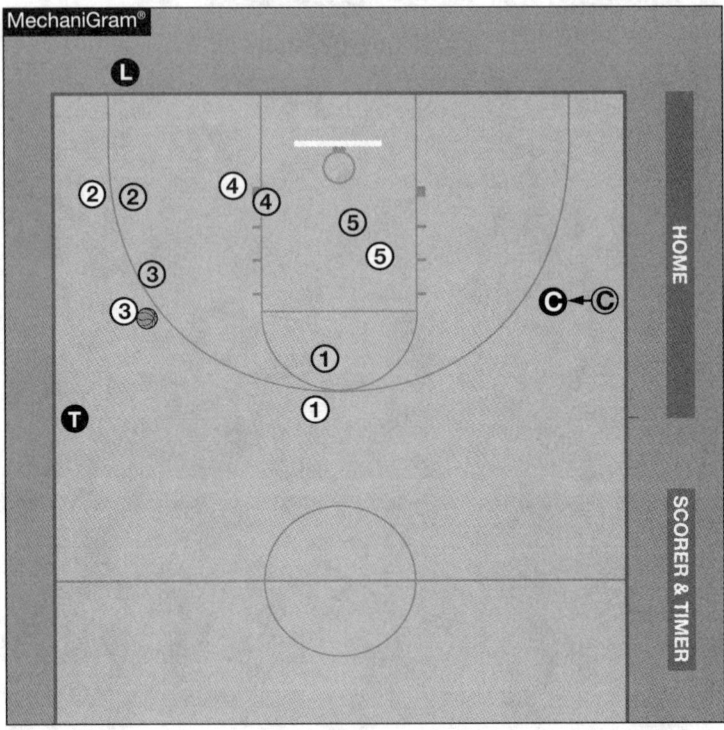

When the majority of the players are on the far side of the lane, the Center may need to temporarily move one or two steps onto the court, as in the MechaniGram. It does not do any good to have the Center stay chained to sideline if there are not any players to officiate.

By moving onto the court one or two steps, the Center is not only closer to the players, but will have a better angle on off-ball fouls.

When the Center is on the court and play comes back toward the Center, simply move back to the sideline and the normal location for the Center position.

OPEN ANGLES

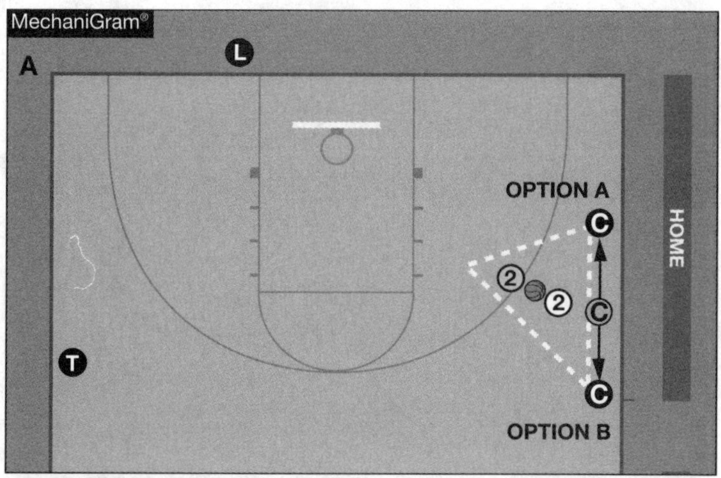

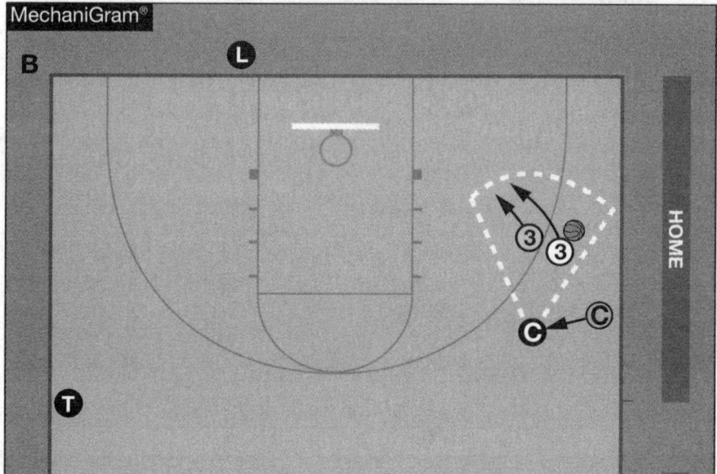

When play comes directly at the Center who is standing on the sideline, most angles and depth are lost. It is difficult to officiate plays when officials are too close to them.

The Center can and should move to maintain an open angle. Otherwise the Center will become straightlined. The Center can step up toward the division line or down toward the end line, as in MechaniGram A.

The same emphasis holds true when an offensive player with the ball in the Center's coverage area turns the corner and drives the lane. The Center must maintain the proper angle on that drive and that may mean moving onto the court a step or two to keep it, as in MechaniGram B. Officials who stay in the same place and do not move often do not see the whole play. Officials should always strive to create the best possible angles.

HELP ON OUT OF BOUNDS

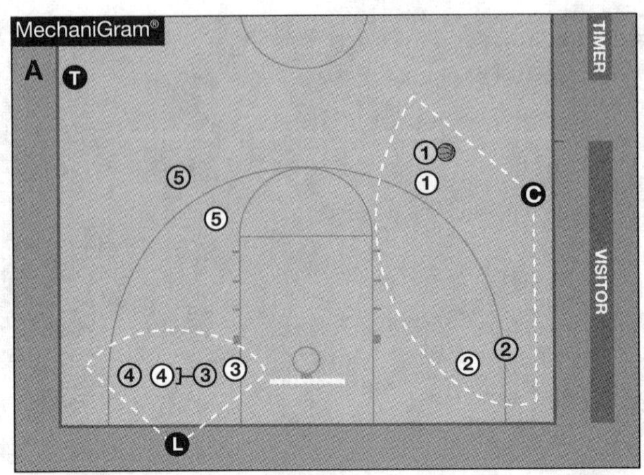

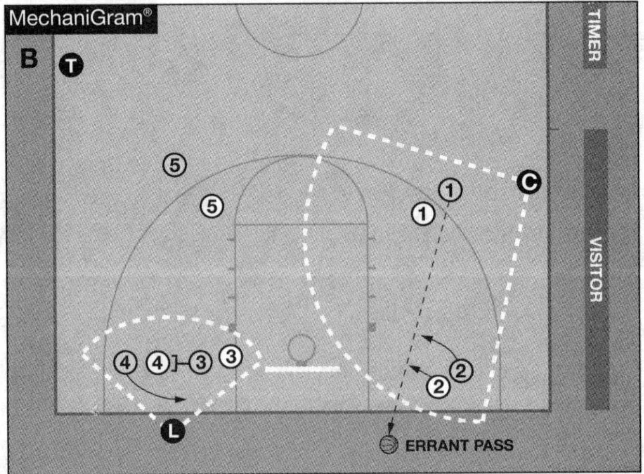

Though rare, there will be instances when action is going to occur and the calling official is not going to know what happened. That occasionally happens on out-of-bounds calls. The Center must be ready to help.

In MechaniGram A, the Lead is watching a screen. The Center has on-ball coverage and is responsible for the ball. In MechaniGram B, the pass is not handled cleanly and goes out of bounds on the end line.

The Lead official, still watching the screen, sees the ball go out of bounds but does not know who touched it last. The Lead should blow the whistle and immediately look to the Center for help to see who caused the out-of-bounds violation. The Center will know which player caused the ball to go out of bounds and should make the call.

Because the Lead was watching the Lead's PCA, and with some communication by the Center, the play can be called correctly, without sacrificing off-ball coverage.

SPIN MOVE

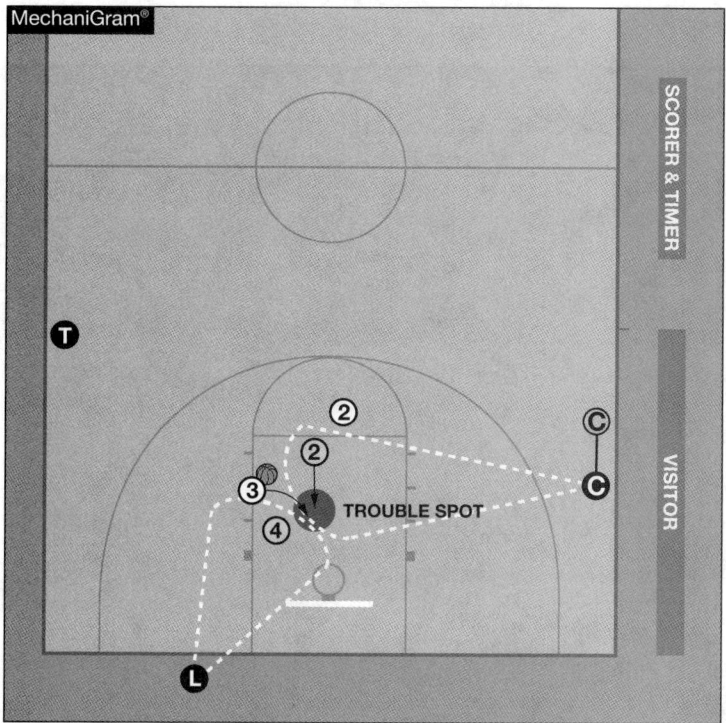

A trouble spot for the Lead develops when a player with the ball on the low block spins toward the middle of the lane away from the Lead. The quick spin move often leaves the Lead straightlined and without a good look on the play.

Many times, a defender near the free-throw line will drop down into the lane and challenge the move toward the basket. This is when the defender will likely slap at the offensive player, trying to poke the ball away. That steal attempt is sometimes a foul — one that goes unseen by the now-straightlined Lead.

The Center must help out and watch the area in the lane when a post player spins away from the Lead. Commonly referred to as the Lead's "backside," the Center has a much better look at the play after penetrating toward the end line for an improved angle, as seen in the MechaniGram.

5.6 The Trail Position

SPACING

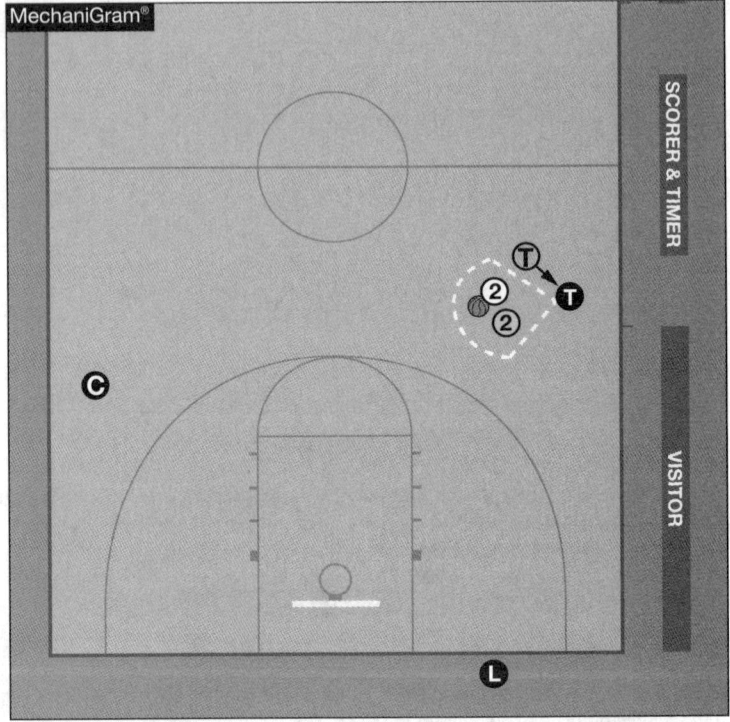

When an official gets too close to a play, that official's view of the play is distorted, as shown in the MechaniGram.

When the official moves, that official creates proper spacing and can see all of the items involved in the play (ball, defender, hands).

OUTSIDE-IN LOOK/INSIDE-OUT LOOK

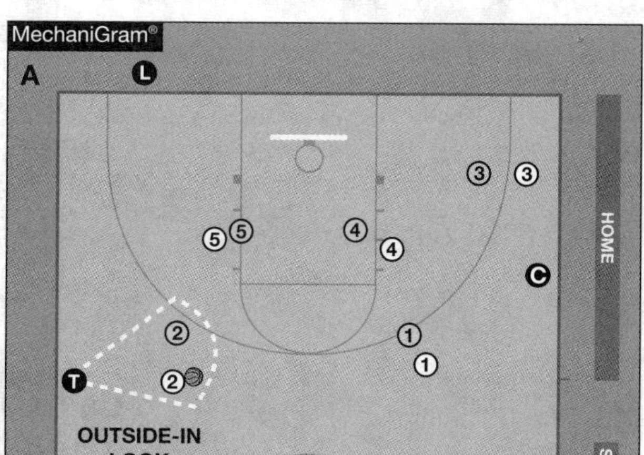

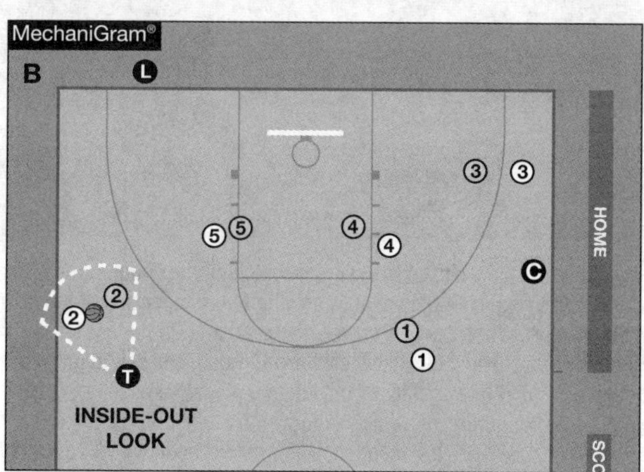

The officials in the Trail and Lead positions will normally officiate all play in a halfcourt game on the strong side. With the ball in the frontcourt above the free-throw line extended, the Trail is responsible for on-ball coverage. The Trail will officiate from the outside-in, assuming a position that is perpendicular to the ball whenever possible, as in MechaniGram A. Officiating from the outside-in allows the Trail to see as many of the 10 players as possible while officiating on the ball. It allows the Trail to dictate the Trail's angle instead of taking the angle given by the players. When there is defensive pressure on the perimeter, before the ball clearly crosses the lane line closest to the Center, the Trail will step onto the court to get a better angle, or open look, on the play.

When the ball is too near the sideline, the official will move onto the court and officiate from the inside-out, as seen in MechaniGram B, or up toward the division line. Once that matchup dissolves, the officials should move back toward the sideline closer to the home position.

MOVEMENT ON JUMP SHOT

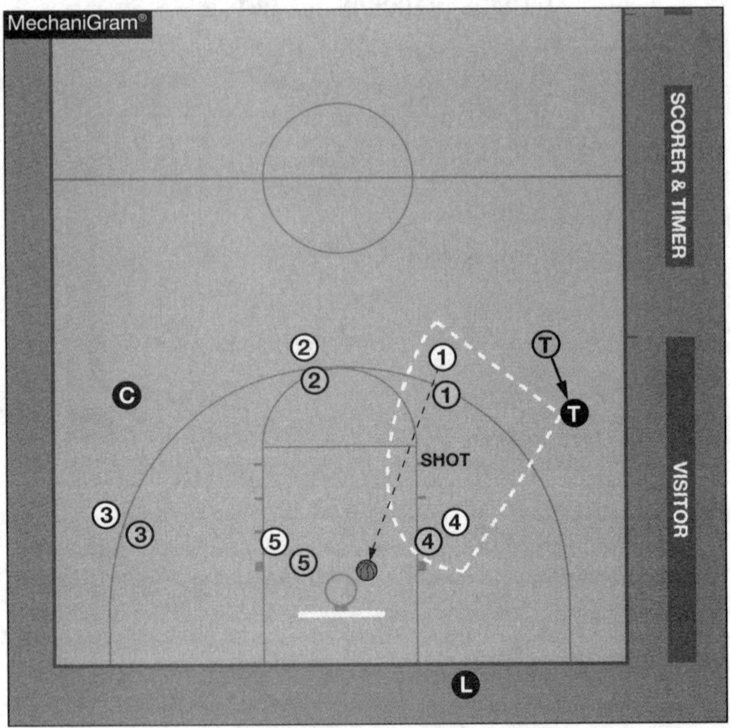

The Trail has more responsibilities than simply watching the shooter. Too often a shot goes up and the Trail's first thought is to start moving to the other end of the floor to avoid getting beat down court. When the Trail leaves, the Lead and Center are left with offensive players crashing the boards and defensive players doing all they can to grab the rebound.

The Trail must help with rebounding action. When a player takes a jump shot within the Trail's coverage area, the first responsibility is to watch the airborne shooter all the way back to the floor to ensure there are no offensive or defensive fouls. While watching that action, the Trail should be moving a couple of steps toward the end line, as shown in the MechaniGram.

Once everything is okay with the shooter and surrounding action, the steps toward the end line allow the Trail to help the Lead by watching rebounding action. A step or two to improve an official's angle is all that is necessary to successfully watch rebounding action. The Trail is likely to see an offensive player pushing (or crashing into) a defensive player from behind — something that is difficult for the Lead to see from the end line.

Resist the urge to sprint to the other end of the floor when the shot goes up. Move toward the end line to get rebounding angles.

CONCENTRATE ON OFF BALL

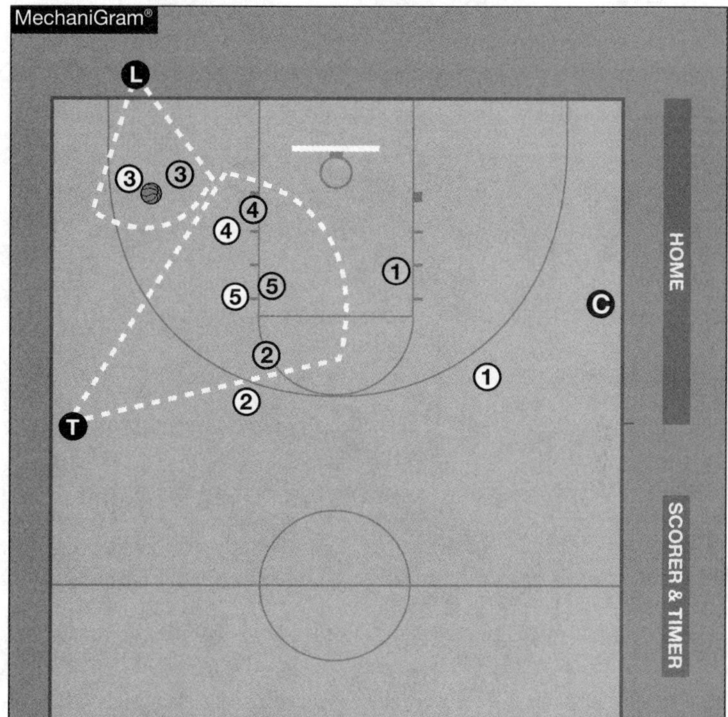

One of the many keys to successful three-person officiating is knowing when to watch off-ball and when not to. When the ball is not in an official's PCA, that official must concentrate on off-ball action.

In the MechaniGram, the Lead has on-ball coverage. The Trail must concentrate off-ball and observe the actions of players away from the ball. If the Trail were to watch the ball while it is in the Lead's PCA, that leaves only the Center to watch the other eight players.

5.7 Rotations

CLOSE DOWN

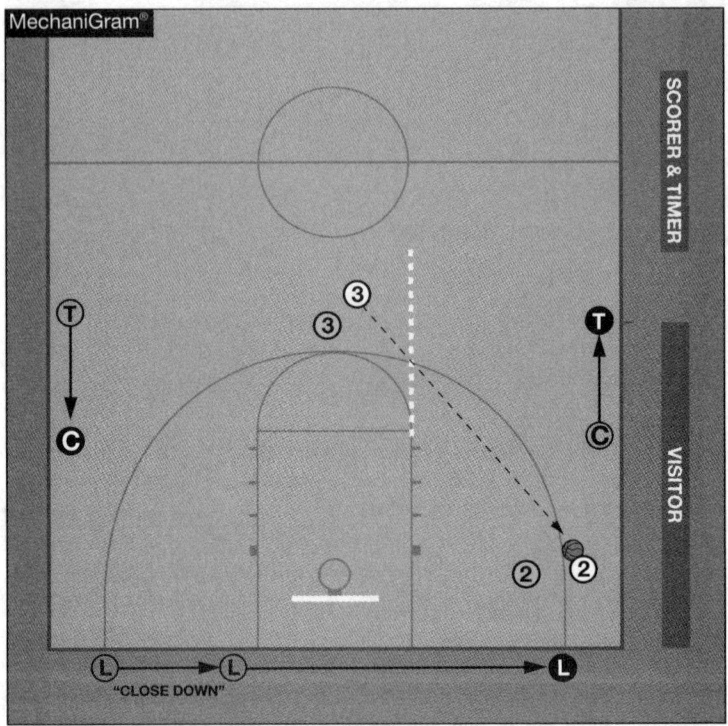

As a guideline and depending on playing action, the Lead should close down and may move laterally to ball side when the ball is near the free-throw lane line extended nearest the Center. When the Lead moves laterally across the end line (initiates a rotation), activity in the lane must still be observed by the Lead.

"Close down" means the Lead moves from an area along the end line on the Lead's side of the court to the free-throw lane line nearest the Lead, as seen in the MechaniGram. Often, closing down means a lateral movement by the Lead of a few feet.

WHEN TO ROTATE

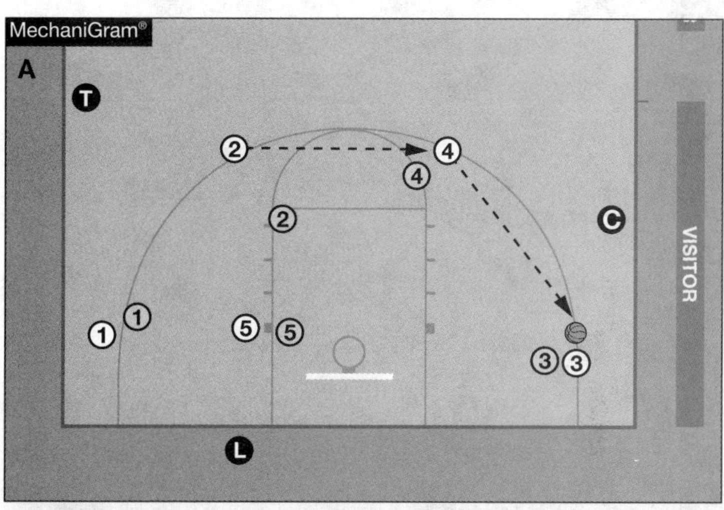

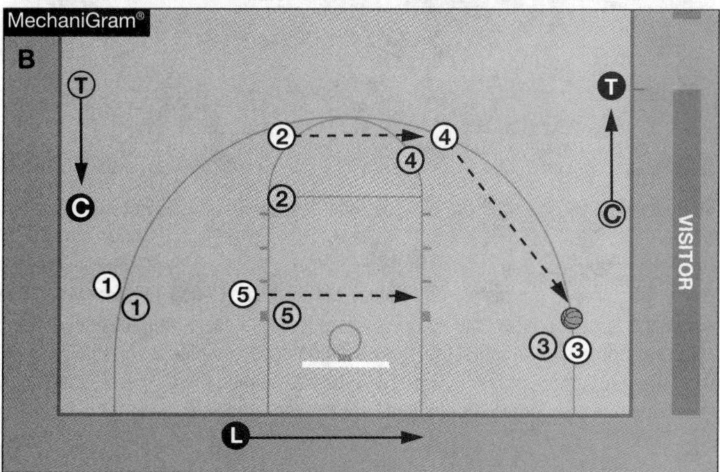

The Lead should rotate when the ball is near the free-throw lane line extended in the Center's coverage area. The Lead must read the playing action and anticipate ensuing plays to rotate properly, as seen in MechaniGram A.

If the ball is on the wing just entering the Center's area and the Lead does not anticipate post action or a drive to the basket, there is no need to rotate.

If the ball is near the free-throw lane line extended and the Lead senses ensuing post-play action (such as a post player moving ball side) as seen in MechaniGram B, the Lead must initiate a rotation to get in better position to officiate the post play. By not rotating, the Lead makes the Center work harder by officiating a lot of action in a short amount of time.

CENTER INITIATES

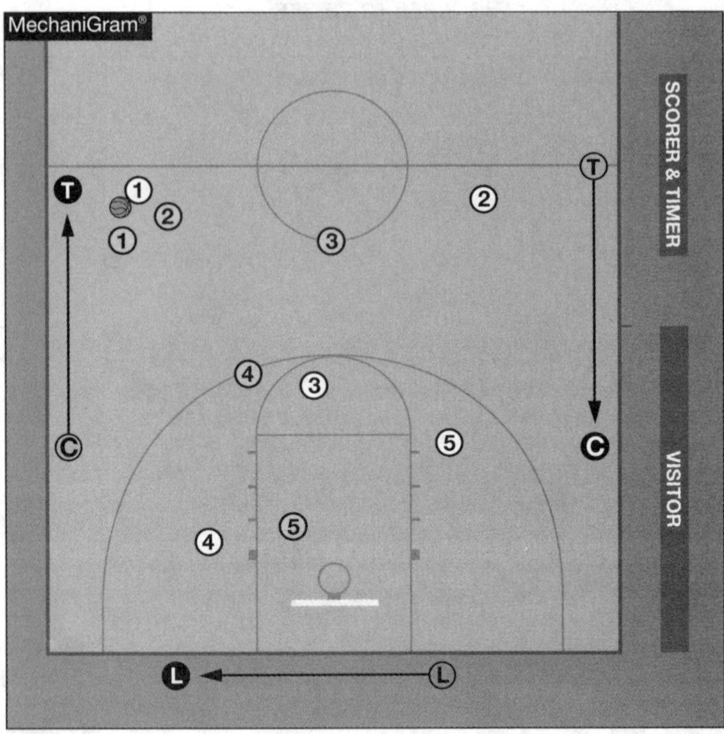

In most cases during a game, the Lead dictates the rotation. However, there is a notable exception.

When a player with the ball is trapped near the division line on the Center's side of the court it is a difficult area to officiate. When that happens, the Center must move up toward the division line to get in better position to officiate that defensive trap, as seen in the MechaniGram. Once that happens, the other two officials must pick up on the Center's movement, then rotate accordingly. With the Center becoming the new Trail, the Trail drops down and becomes the Center and the Lead shifts over to ball side.

CENTER STAYS ON BALL

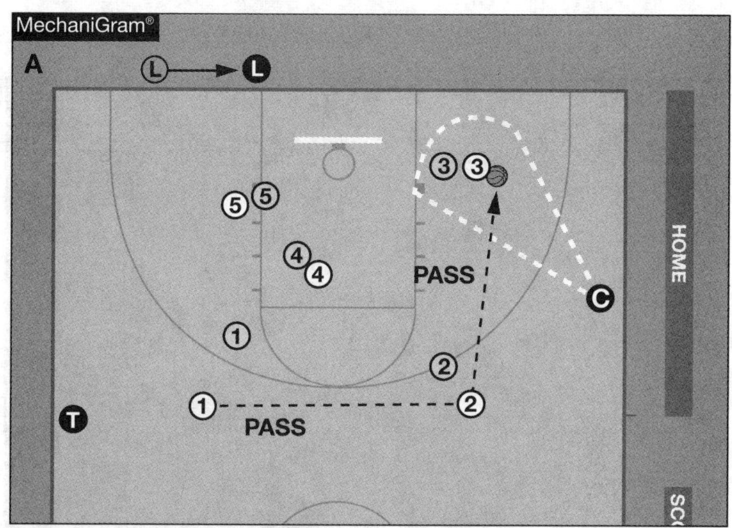

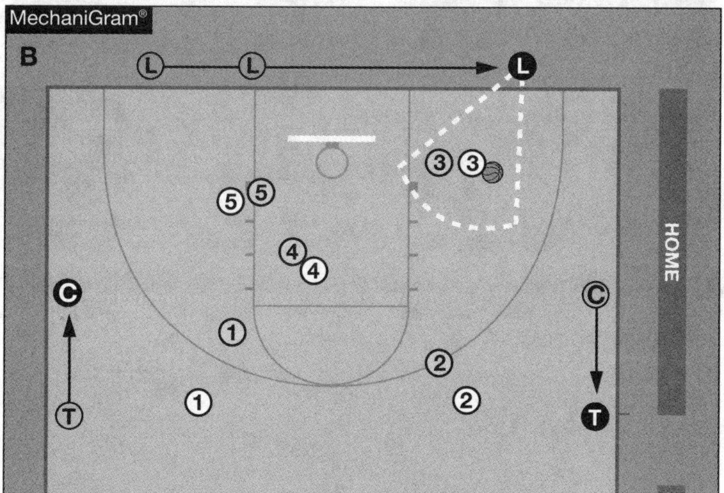

The Center must officiate all the action when the ball is near the free-throw lane line extended nearest the Center until the Lead can move laterally across the floor to accept responsibility to cover the play, as seen in MechaniGram A.

The Center will probably be officiating on the ball prior to any rotation for a brief period of time. In order to maintain better coverage, the Center may need to pause while rotating to Trail. Temporarily, there are two Center officials. Complete the rotation when play permits, as in MechaniGram B.

5.8 Transitions

BACKCOURT TO FRONTCOURT

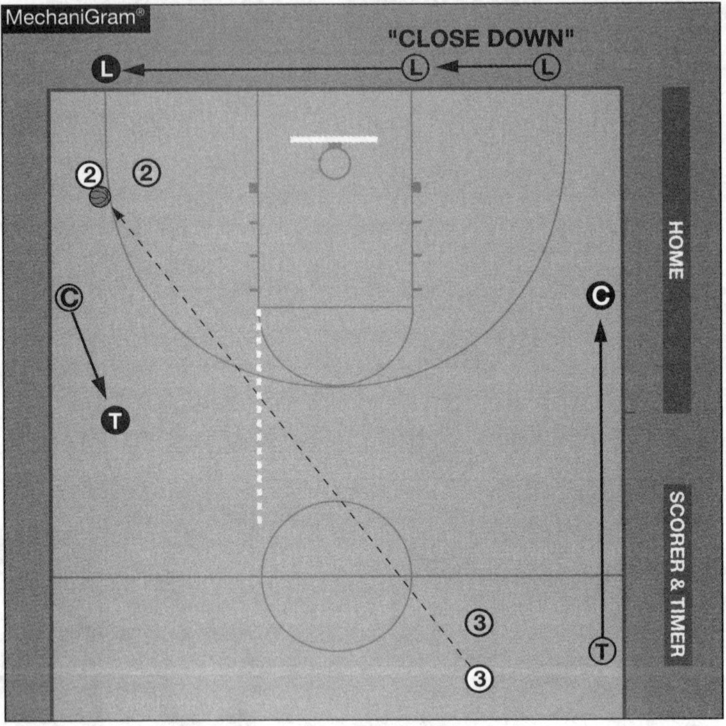

The Lead may rotate ball side once all three officials or the ball and all 10 players are in the frontcourt. That makes for a smooth rotation and ensures that all three officials are aware a rotation may take place.

DO NOT BAIL OUT AFTER BASKET

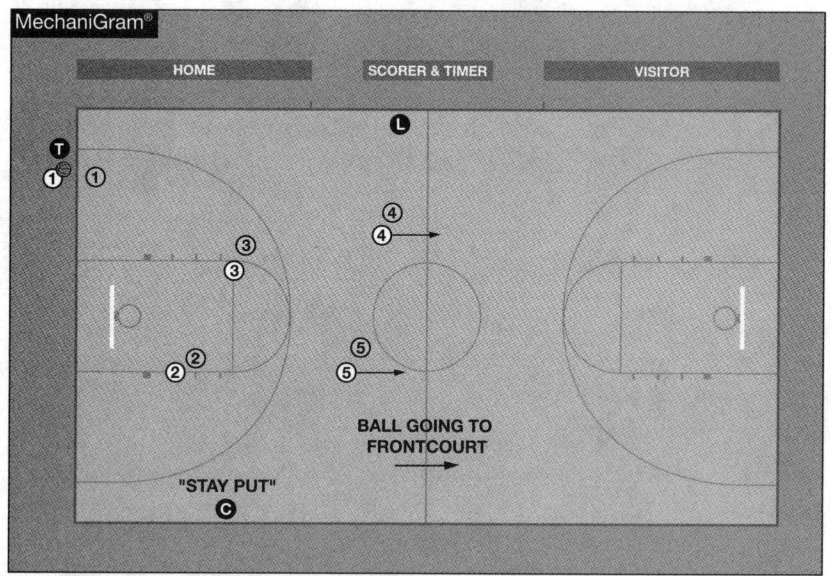

After a goal is scored, players are in a hurry to get to the other end of the court, unless the team that just scored is pressing. It is at that moment when the Center cannot be moving downcourt like the players.

With the Center staying in the same relative location, as seen in the MechaniGram, the Center helps the new Trail officiate players moving to receive the ensuing throw-in pass.

If a team does press, then the Center is already in perfect position to officiate the fullcourt pressure.

The Center should stay in position after a successful goal just long enough to observe there will not be any problems the new Trail cannot handle with ease. Then the Center can move down the court at the same rate as the players. However, if players' actions dictate the Center to stay a bit longer, do so.

TRAIL IN TRANSITION

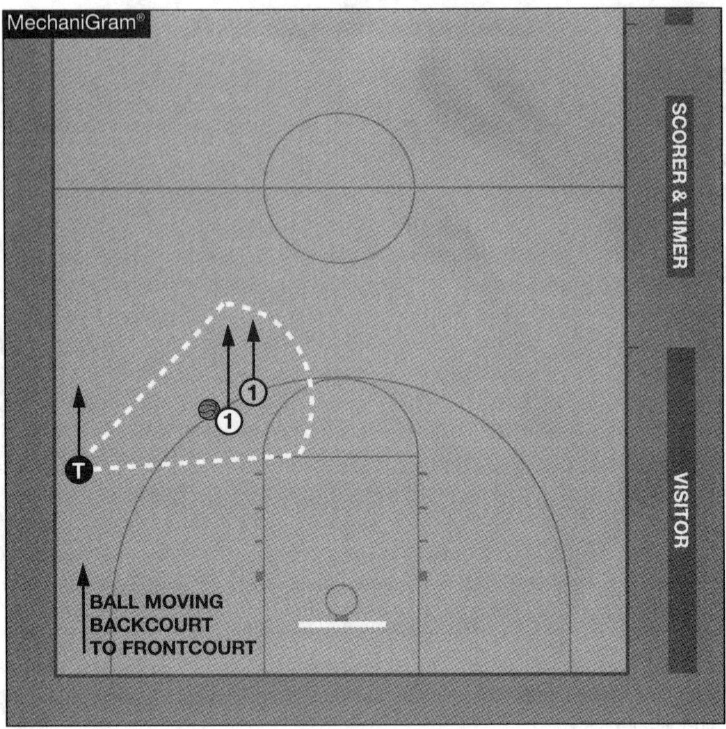

Following a change in possession, the new Trail should follow the players up court and be off toward the side. The Trail should trail the players. The Trail is responsible for all one-on-one situations until it reaches the frontcourt.

TRAIL MOVES ONTO COURT

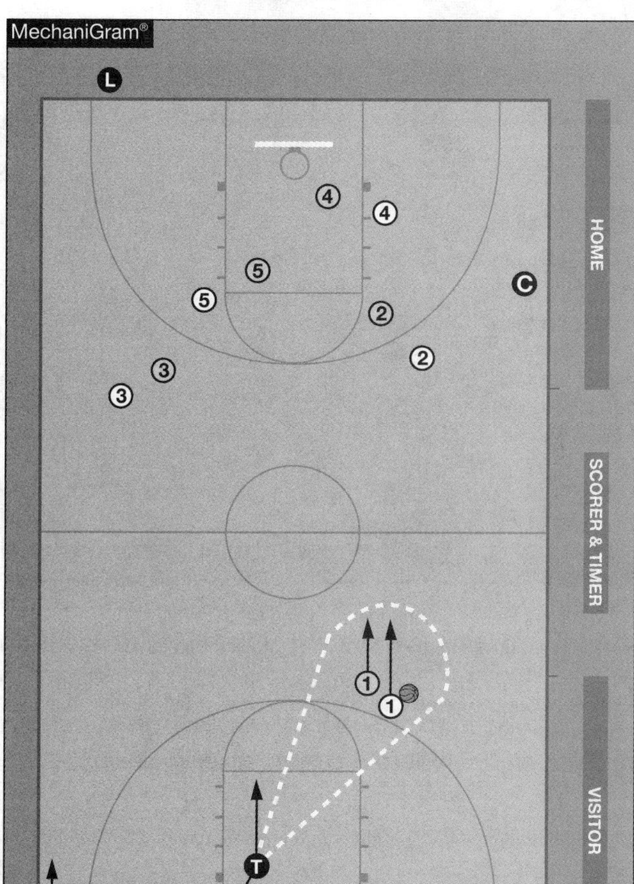

If there is one player providing defensive pressure, the Trail must move onto the court to have a clear view of the play. That may require the Trail moving up the middle of the court toward the Center's side to get the best angle on the play. When the ball reaches the frontcourt, normal frontcourt responsibilities apply.

AFTER A TURNOVER

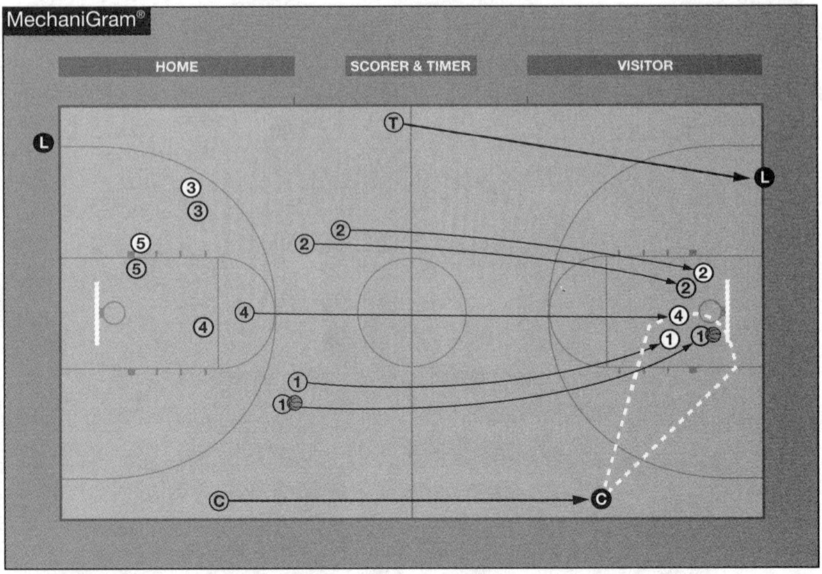

Fast-break action is shared among the Lead and Center officials.

Much like frontcourt drives to the basket, the Lead and Center are responsible for action that originates from their side of the lane, even on fast breaks. In the MechaniGram, the new Lead is blocked out and cannot see the drive to the basket clearly. That is the action the Center must officiate.

If a play happens, officials should move to get the proper angles and officiate as needed.

ONE-ON-ONE

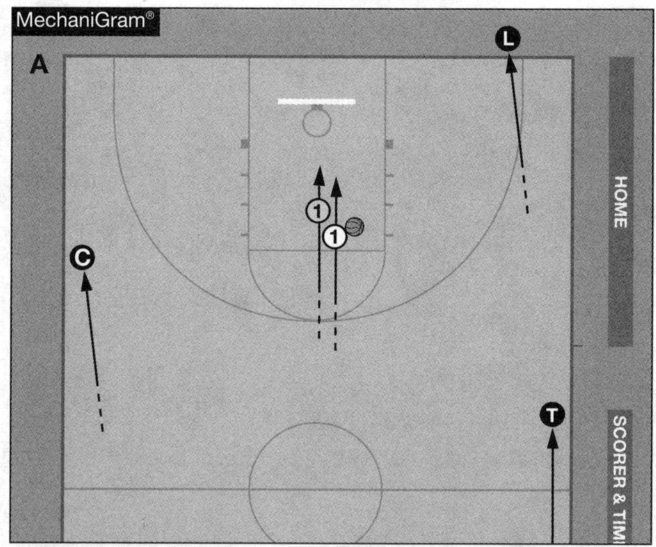

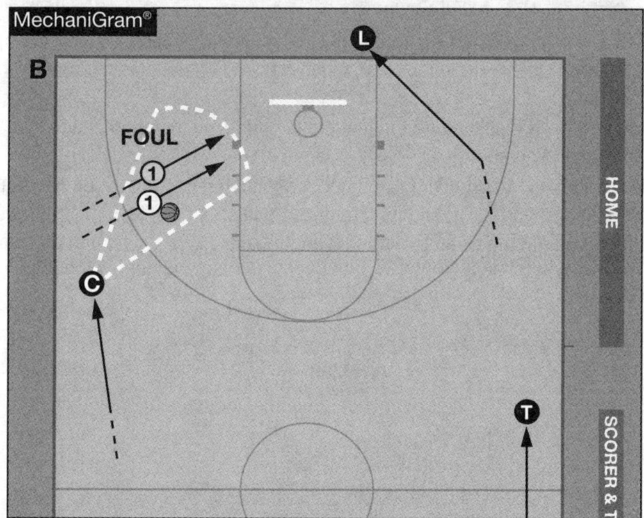

During a fast break one-on-one situation, the Center and Lead need to stay wide if the play is down the middle of the floor as in MechaniGram A. If there is a foul in the lane and a double whistle, it is the Lead's call to take or give up.

In one-on-one situations, with the play originating in Center's area and a foul committed on the drive to the basket, the Center makes the call as in MechaniGram B. If there is a double whistle on the play, the Center will take ownership of the PCA and make the ruling.

TROUBLE SPOT

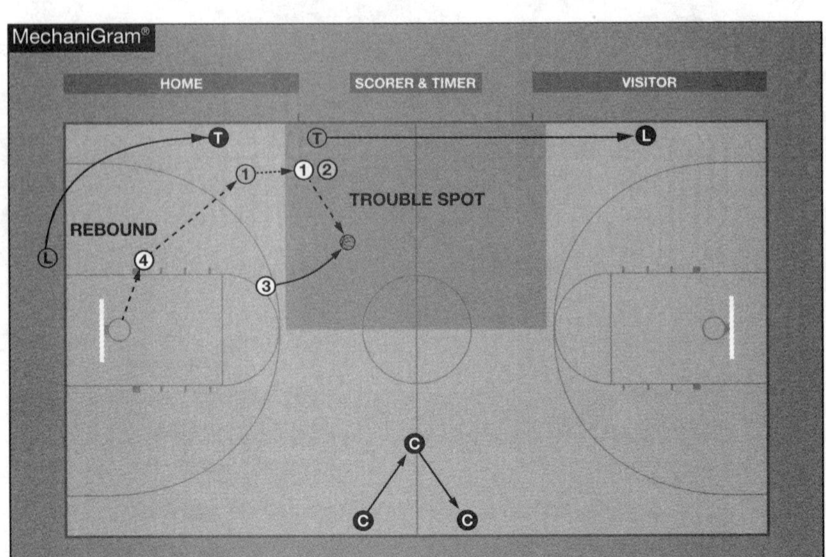

The same pass/crash principles that apply in the lane area apply all over the court. One trouble spot for officials is the pass/crash when a team in transition starts a fast break up the court.

The new Trail must quickly read the fast break and move toward the sideline. That play is the new Trail's call to make.

However, if the new Trail gets blocked out or cannot get into a position to see the play in its entirety, the call or no-call will rest on the shoulders of the Center. The Center can temporarily move onto the court to help. If there is no foul or violation and play continues, the Center can move back to the normal sideline position (as shown in the MechaniGram).

CENTER BUMPED

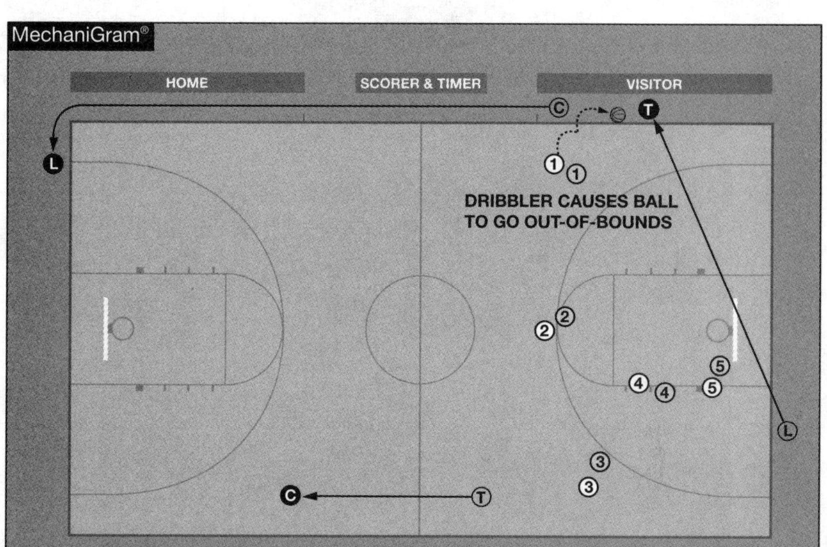

When an offensive violation occurs in the Center's coverage area, the Center should stop the clock, signal the violation and the direction, then point to the spot for the throw-in. Next — after checking that there are no problems — the Center should hustle down court while viewing the action behind and become the new Lead official.

The Lead should watch the Center's signals and should move toward the spot for the throw-in and administer it. The Lead has now become the new Trail. The Lead "bumped" the Center down court and the Center moving to Lead goes the length of the court. The Trail will move to become the new Center.

CENTER RESPONSIBLE FOR BALL

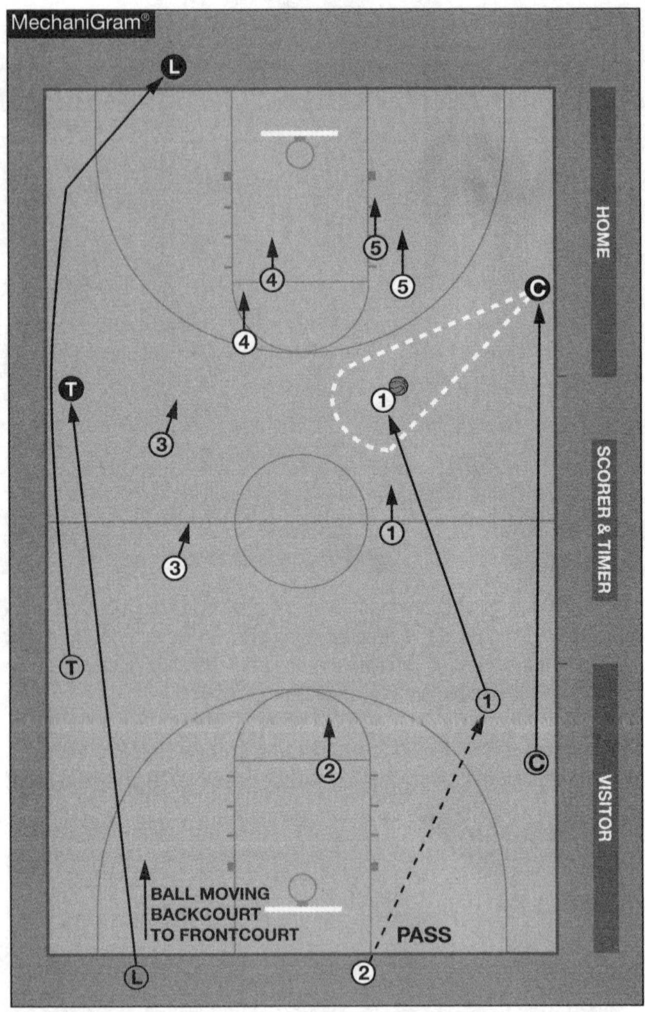

If the ball is at the free-throw lane line extended nearer the Center's position, the Center is responsible for on-ball coverage as soon as the ball crosses the division line, as seen in the MechaniGram.

LEAD CLOSES DOWN IMMEDIATELY

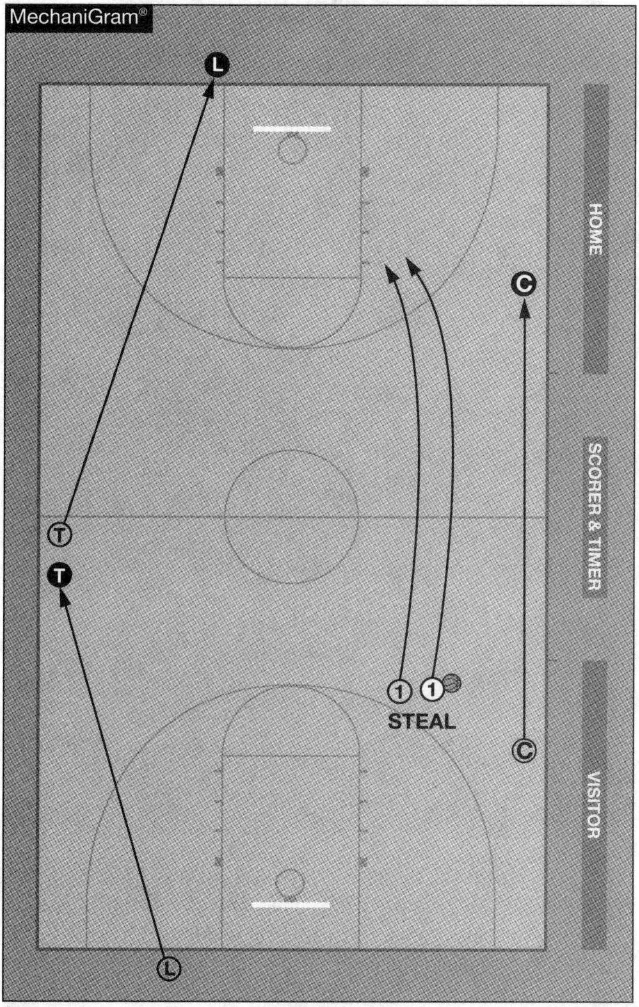

When there is a change of possession and the ball is on the Center's side of the court, the new Lead can go immediately to the close-down position along the end line. There is no need for the Lead to go to the end line, then move to the close-down position. Officials should avoid potential passing lanes.

LEAD HELPS

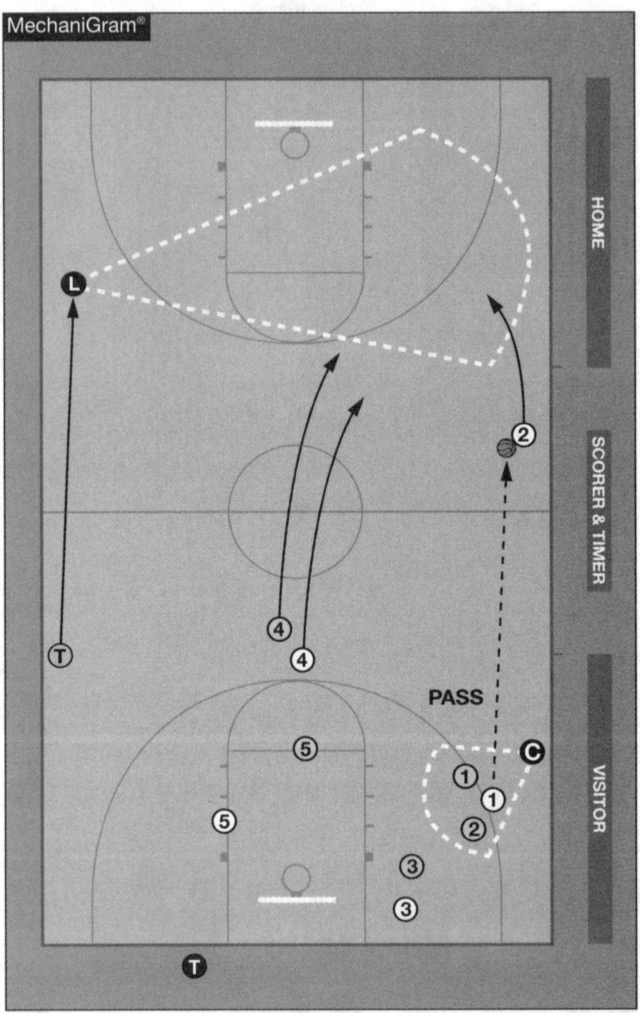

If defensive pressure is applied which causes the Center to assist in the backcourt, the new Lead must hesitate near the free-throw line extended or higher if necessary and assist with any action as seen in the MechaniGram.

SIDELINE RESPONSIBILITY

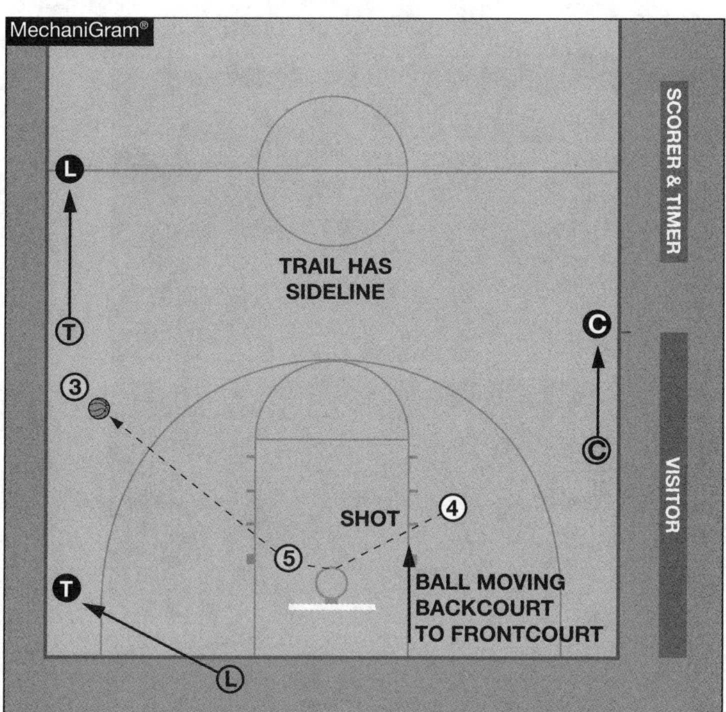

When there is a quick outlet pass after a rebound, the new Trail sometimes cannot cover sideline responsibilities immediately. Help is needed from the new Lead. The new Trail has primary sideline responsibility should the ball go out of bounds. The new Lead offers secondary coverage.

If a long pass goes out of bounds downcourt ahead of the new Lead, the new Lead has primary coverage.

5.9 Throw-ins

ADMINISTERING OFFICIALS

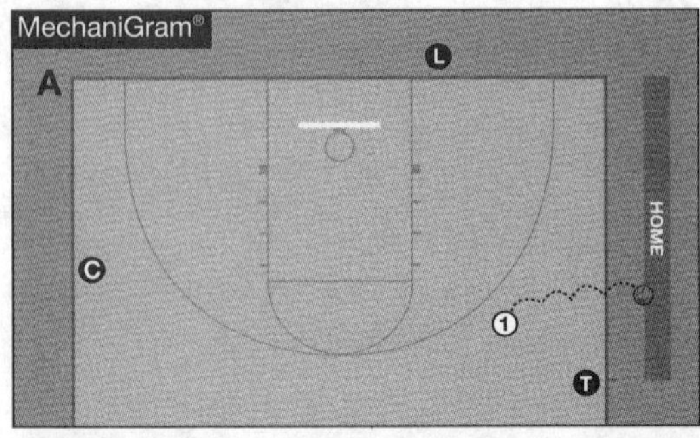

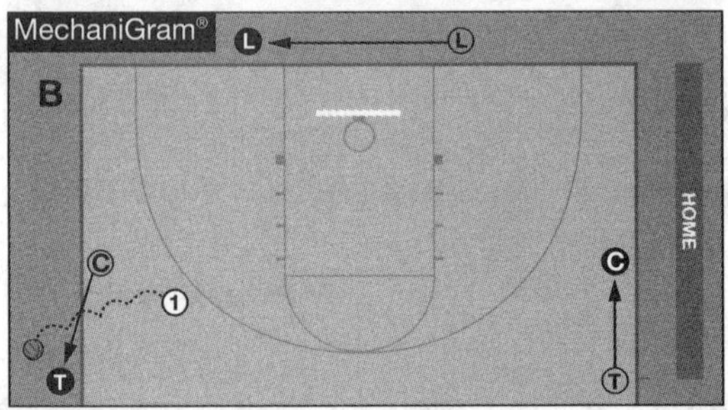

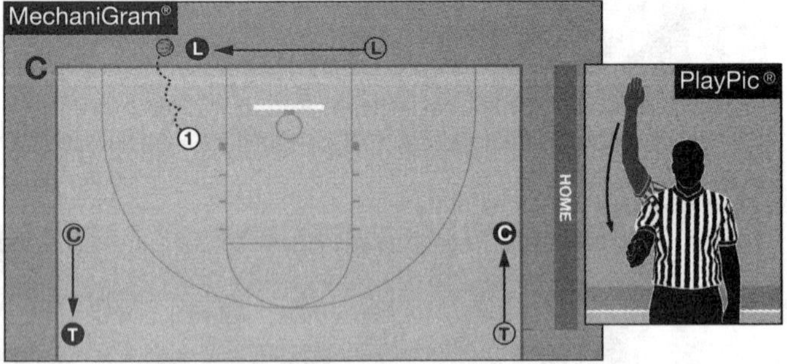

All throw-ins will be handled by the covering official.

In MechaniGram A, the ball goes out of bounds on the Trail's sideline. The Trail is the administering official no matter how close the ball is on the sideline to the end line.

In MechaniGram B, the ball goes out of bounds on the Center's sideline. The Center administers the ensuing throw-in and becomes the new Trail. Because two officials are needed on the same side of the court as the throw-in, the Lead moves across the end line. The Trail slides down to become the new Center.

In MechaniGram C, the ball goes out of bounds on the Lead's end line on the other side of the lane. The Lead moves across the end line and administers the ensuing throw-in. The Center slides toward the division line, becomes the new Trail and mirrors the Lead's "start clock" signal (Signal 1). The Trail slides down and becomes the Center.

LEAD POSITION

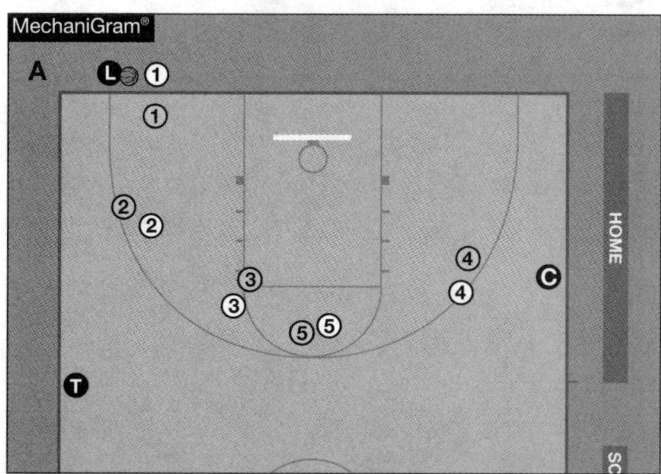

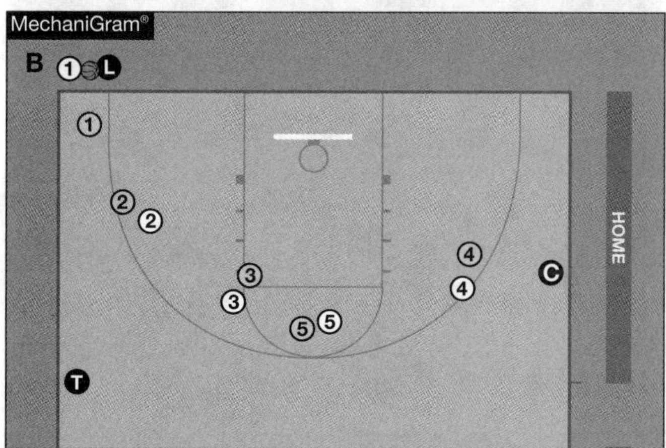

For frontcourt end line throw-ins, the Lead may be on either side of the thrower, based on the best view of the play. In MechaniGram A, the Lead is on the outside between the player and the sideline. In MechaniGram B, the Lead is on the inside between the player and the basket.

The Lead should hand the ball to the thrower on all frontcourt end line throw-ins.

To assist the timer, the Trail shall mirror the Lead's stop- (Signal 1) and start-clock (Signal 2) signals for frontcourt end line throw-ins.

The change gives the Center increased importance. Since it is possible that two officials will now be involved in the restarting of the game clock, the Center needs to concentrate more than ever on off-ball coverage.

WHEN TO BOUNCE

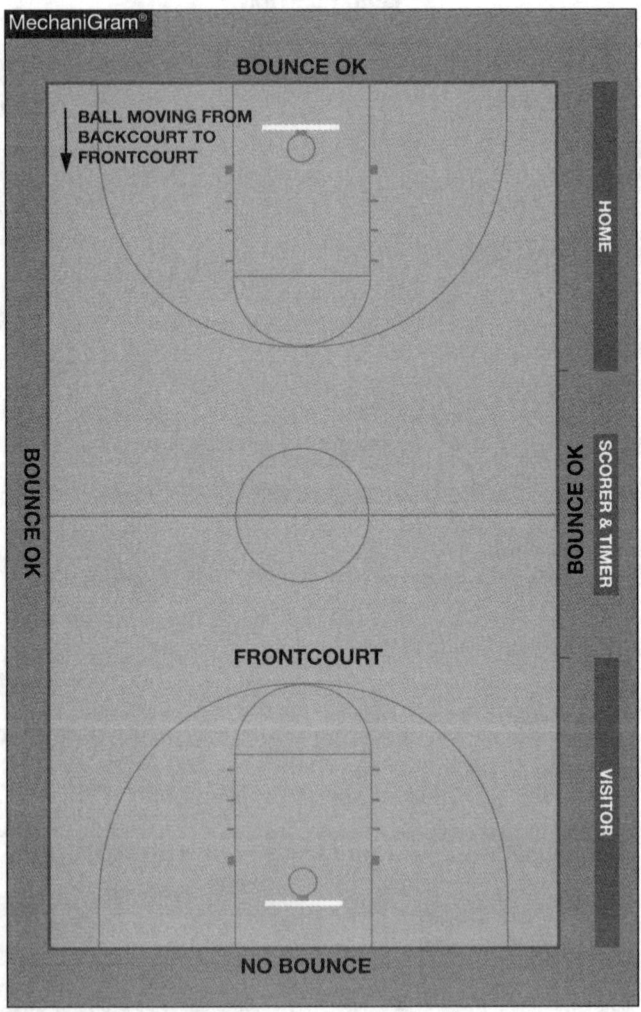

The official administering the throw-in has two ways of giving the ball to the thrower: handing or bouncing the ball. Which method depends upon where the throw-in takes place, as seen in the MechaniGram.

All throw-ins on the frontcourt end line are to be administered by handing the ball to the thrower.

The Trail should bounce the ball to the thrower in the backcourt, unless there is defensive pressure, in which the Trail should hand the ball to the thrower.

BACKCOURT THROW-IN

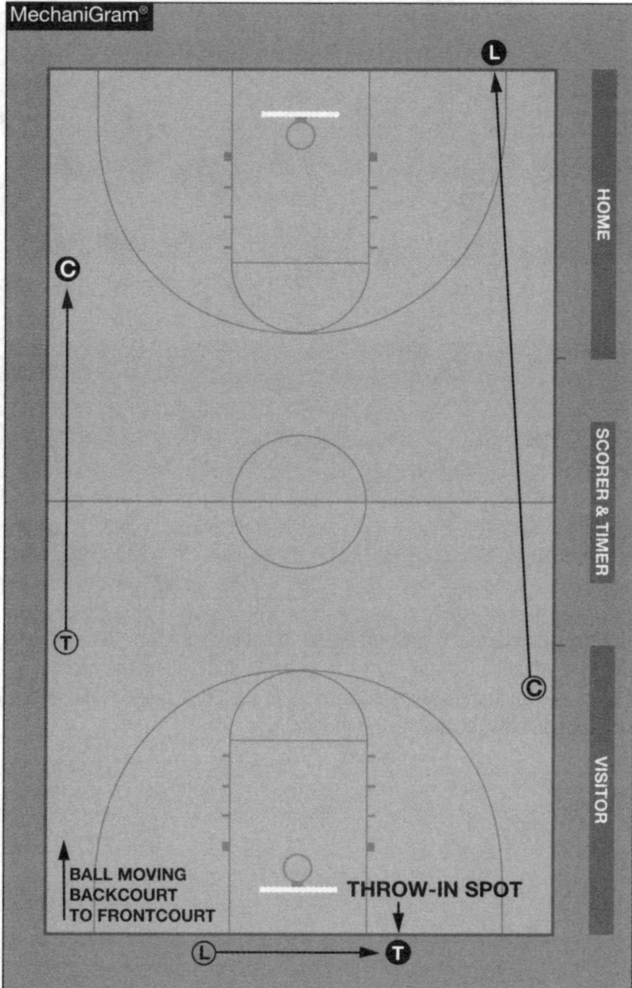

If the administering official is on the opposite side of the lane from the inbound spot, the administering official should move across the lane and refrain from bouncing the ball across the lane. The old Center moves downcourt and becomes the new Lead. The old Trail moves downcourt and becomes the new Center. The old Lead moves across the lane and becomes the new Trail.

If play is resumed after a stoppage (charged time-out, injury, etc.) with a throw-in along the end line after a successful goal, the administering official should use Signal 8 to indicate the thrower may move along the end line since the throw-in is not a designated spot throw-in.

DESIGNATED SPOTS IN THE FRONTCOURT

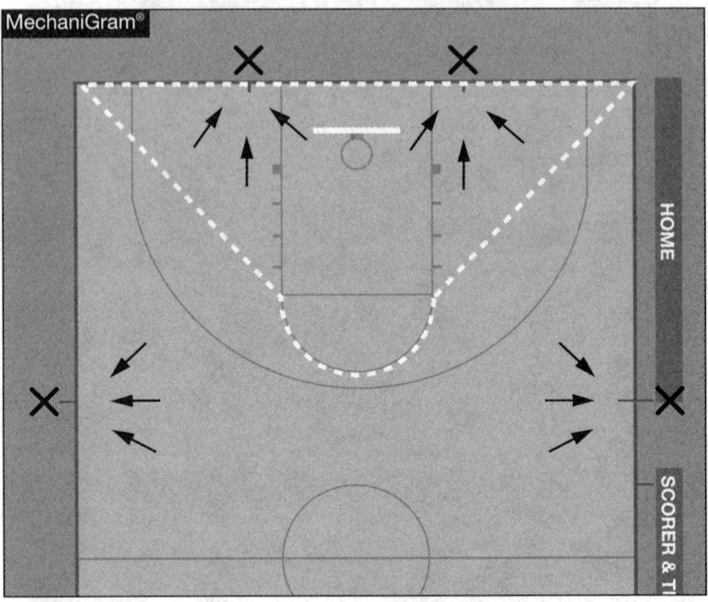

If there is a designated-spot frontcourt throw-in caused by a foul, violation or a stoppage (i.e. an inadvertent whistle or a time-out). the throw-in spot will be the nearest of the four designated spots shown in the MechaniGram: either the 28-foot line along either sideline or the three-foot spot outside the lane along the end line.

5.10 Reporting Fouls and Switching

FOUL REPORTING AREA

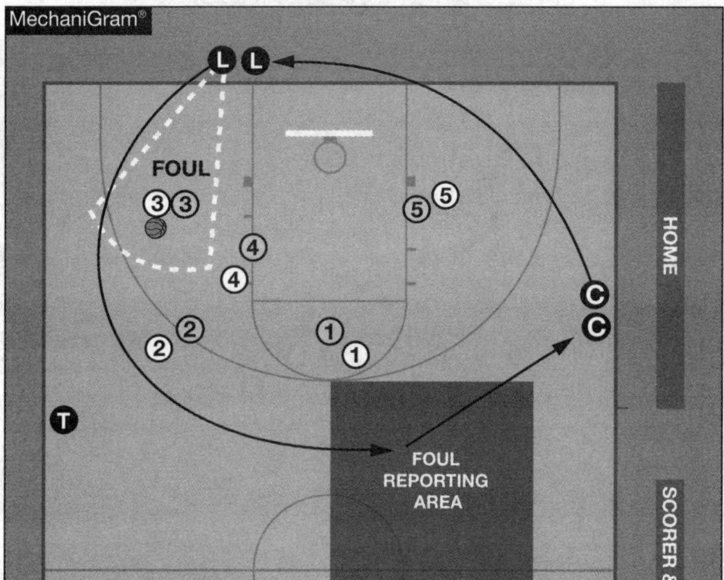

In the MechaniGram, the Lead has called a foul on the defender in the low post. At that time, the Lead must do a number of things:

1. Delay momentarily after signaling the foul at the spot to ensure there is no continuing action or inappropriate conversation among the players.
2. Do not worry about the basketball. Many times the ball will bounce away from the area. It is not the responsibility of the official to chase it. Going after the ball leaves players unattended.
3. Once the immediate area appears calm, the Lead clears all the players by running around them toward the reporting area. Officials should not run through a crowd and lose sight of the players.
4. Stop and square up to the scorer's table in the reporting area. Make eye contact with the scorer before communicating and do not get too close to the table.
5. Give clear, crisp signals.

The non-ruling officials also have specific duties during the dead ball:

1. Keep all players in view. Close down toward the crowd of players slightly — maybe just a step or two depending on where the players are. During that dead-ball time, officials can prevent many extracurricular illegal activities from brewing into bigger problems. Officials should use their voices to let players know they are there; the mere presence of an official can help prevent a problem from occurring.
2. If the players appear calm, begin moving toward the throw-in spot or begin preparing players for free throws. Officials should move slowly, with their heads up, watching the players as they move. Officials should have the players ready for the next play, so that the ball will get back in play quickly and smoothly.

TABLE SIDE LEAD CALLS FOUL, NO FREE THROWS

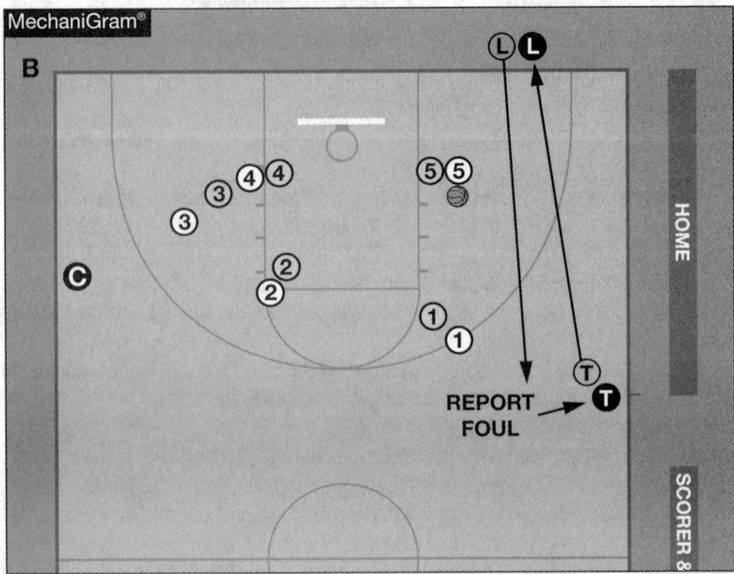

When a foul is called by the table side Lead, two officials, the Lead and Trail, will be involved in the switch. The Lead reports the foul, stays table side and become the new Trail. The old Trail fills the vacated spot and becomes the new Lead. The Center does not switch and stays in the same position.

LEAD OPPOSITE CALLS FOUL, NO FREE THROWS

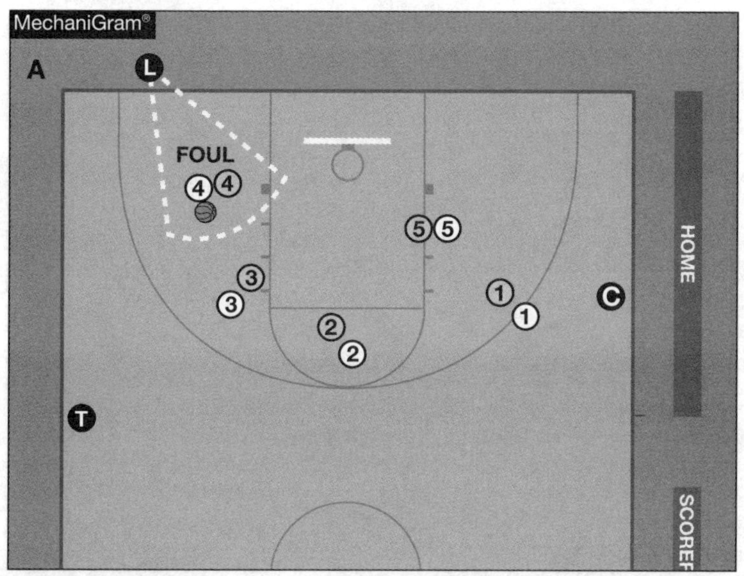

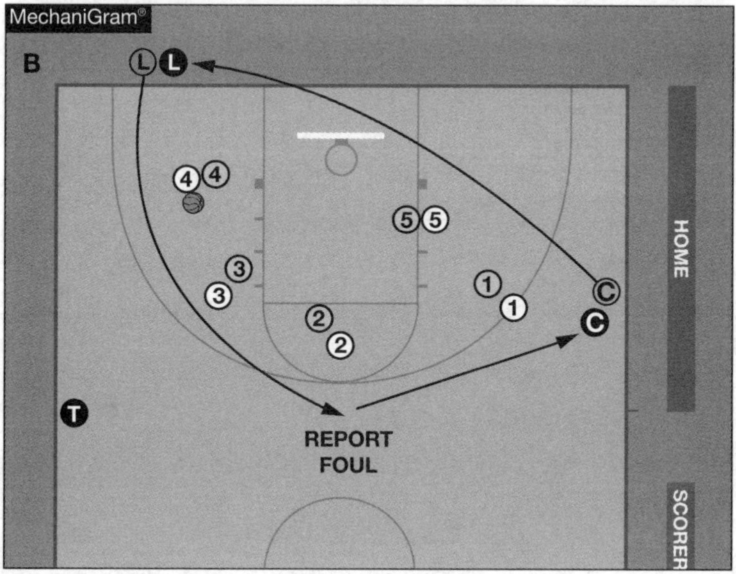

When a foul is called by the Lead opposite the table, two officials, the Lead and Center, switch. The Lead reports the foul, goes table side and becomes the new Center. The old Center fills the vacated spot and becomes the new Lead. The Trail does not switch and stays in the same position.

TABLE SIDE CENTER CALLS FOUL, NO FREE THROWS

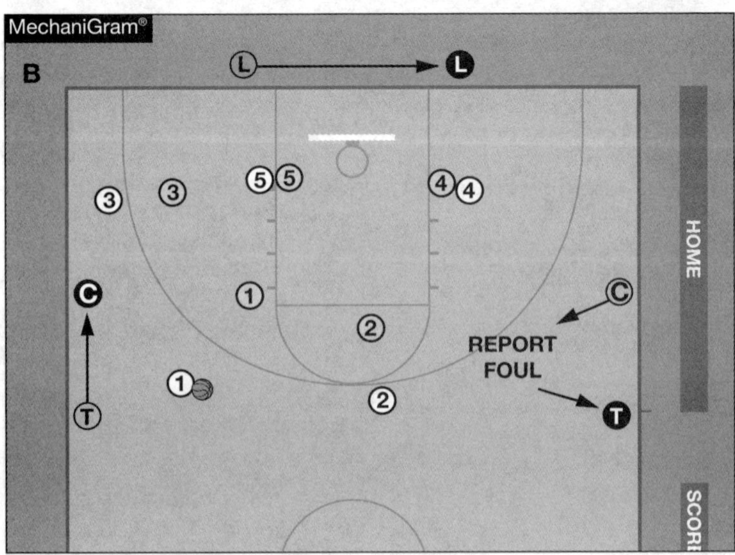

When a foul is called by the table side Center and there are no free throws, there is no switch even though all officials will be moving. The Center reports the foul, stays table side, moves up and becomes the new Trail. The Lead stays as the Lead and moves along the end line to the strongside for the throw-in. The Trail slides down and becomes the new Center.

CENTER OPPOSITE CALLS FOUL, NO FREE THROWS

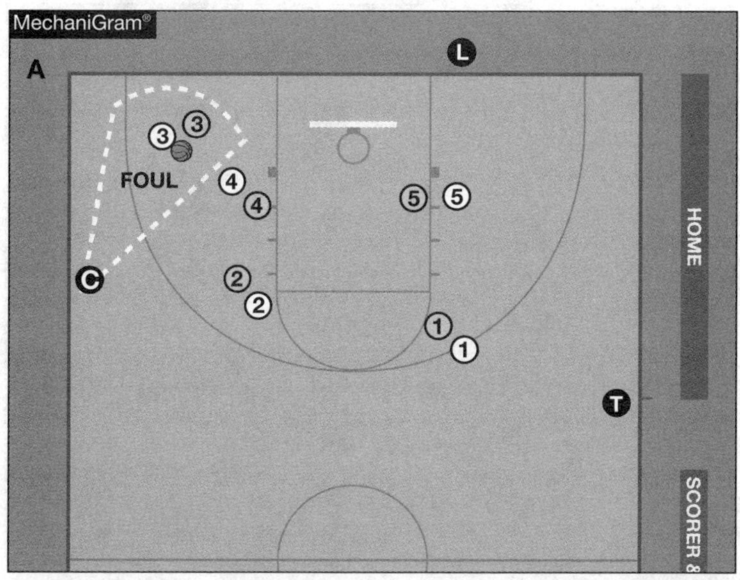

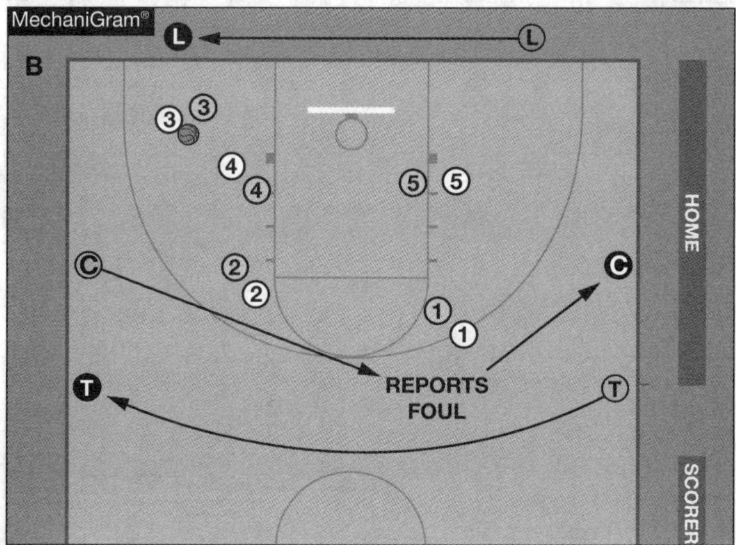

When a foul is called by the Center opposite the table and there are no free throws, all three officials will be moving. The calling official, or Center, reports the foul and goes table side, remaining the Center now on the other side of the court. The Lead stays as the Lead and moves along the end line to the strongside for the throw-in. The Trail moves across the court and remains the Trail.

TABLE SIDE TRAIL CALLS FOUL, NO FREE THROWS

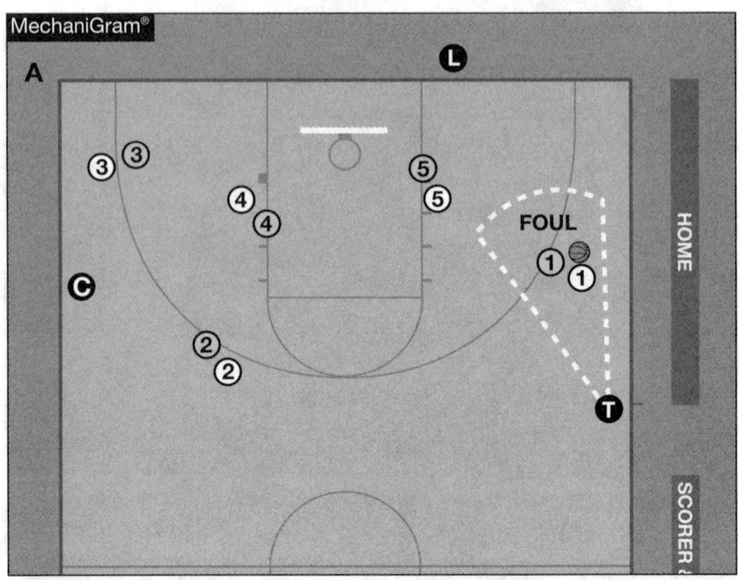

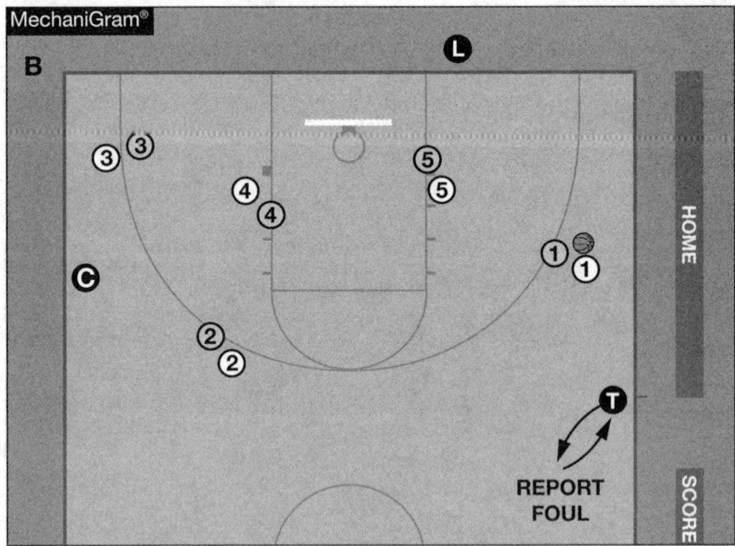

When a foul is called by the table side Trail, there is no switch. The Trail simply reports the foul and stays in the same location. The Center and Lead do not move.

TRAIL OPPOSITE CALLS FOUL, NO FREE THROWS

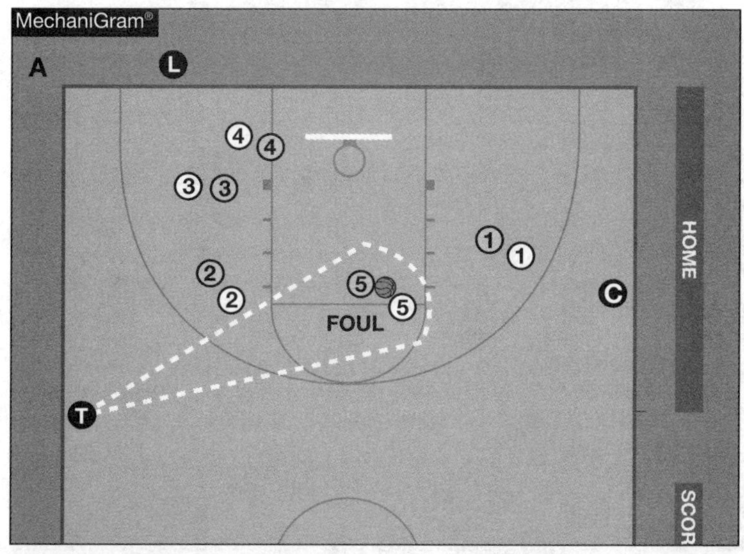

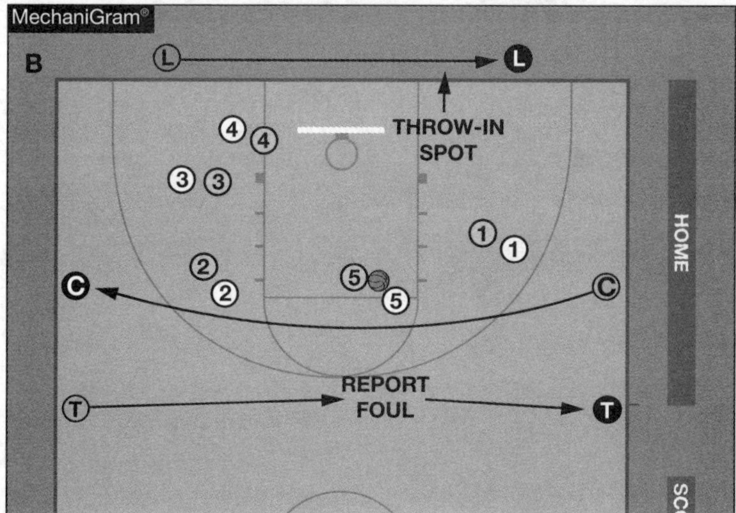

When a foul is called by the Trail opposite the table and the ensuing throw-in is table side, all three officials will be moving (although only two actually switch positions). The Trail reports the foul, goes table side and remains the Trail. The old Center moves opposite the scorer's table and remains the Center. The Lead simply moves along the end line to administer the throw-in but will be on a different side of the court.

TABLE SIDE LEAD CALLS FOUL, FREE THROWS

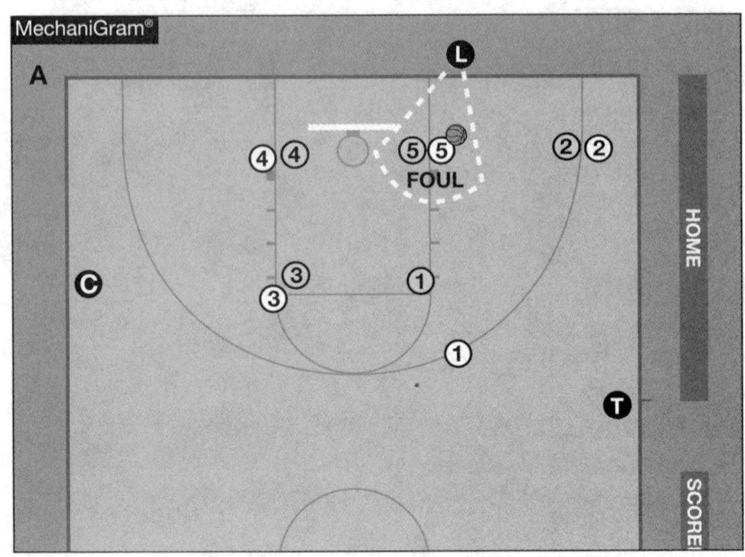

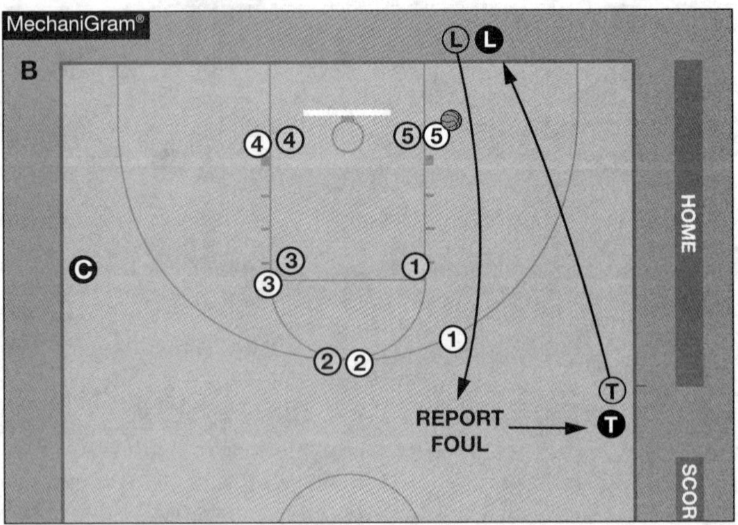

When a foul is called by the table side Lead and there are free throws, the Lead and Trail are involved in the switch. The Lead reports the foul, stays table side and becomes the new Trail. The old Trail fills the vacated spot, becomes the new Lead and administers the free throws. The Center does not switch and stays in the same position.

LEAD OPPOSITE CALLS FOUL, FREE THROWS

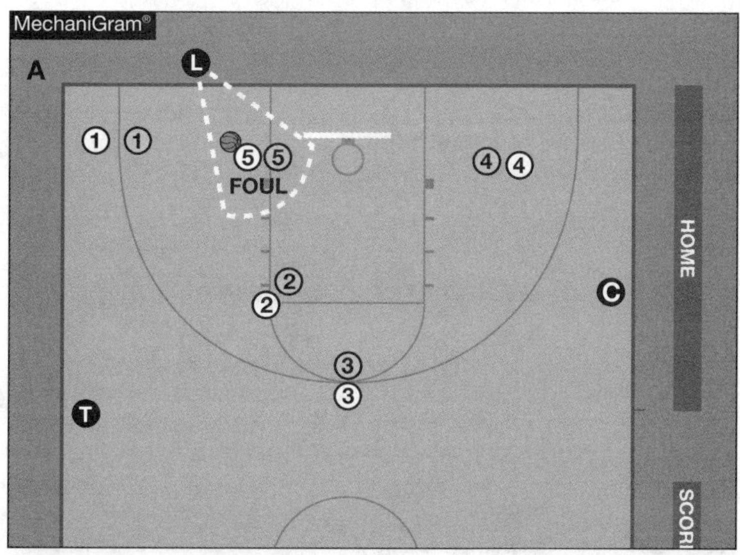

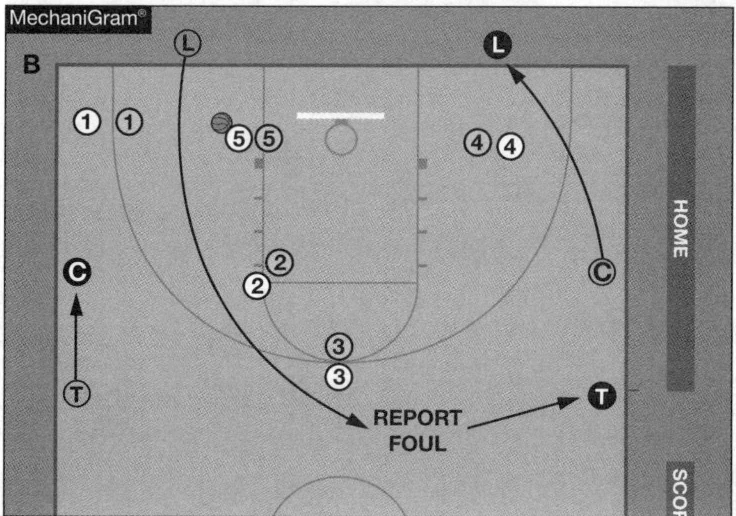

When the Lead is opposite the table, calls a foul and there are free throws, the Lead and Center switch. The Lead reports the foul, moves across the court and becomes the new Trail. The Center fills the spot the Lead vacated and will administer free throws. The old Trail stays opposite the table, slides down and becomes the new Center.

TABLE SIDE CENTER CALLS FOUL, FREE THROWS

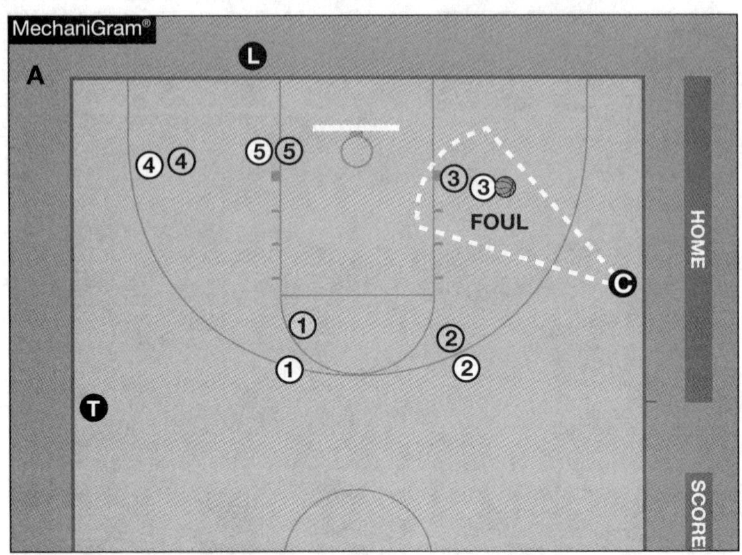

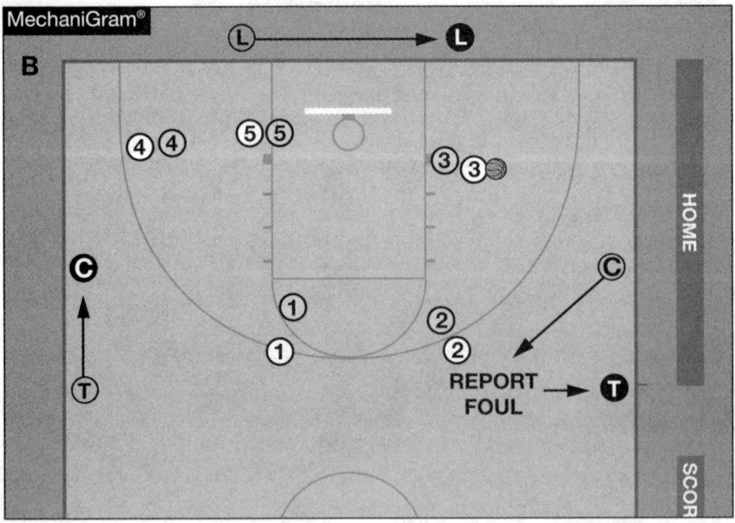

When a foul is called by the table side Center and there will be free throws, there is no switch. The Center will report the foul, stay table side and become the new Trail. The Trail slides down to become the new Center. The Lead moves along the end line to the strongside, stays as the Lead and administers the free throws.

CENTER OPPOSITE CALLS FOUL, FREE THROWS

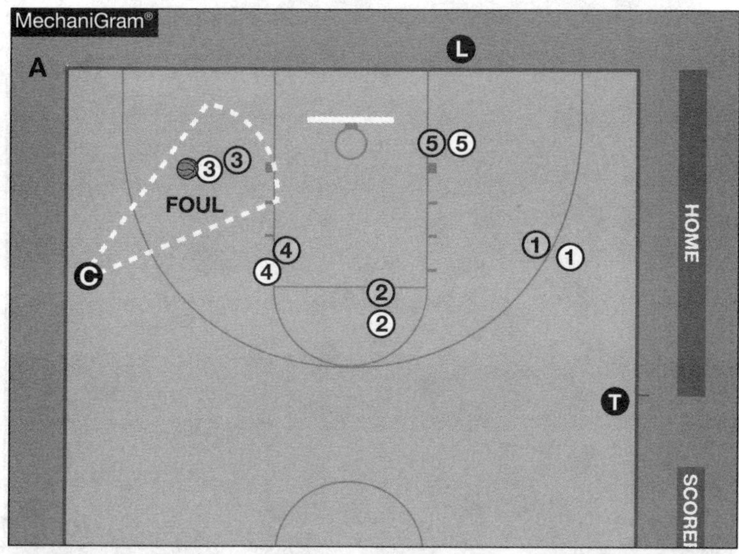

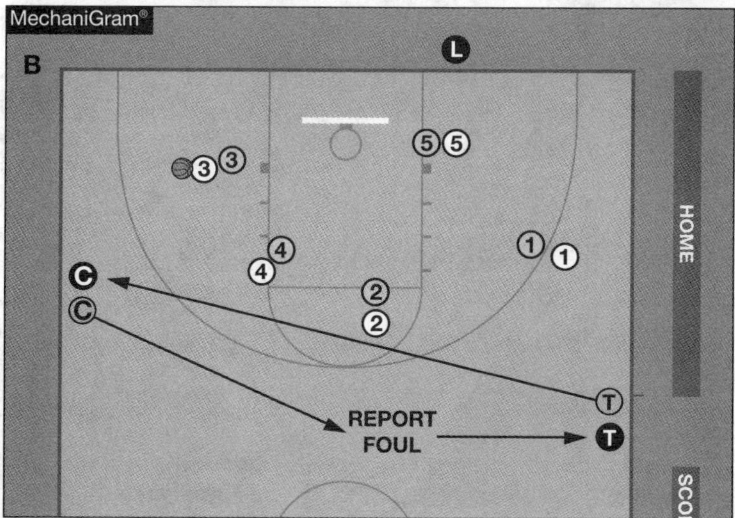

When a foul is called by the Center opposite the table and there are free throws, the Trail and the Center switch. The Center reports the foul, goes table side and becomes the new Trail. The Trail fills the spot vacated by the Center and becomes the new Center. The Lead does not move.

TABLE SIDE TRAIL CALLS FOUL, FREE THROWS

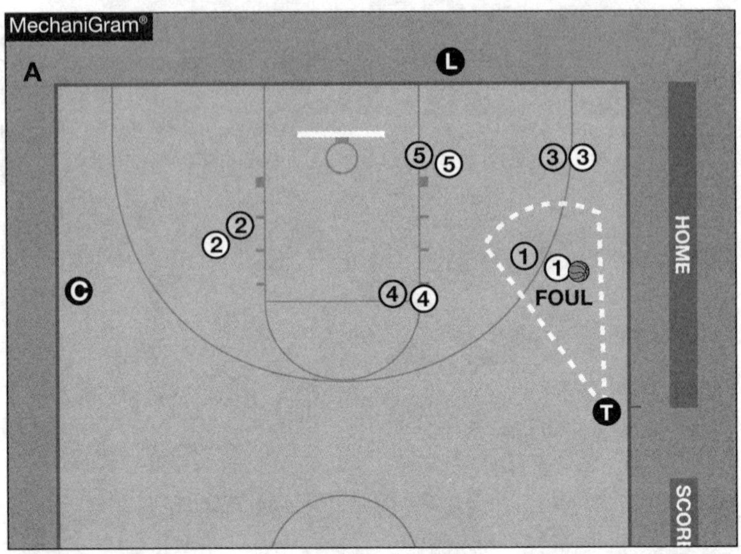

When a foul is called by the table side Trail and there are free throws, there is no switch. The Trail reports the foul, stays table side and stays as the Trail. The Center and the Lead do not move.

TRAIL OPPOSITE CALLS FOUL, FREE THROWS

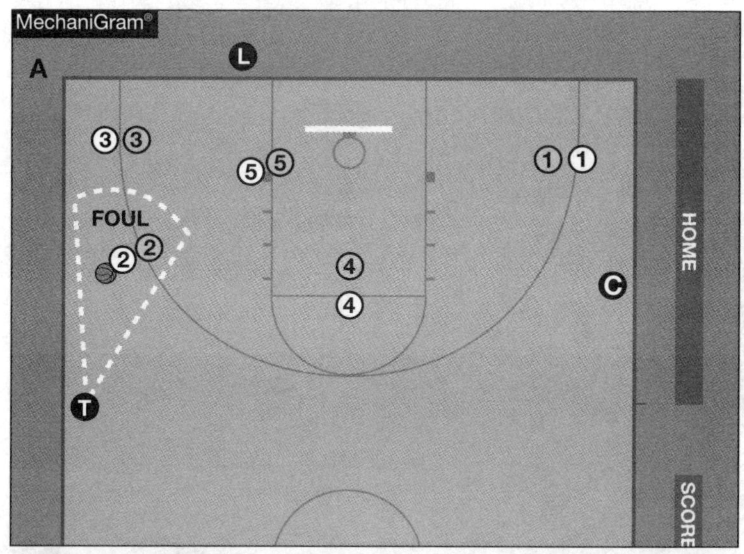

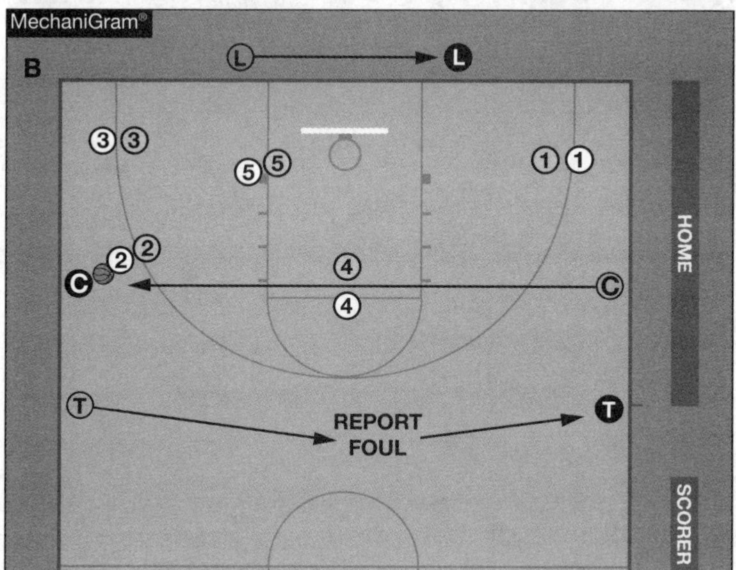

When a foul is called by the Trail opposite the table and there are free throws, the Trail and the Center switch. The Trail reports the foul, goes table side and becomes the new Trail. The Center fills the spot vacated by the Trail and becomes the new Center. The Lead moves along the end line, stays the Lead and administers the free throws.

TABLE SIDE LEAD CALLS FOUL ON OFFENSE, NO FREE THROWS

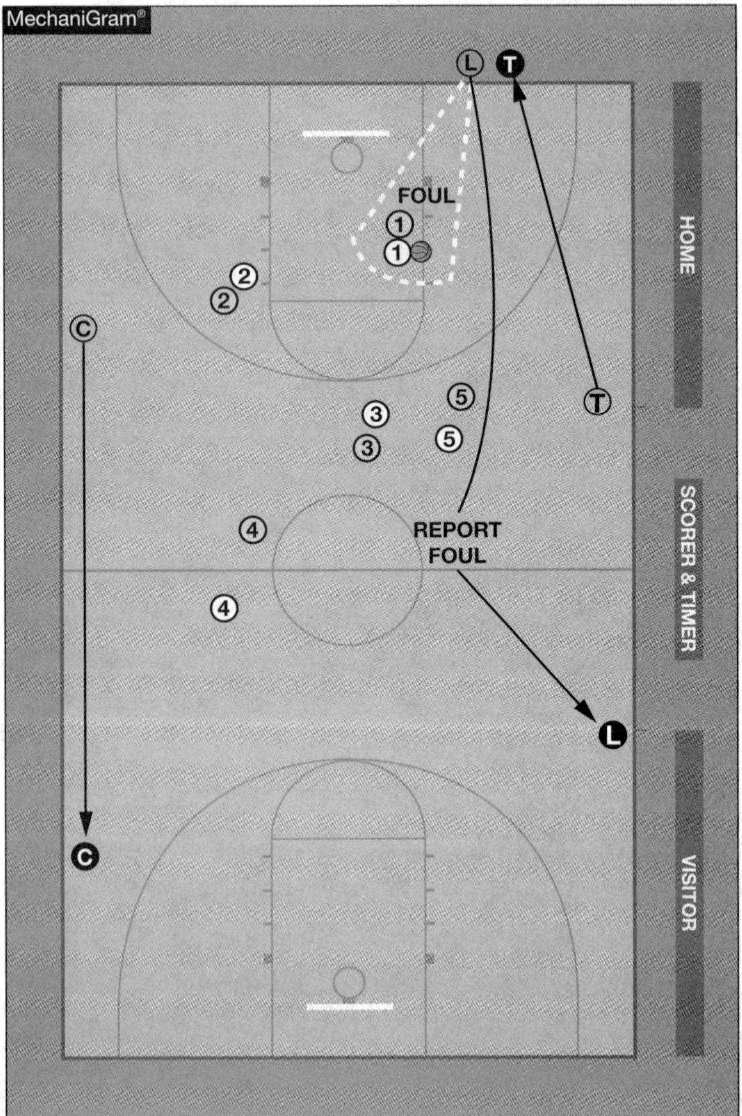
MechaniGram®
L
T
FOUL
1
1
2
2
C
5
3
3
5
T
4
REPORT
FOUL
4
L
C
HOME
SCORER & TIMER
VISITOR

When a foul is called on the offense by the table side Lead and there are no free throws, there is a switch. The Lead reports the foul and remains the Lead. The Trail moves to the end line to administer the throw-in and remains the Trail while the Center moves down court and stays the Center.

LEAD OPPOSITE CALLS FOUL ON OFFENSE, NO FREE THROWS

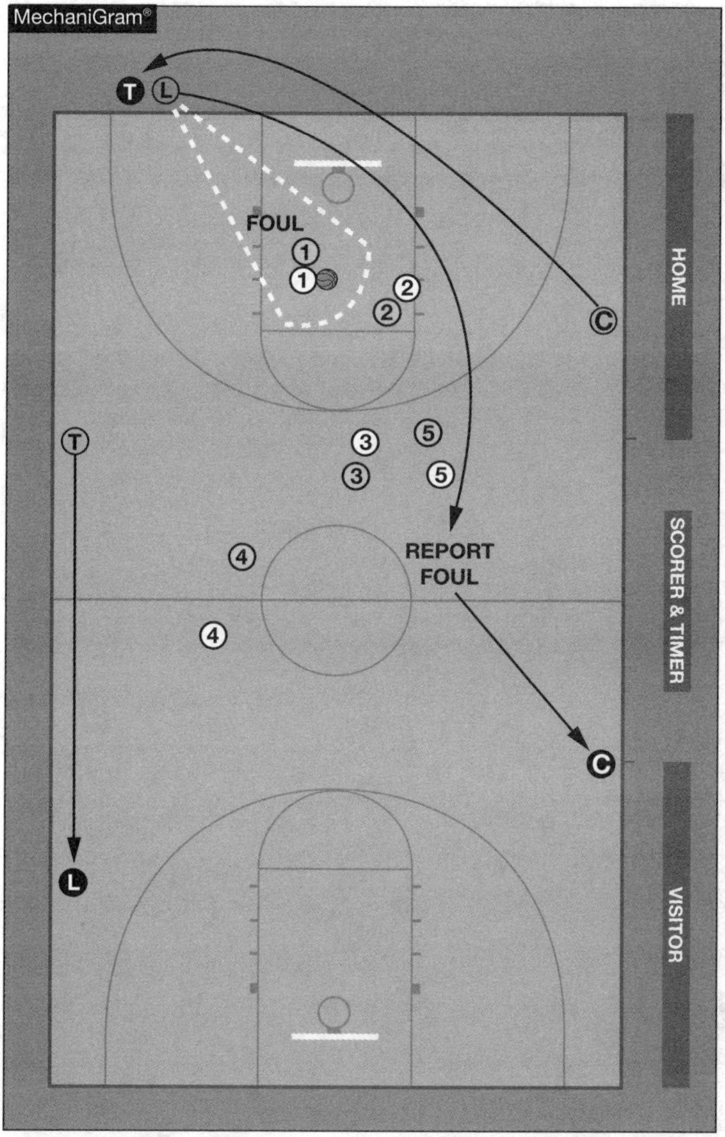

MechaniGram®

FOUL

REPORT FOUL

HOME

SCORER & TIMER

VISITOR

When the Lead opposite the table calls a foul on the offense and there are no free throws, there is a switch. The Lead reports the foul and becomes the new Center. The old Center moves to the end line in place of the old Lead to administer the throw-in and becomes the new Trail while the Trail moves down court and becomes the new Lead.

TABLE SIDE CENTER CALLS FOUL ON OFFENSE, NO FREE THROWS

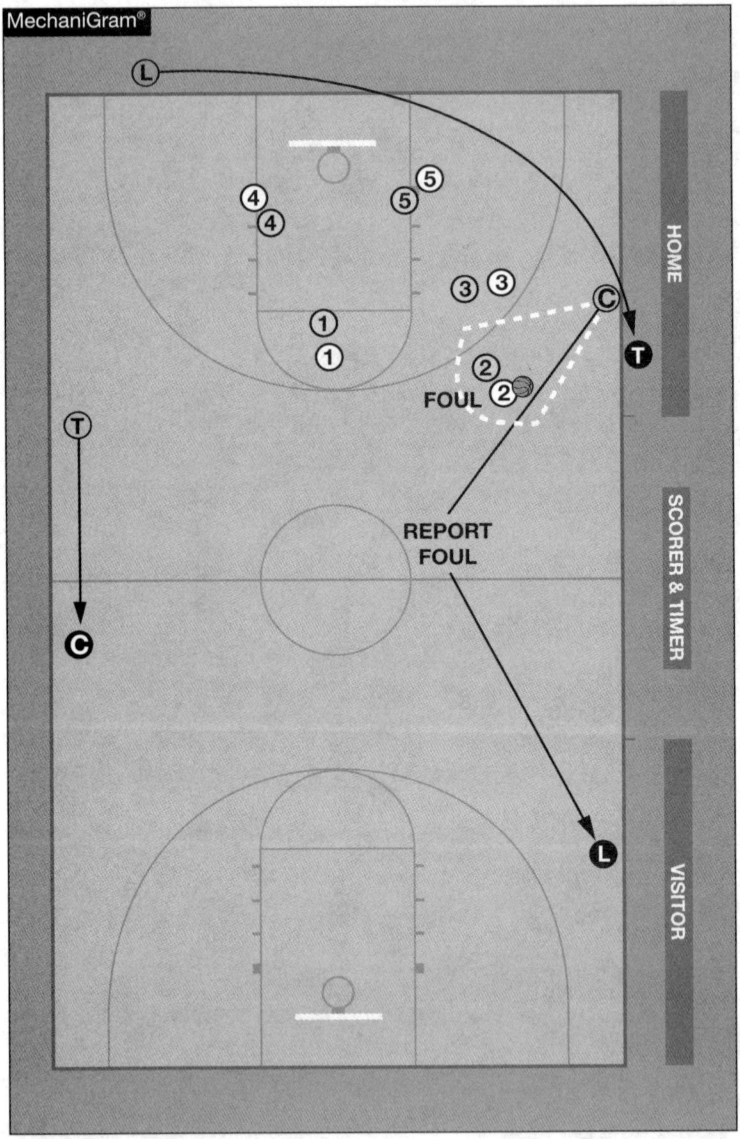

When the table side Center calls a foul on the offense and there are no free throws, the Center reports the foul, stays table side and becomes the new Lead. The old Trail moves down the court and becomes the new Center. The old Lead moves across the court and becomes the new Trail. The officials slide the same as they would as if a violation were called.

CENTER OPPOSITE CALLS FOUL ON OFFENSE, NO FREE THROWS

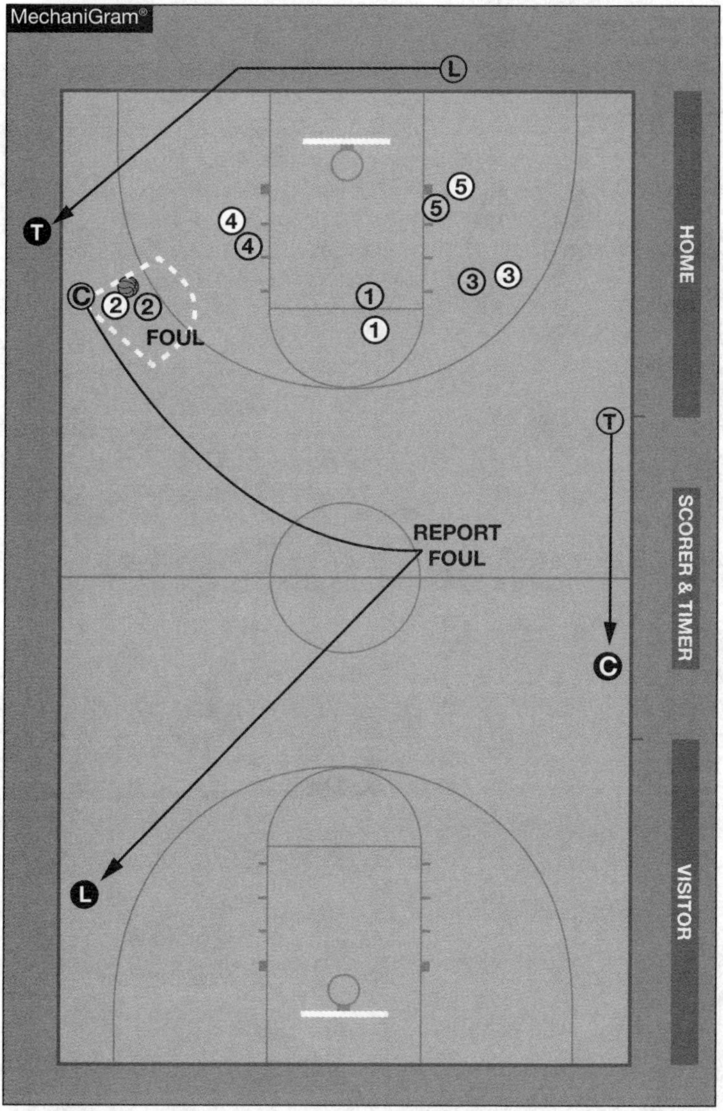

MechaniGram®

L
T
5 5
4 4
3 3
C 2 2
1 1
FOUL
HOME
T
REPORT FOUL
SCORER & TIMER
C
L
VISITOR

When a foul is called on the offense by the Center opposite the table and there are no free throws, there is no switch. The Center reports the foul but does not go table side. Instead, the Center stays opposite the table and becomes the new Lead. The old Lead moves across the court to administer the ensuing throw-in and becomes the new Trail. The old Trail slides downcourt and becomes the new Center. The officials slide as if there were a violation called.

TABLE SIDE TRAIL CALLS FOUL ON OFFENSE, NO FREE THROWS

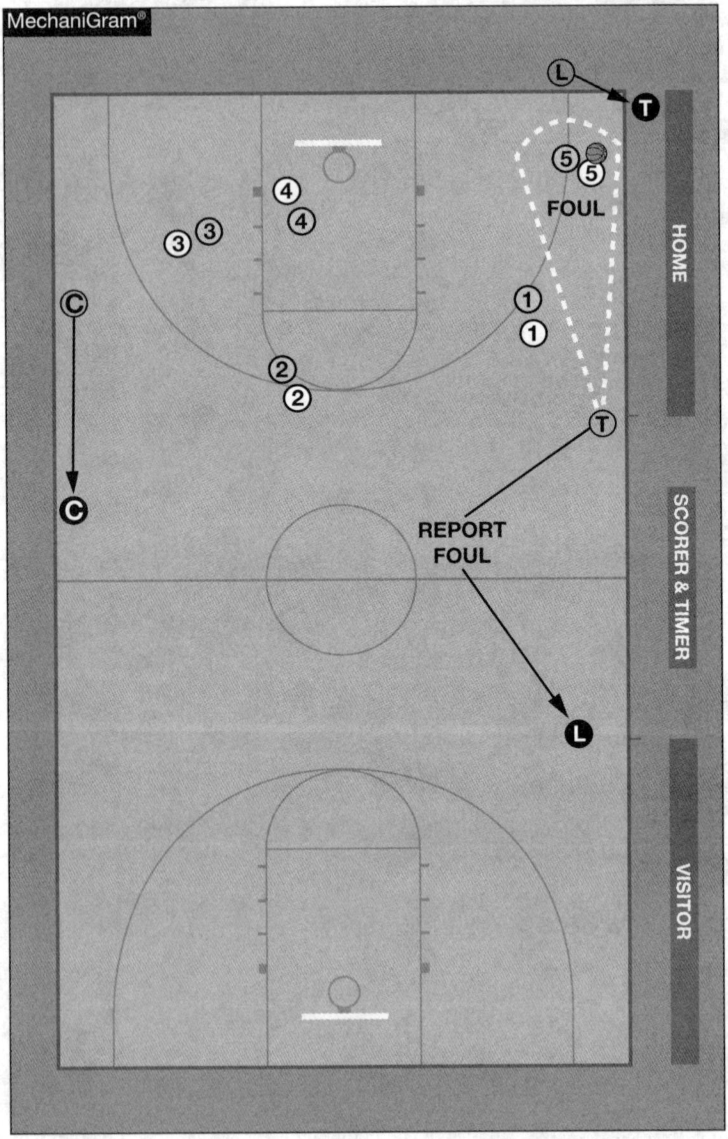

When a foul is called on the offense by the table side Trail and there are no free throws, there is no switch. The Trail reports the foul, moves downcourt, stays table side and becomes the new Lead. The old Lead administers the throw-in and becomes the new Trail. The Center stays the Center and moves downcourt. The officials slide as if there was a violation called.

TRAIL OPPOSITE CALLS FOUL ON OFFENSE, NO FREE THROWS

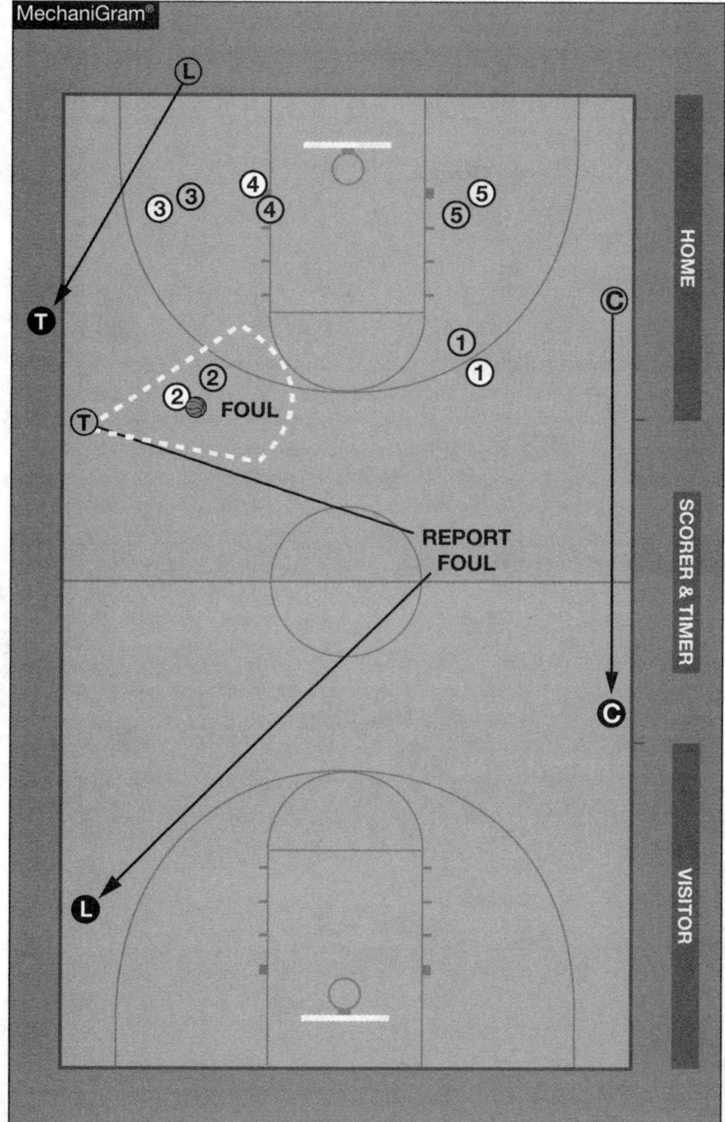

When a foul is called on the offense by the Trail opposite the table and there are no free throws, there is no switch. The foul is treated like a violation. The Trail reports the foul but does not go table side. Instead, the old Trail stays opposite the table and becomes the new Lead. The old Lead moves to administer the ensuing throw-in and becomes the new Trail. The old Center slides downcourt and stays the Center.

TABLE SIDE LEAD CALLS FOUL ON OFFENSE, FREE THROWS

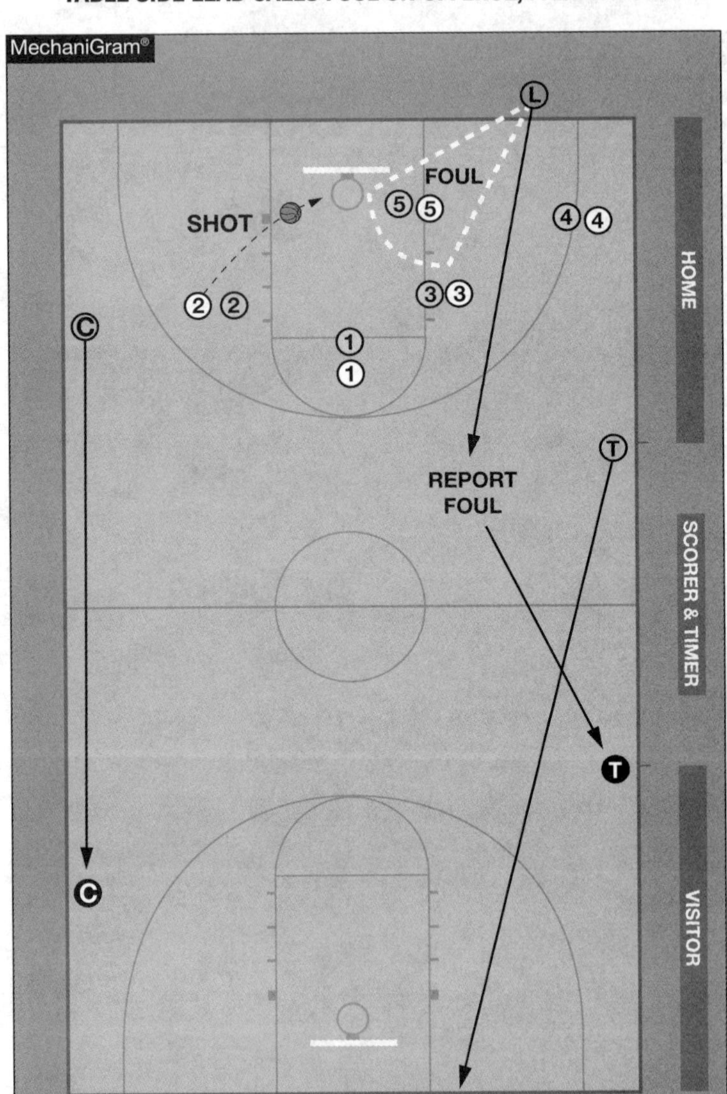

When the table side Lead calls a foul on the offense and there are free throws, there is no switch. The officials slide down the court. The Lead reports the foul, stays table side and becomes the new Trail. The old Trail slides down and becomes the new Lead. The Center slides down and stays the Center.

LEAD OPPOSITE CALLS FOUL ON OFFENSE, FREE THROWS

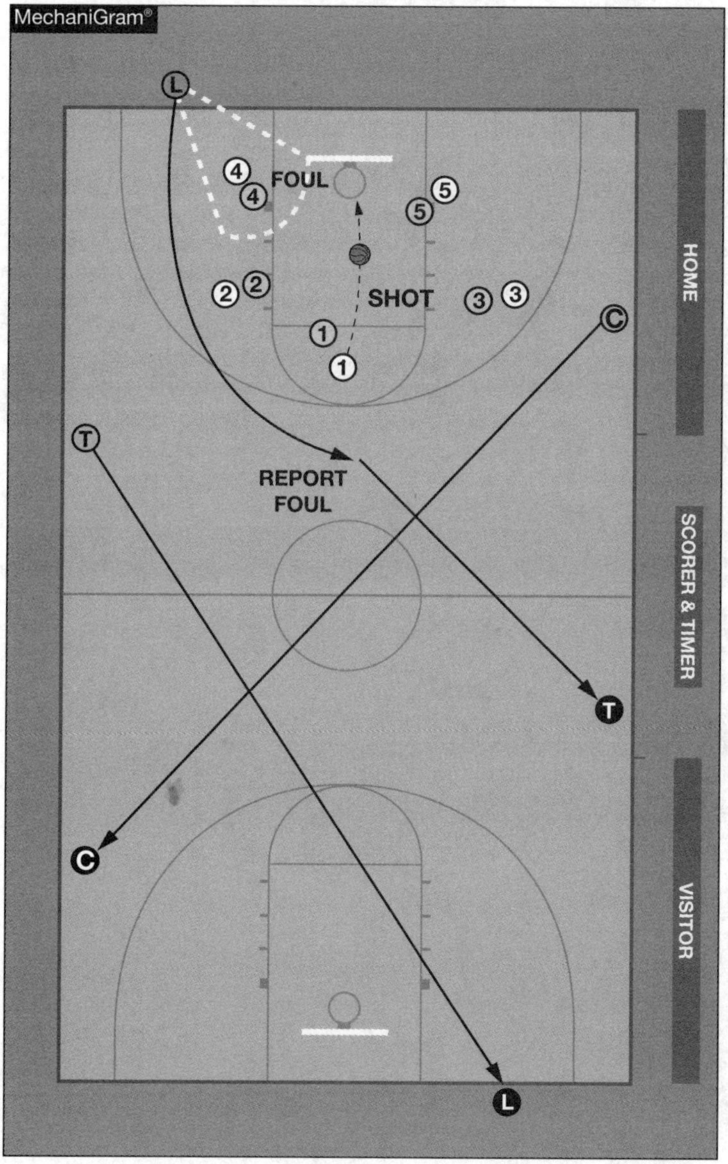

MechaniGram®

FOUL

SHOT

REPORT FOUL

HOME

SCORER & TIMER

VISITOR

When the Lead is opposite the table, calls a foul on the offensive team and there are free throws, all three officials will be moving. The Lead reports the foul, moves across the court and becomes the new Trail. The old Trail moves across the court and becomes the new Lead. The Center moves across the court and stays the Center.

TABLE SIDE CENTER CALLS FOUL ON OFFENSE, FREE THROWS

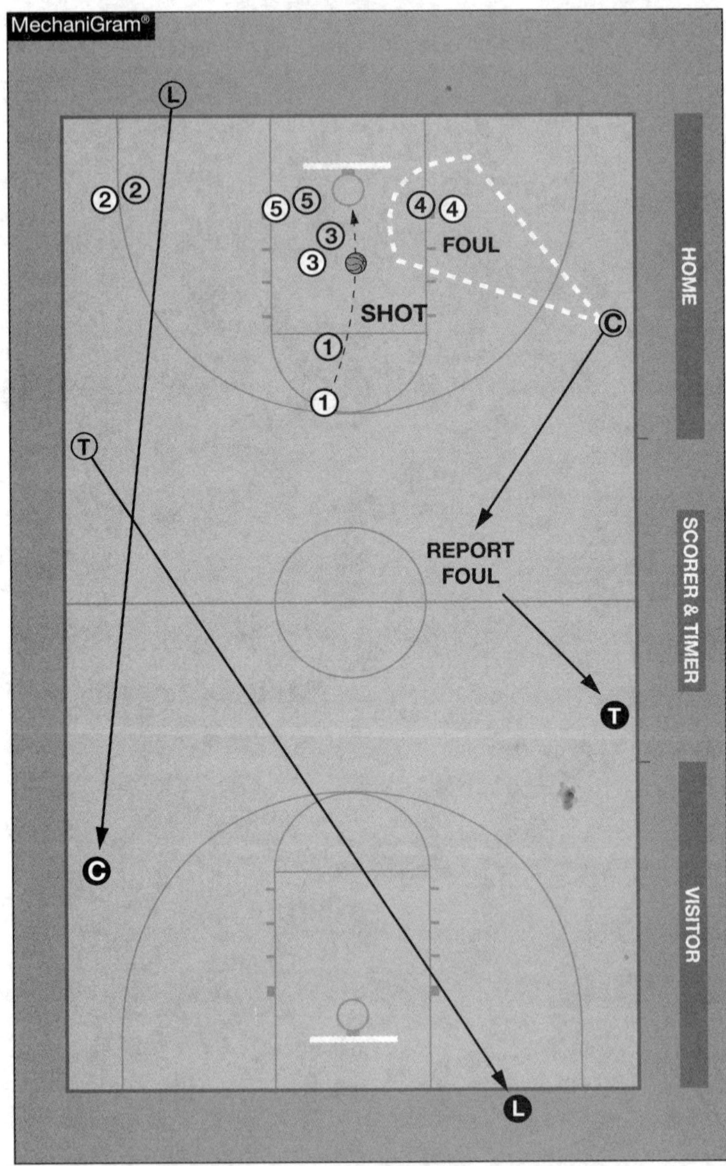

When the table side Center calls a foul on the offense and there are free throws, all three officials will be moving. The Center reports the foul, stays table side and becomes the new Trail. The old Trail moves across the court and becomes the new Lead. The old Lead slides down and becomes the new Center.

CENTER OPPOSITE CALLS FOUL ON OFFENSE, FREE THROWS

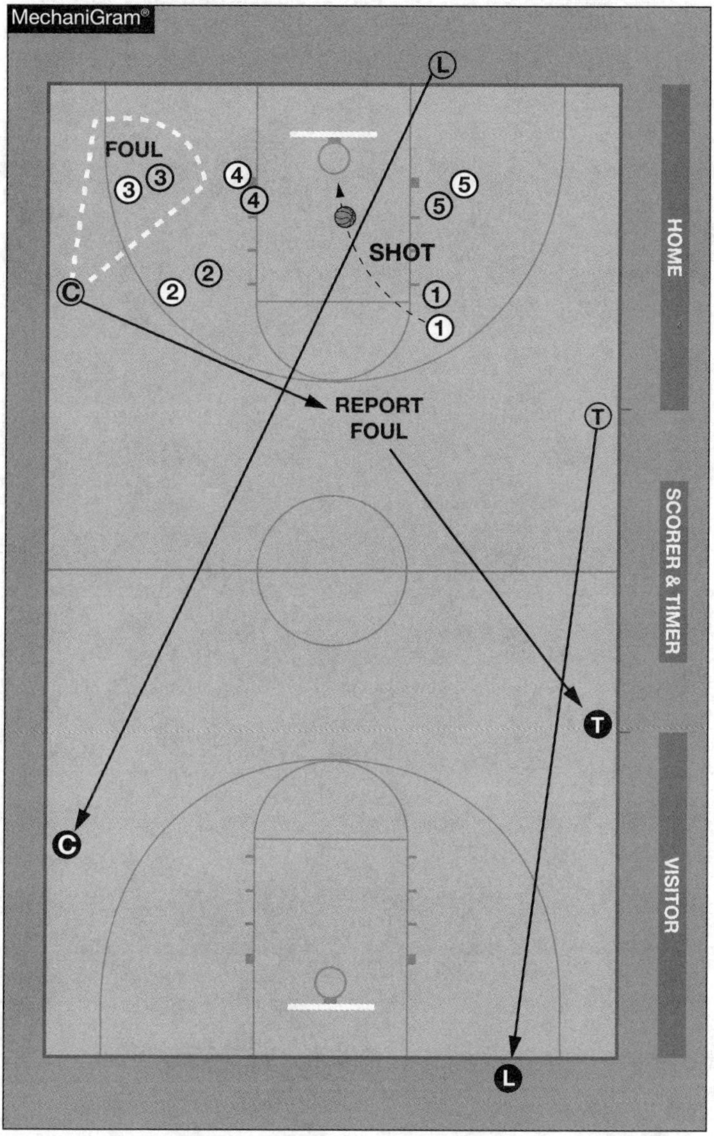

When a foul is called on the offense by the Center opposite the table and there are free throws, all three officials will be moving. The Center reports the foul and goes table side to become the new Trail. The old Trail moves downcourt and becomes the new Lead. The old Lead moves down and across the court to become the new Center.

TABLE SIDE TRAIL CALLS FOUL ON OFFENSE, FREE THROWS

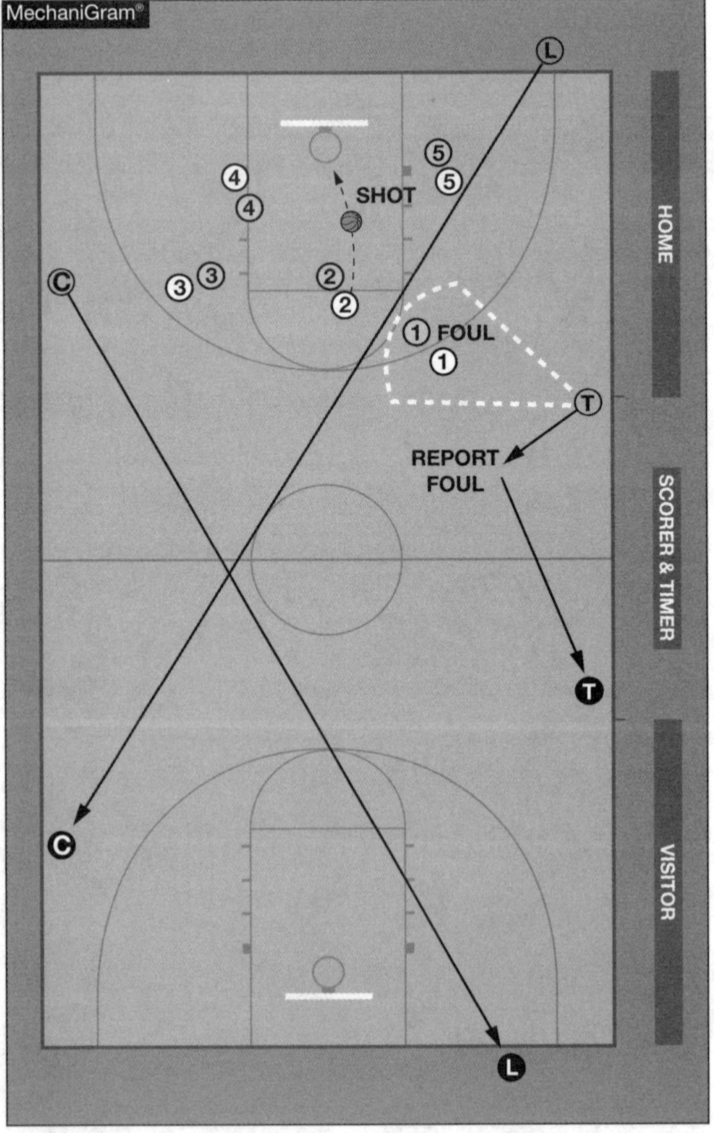

When a foul is called on the offense by the table side Trail and there are free throws, all officials will be moving. The Trail reports the foul, stays table side and continues to be the Trail. The old Center moves down and across the court to become the new Lead. The old Lead moves down and across the court to become the new Center.

TRAIL OPPOSITE CALLS FOUL ON OFFENSE, FREE THROWS

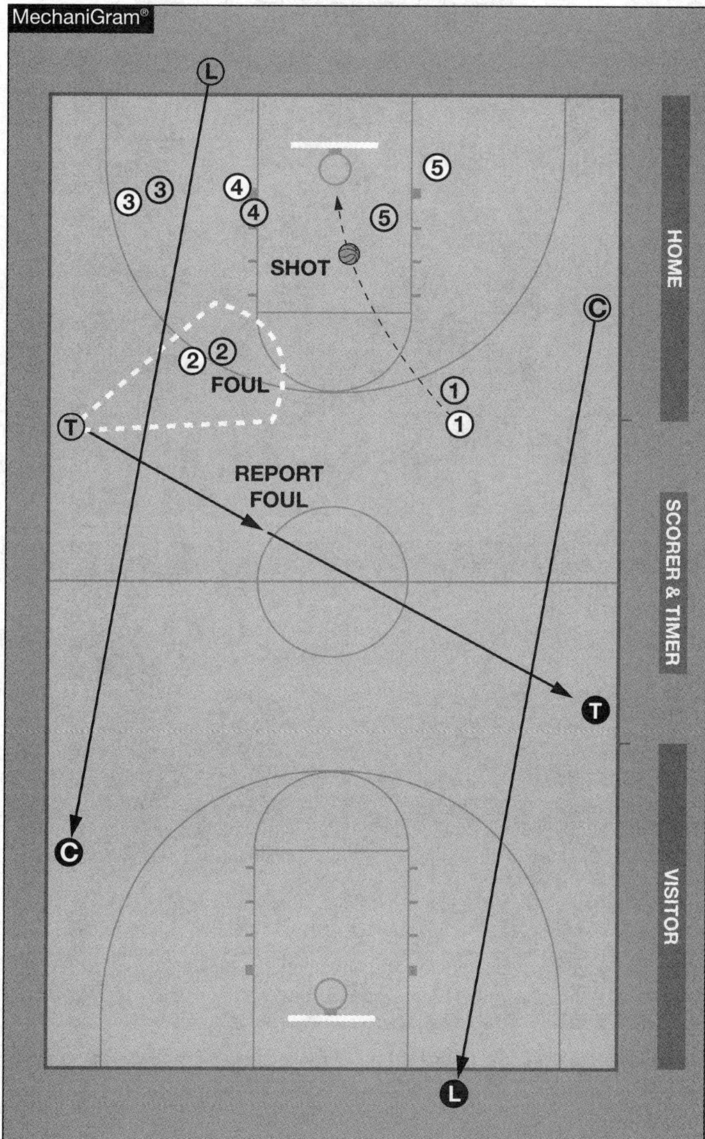

When a foul is called on the offense by the Trail opposite the table and there are free throws, all officials will be moving. The Trail reports the foul, goes table side and stays the Trail. The old Center moves downcourt and becomes the new Lead. The old Lead moves downcourt and becomes the new Center.

NOTIFY COACH OF DISQUALIFIED PLAYER

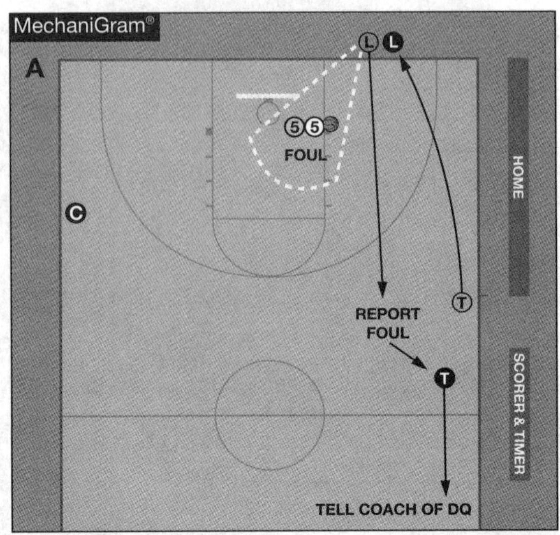

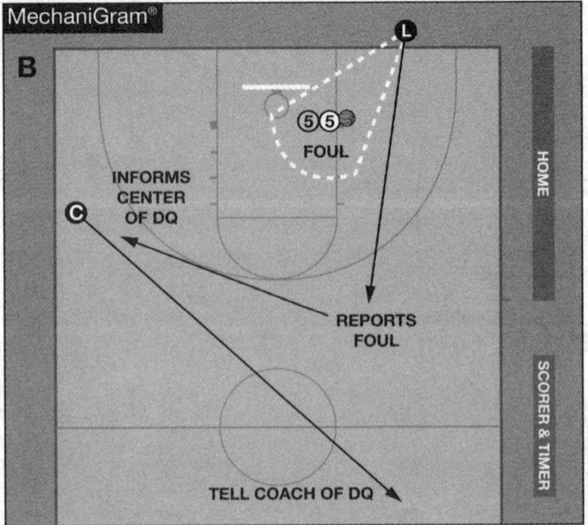

When a player fouls out, the calling official is responsible for notifying the coach, having table personnel start the 20-second substitution clock and informing the player, as in MechaniGram A.

If informing the coach of the disqualified player could be confrontational, the calling official does not have to stay table side. When informed by the table of the player's disqualification, the calling official can go opposite the table. The official who is opposite, either the Trail or Center, should notify the coach, as in MechaniGram B.

Any official has the same option of going opposite to avoid a confrontation, such as after a technical foul or ejection.

5.11 Free Throws

COVERAGE

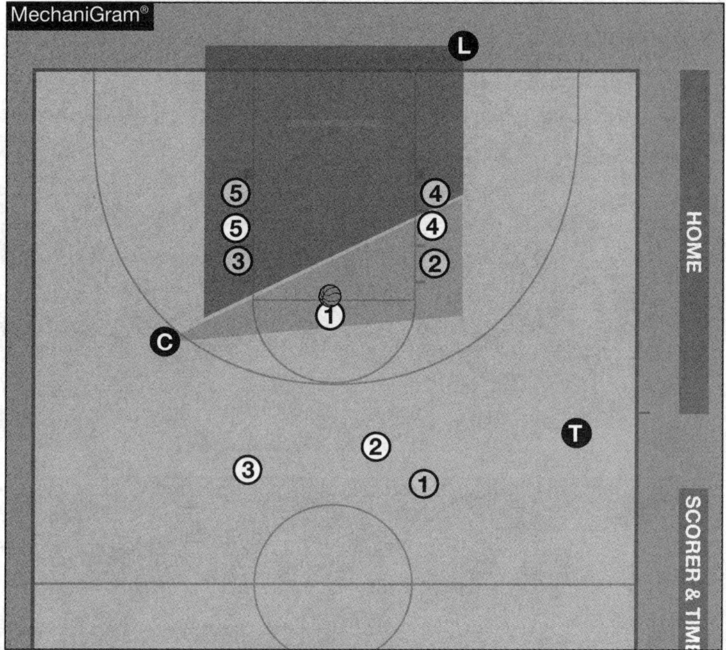

The Lead watches players on the opposite lane line (closer to the Center) for potential violations, etc. The Lead also watches the lane space nearest the end line on the lane line nearest the Lead. The Lead is the administering official during all free throws and is to bounce the ball to the thrower before backing out of the lane. For all free throws, the Lead should be approximately 4 feet from the nearer lane line and well off the end line.

The Center observes players on the opposite lane line (closer to the Lead) except the opposite low block area. The Center also watches the free-throw shooter. The Center administers a silent and visible 10-second count with the arm farthest from the basket using "wrist flicks." When showing a visible count as a Center during a free-throw attempt, the count should be less demonstrative than a normal visible count so as to not distract the shooter and draw unnecessary attention to the official.

On the last free throw, the Center uses the "stop clock" signal (Signal 2) immediately after the shooter releases the shot. Use the same arm (farthest from the basket) to ensure the timer clearly sees the signal. During the flight of the try and with the arm still raised, close down slightly toward the end line. That movement ensures good angles on rebounding action. If the shot is good, lower the arm. If the shot is no good and the ball is to remain live, use the "start clock" signal (Signal 1) as soon as the ball is touched by or touches a player.

The Trail watches all lane activity to assist the Lead and Center, but also watches any action above the three-point arc.

There is no need to signal a successful free throw.

TRAIL POSITIONING

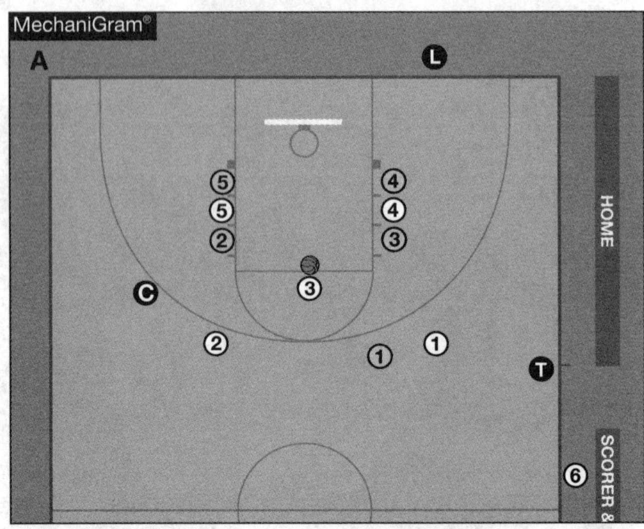

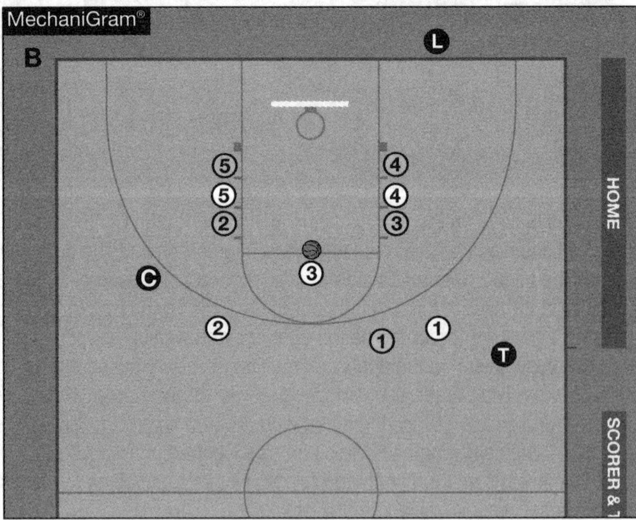

On multiple free throws, the Trail shall be positioned near the 28-foot mark for the first of two (or first two of three) free throws, as shown in MechaniGram A. The Trail should take a position approximately 28 feet from the end line just inside the table side boundary. If possible, the Trail should not obstruct the view of the scorer, timer and team benches. The Trail is primarily responsible for holding and beckoning substitutes and any other table activity. The Trail should also observe all players in the backcourt.

If necessary to get away from a boisterous coach or volatile situation, the Trail may move onto the court, as shown in MechaniGram B.

CENTER/TRAIL MOVEMENT

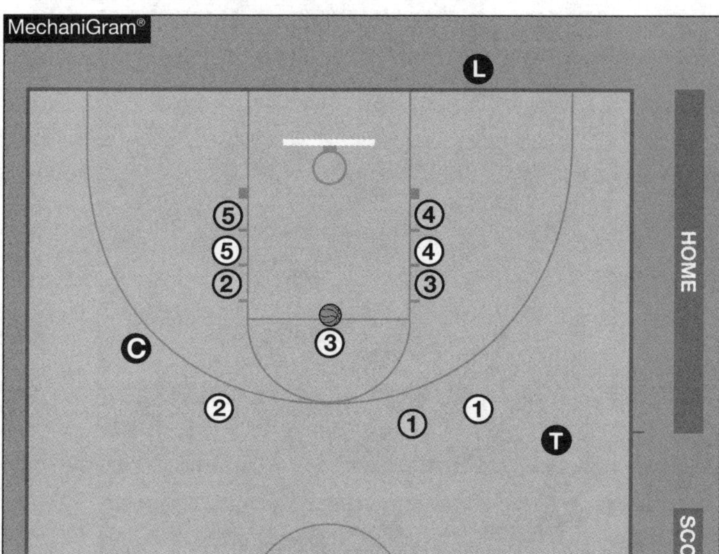

During the flight of the last free throw, the Center and Trail close down slightly toward the end line. That movement ensures good angles on rebounding action. The Center is responsible for weak-side rebounding and the Trail is responsible for strong-side rebounding.

TECHNICAL FOUL

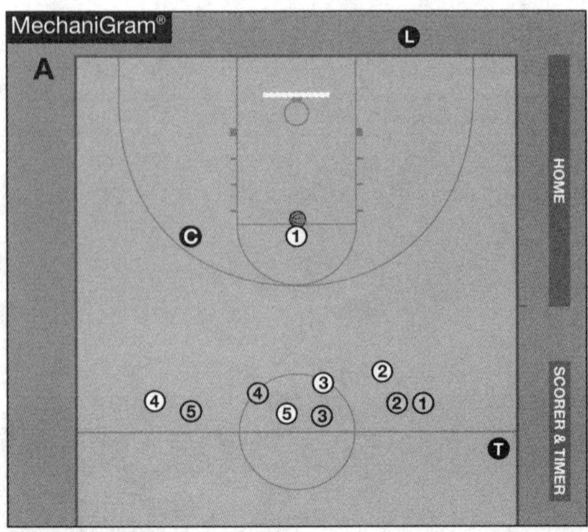

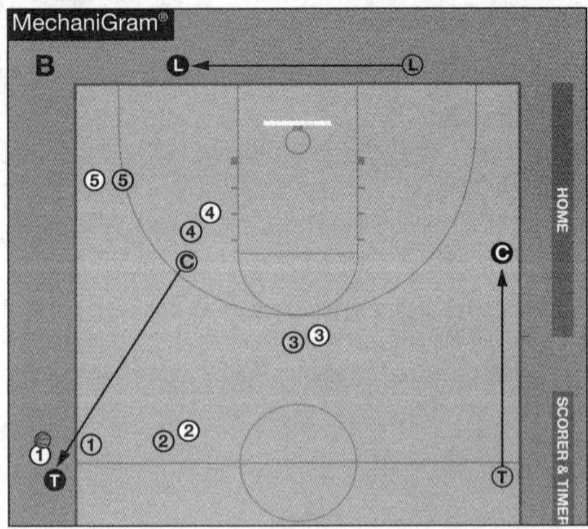

When a technical foul is called, the three officials should switch, just as they would with any foul. Technical foul free throws are administered in the same manner as other free throws: the Lead administering the free throws, the Center observing the free-thrower and the Trail on or near the division line to observe the remaining nine players, as seen in MechaniGram A.

After all free throws have been attempted, the Center will move up the court to the division line and administer the throw-in opposite the scorer's table, becoming the new Trail. The Trail will move down toward the end line to become the new Center and the Lead will move along the end line to balance the floor, as seen in MechaniGram B.

The calling official always has the option of going opposite if the situation is potentially heated.

Note: Non-shooting players do not have to be behind the division line.

5.12 Substitutions

HANDLING SUBSTITUTIONS

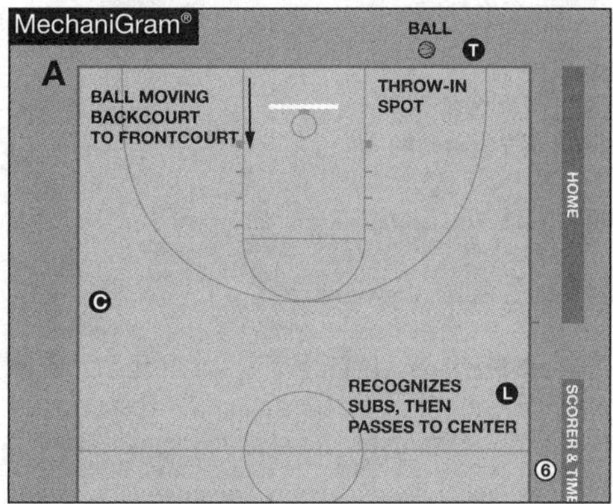

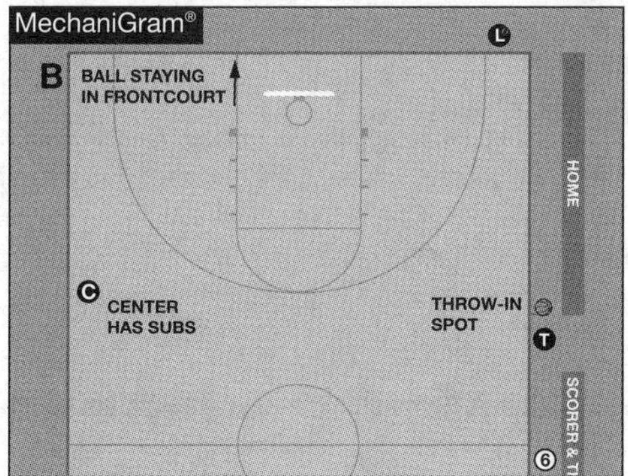

When substitutions are coming into the game, the official responsible depends on the location of the officials and where and how the ball will become live. During all substitutions, the responsible official should blow the whistle (if needed to get attention) and hold the "stop clock" signal (Signal 2) while beckoning substitutes.

- Throw-in with the ball staying in the frontcourt: In most situations, the official nearest the table is responsible.
- Throw-in with ball going from backcourt to frontcourt: If table side, the new Lead beckons the substitutes and then passes substitution responsibilities on to the Center, as seen in MechaniGram A. If the new Lead is opposite the table, the Center has all substitution responsibilities.
- Prior to last free throw: The Trail has substitution responsibilities.
- Trail administering throw-in table side: The Center has substitution responsibilities even though the Center is across the court from the scorer's table as seen in MechaniGram B. The Trail may not see the substitutes and the Center has the best view of the scorer's table.
- Trail administering throw-in opposite the table: The Center has substitution responsibilities.

The key to smooth substitutions is for all officials to have good communication, including eye contact.

OFFICIALS' PREGAME CONFERENCE

The following pregame conference is designed for a crew of three but can be adjusted accordingly for a crew of two:

A. Review New Rules

B. Review New Points of Emphasis

C. Review New Mechanics and Signal Changes

D. Review Previous Year's Rules Changes

E. Conference with Table Officials: Equipment; special court considerations; new rules

1. Scorer: Reporting; good eye contact; substitutions; substitution for disqualified/injured player; give disqualification information immediately; confirmation that game is over and there are no problems.
2. Timer: Time-outs, interval for disqualification or injury.

F. Game Management

1. Review all dead-ball situations.
2. The guidelines regarding hand-checking, post play, illegally bumping cutters, traveling, palming the ball, illegal screens, three seconds and off-the-ball coverage must be emphasized in the pregame meeting before every game.
3. Stay consistent as a crew throughout the game.
4. Stay with the play after ruling a foul or a violation.
5. Know game situations.

G. Clock Management: Check game clock; starting and stopping; be aware of mistakes/malfunctions.

H. Basic Rotation/Court Coverage:

1. On-/off-ball coverage/areas of intersection.
2. All officials in frontcourt before Lead rotates. Lead may use accelerated pace in rotation – doesn't have to finish, but do not stop in Center of lane. Do not rotate when a try for goal is in flight, stop and return. Late rotations put crew members in poor rebounding coverage.
3. Officiate the new area of responsibility immediately.

   EXCEPTION: If the Center has started the five-second closely guarded count and the Lead has rotated to the Center side, the Lead needs to continue to officiate in the free-throw lane until the Center stops the five-second count. Be patient in starting the five-second count.
4. Free-Throw Coverage

I. Lead Position:

1. In transition – wide-angle (2-3 steps inside arc) or close-down (1 step outside lane) position, two or three steps off end line.
2. Take a position near the free-throw lane line extended – May step into free-throw

lane extended one or two steps on drives from Center's side or down middle; primary coverage for Center; secondary coverage for Lead.
3. Primary focus is post play – stay in your PCA, may assist where official's PCA overlap when OBVIOUS.

J. Center Position:

1. Establish home position – free throw line extended and on or near the sideline.
2. Move to improve angles of coverage: movement area typically goes top of free throw semi-circle to second lane space.
3. Drive to basket, officiate the play all the way to the basket.
Includes primary, secondary and all defenders.

K. Trail Position:

1. Establish home position – near 28-foot mark and on or near the sideline.
2. Trail must officiate in the post when the Lead picks up ball at the free throw line extended and below.
3. Officiate where Lead cannot; stay wide; move to improve angles of coverage; monitor secondary defenders on drives to the basket.
4. Free Throw – Position at the 28-foot mark unless players in backcourt; the Trail must trail players in transition.

L. Double Whistles:

1. Do not assume your partner's ruling, confirm/affirm.
2. Double whistles belong to primary; release or help when requested.

M. Crew Communication:

1. Competitive or potential match-up concerns.
2. Help rulings: out of bounds, 2- vs. 3-point try, tipped ball, count/cancel field goal.
3. Signals – the language of the game.
4. Shooters – confirm who they are.
5. Warnings to head coaches, delay warnings are recorded in the scorebook.
6. Time-outs: get together, especially late in the game - quarter-ending situations, resumption of play.
7. Last-second try for goal.

N. Challenging Rulings/Situations:

1. Jump ball and held balls.
2. Illegal screens; consider location and timing of the screener.
3. Traveling; identify the pivot foot.
4. Out-of-bounds; request or offer help.
5. Tripping.
6. Illegal or excessive contact – defense and offense.
7. Secondary defenders.
8. Double personal/technical fouls; intentional; flagrant; fights.
9. Consider intentional fouls on fast-break situations.
10. Always know the location/status of the ball and player.

O. Free Throw Administration:

1. Players occupying free-throw lane line spaces may enter the free-throw lane upon the release of the ball. Do not permit players in early – on the lane lines, enter on release; all others enter when ball contacts ring.
2. Lead – administers all free throws, responsible for near free-throw lane line space and all spaces along the opposite free-throw lane line.
3. Trail – responsible for table officials, substitutes, perimeter rebounding, goal tending, basket interference.
4. Center – responsible for free thrower, opposite free-throw lane line spaces two and three, goal tending, basket interference, starting clock when an unsuccessful free throw is legally touched.

P. Time-Out Responsibilities:

1. Reporting, to the scorer, the team and player or head coach requesting/being granted the time-out and the type of time-out.
2. Reporting warning horns to the head coach and players.
3. Positions during time-outs.

Q. Crew Discussion:

1. Rules questions/clarifications.
2. Game situations.
3. Officiate PCA when ball goes away, PCAs and field of vision zones.
4. Patient whistle: blocked shots, rebound situations, rulings out of your PCA must be obvious.
5. Concentrate and focus throughout the entire game.
6. Game horn sounding: If the horn is sounded, officials may recognize it and stop play with a whistle, even to the extent of declaring that the ball did not become live because of the whistle. The horn may be ignored if it is sounded after the throw-in has started.

R. Conference/State Requirements:

1. Uniform
2. Reports
3. State Championship End-of-Game Monitor Review: A state association may permit game or replay officials to use a replay monitor during state championship series contests to determine if the ball is released on a try for goal at the expiration of the game clock in the fourth quarter or any extra period (0:00 on game clock) should be counted and if so, determine if it is a two- or three-point goal.
   a. Obtain instructions from the state association/tournament director regarding specific guidelines and procedures for use with this rule.
   b. The covering official should always signal and communicate this ruling on the court prior to any monitor review.

OFFICIALS
CODE OF ETHICS

Officials at an interscholastic athletic event are participants in the educational development of high school students. As such, they must exercise a high level of self-discipline, independence and responsibility. The purpose of this Code is to establish guidelines for ethical standards of conduct for all interscholastic officials.

- **Officials** shall master both the rules of the game and the mechanics necessary to enforce the rules, and shall exercise authority in an impartial, firm and controlled manner.

- **Officials** shall work with each other and their state associations in a constructive and cooperative manner.

- **Officials** shall uphold the honor and dignity of the profession in all interaction with student-athletes, coaches, athletic directors, school administrators, colleagues, and the public. This includes, but is not limited to, positive verbal and nonverbal communication with coaches, bench personnel and players.

- **Officials** shall avoid the use of alcohol, drugs, and tobacco products beginning with the arrival at the competition site until departure following the completion of the contest.

- **Officials** shall prepare themselves both physically and mentally, shall dress neatly and appropriately, and shall comport themselves in a manner consistent with the high standards of the profession.

- **Officials** shall be punctual and professional in the fulfillment of all contractual obligations.

- **Officials** shall remain mindful that their conduct influences the respect that student-athletes, coaches and the public hold for the profession.

- **Officials** shall, while enforcing the rules of play, remain aware of the inherent risk of injury that competition poses to student-athletes. Where appropriate, officials shall inform event management of conditions or situations that appear unreasonably hazardous.

- **Officials** shall take reasonable steps to educate themselves in the recognition of emergency conditions that might arise during the course of competition.

- **Officials** shall maintain an ethical approach while participating in forums, chat rooms and all forms of social media.

Signal Chart: Starting and Stopping Clock

Start Clock

Stop Clock

Stop Clock for Held Ball

Stop Clock for Foul

Stop Clock for Foul (Optional 'Bird Dog')

Signal Chart: Information

Directional Signal

Throw-in and Free-Throw Designated Spot/ Violation

Move Along the Endline

Visible Count

Beckoning Substitutes

Signal Chart: Information

60-Second Time-out

30-Second Time-out

Not Closely Guarded

Tipped Ball

Signal Chart: Shooting/Scoring

No Score

Goal Counts

Point(s) Scored:
Use 1, 2 or 3 fingers after Signal 16

3-Point Attempt Score
3-Point Attempt Made

Signal Free Throw Attempts

Signal Chart: Violations

Delayed Lane Violation

Traveling Violation

Illegal Dribble

Palming/Carrying Violation

Back Court Violation

Signal Chart: Violations

3-Second Violation

5-Second Violation

10-Second Violation

Excessively Swinging Arm(s)/Elbow(s)

Kicking

Signal Chart: Fouls

Illegal Use of Hands

Hand Check

Holding

Blocking

Pushing/Charging

Player-Control/ Team-Control Foul

Signal Chart: Fouls

Intentional Foul

Double Foul

Technical Foul